GUNSHOTS & GOALPOSTS

The Story of Northern Irish Football

BENJAMIN ROBERTS

Revised Second Edition, November 2017.

If you want to contact me with any feedback, anecdotes, offers of work, or anything else you can find me on Twitter @benjamarkr and via email at benjaminmarkroberts@gmail.com, as well as keeping up to date with the Gunshots & Goalposts project at facebook.com/GunshotsAndGoalposts and polifootmedia.com

CONTENTS

AUTHOR'S NOTES

ON LANGUAGE

The term Northern Ireland is used throughout this book to refer to the FIFA recognised team of that name, as well as the political entity which is currently part of the United Kingdom. It has been chosen not to offend one community nor to give succour to another, but simply to reflect the present realities of the sporting and diplomatic realms in which it was written.

There are numerous other descriptors used to denote the collection of counties which constitute the area on the island of Ireland which is the subject of this book. Each of these are used sporadically in the absence of a definitive term which would be satisfactory to everyone who might be interested in reading this book. If there were a perfect word to use, then this entire book would most likely not exist. In essence, that's the point: words and how they are used are important everywhere but especially so in the part of the world addressed over the coming pages. Some readers may grimace at one turn of phrase, others will wince at another. A case in point is the name of the second largest city within the borders of Northern Ireland, and the county of which contains it: the former is referred to as Derry (as was common, even among unionists, until the 1960s) throughout, and the latter as Londonderry.

On a stylistic note; unionist, nationalist and republican are only capitalised when referring to explicitly party political actors or organisations.

ACKNOWLEDGEMENTS

My thanks is not limited to but includes: my parents Dave and Sharon Roberts, who edited the manuscript and contributed suggestions as to its content.

To my brother, Joel Roberts, who provided material support which aided the research of this book, particularly the latter chapters.

To Vyki Hendy, who designed the cover for this book and put up with my minor alterations on the way. She can be found @PaintbrushMania on Twitter and at www.vykihendy.com

To Lefkos Kyriacou, who graciously provided the map which forms part of the digital edition of this book.

To Tim Marshall and Paddy Agnew, who took the time to read this book before it came out and provide kind words for the back cover and promotional material.

To all the authors mentioned throughout the text and credited in the bibliography, whose work and insights have formed the narrative of this work.

And finally, to Beth Oliver, who is either my fiancée or wife depending on when you read this. She endured me boring her with obscure details about men she'd never heard for over a year.

I

NINETEEN TWELVE AND ALL THAT

PITCH BATTLE I - Belfast Celtic 0-1 Linfield (match abandoned), 12 September 1912

Belfast's football journalists had given no hint of what was to come. They had little reason to expect anything other than an exciting game between Belfast's great rivals: the *Irish News* had reported that a 'great match' was due to take place in 'genial weather'. Half an hour before the 3.30pm kick-off 20,000 fans were already in the ground, most of them blissfully unaware of what was about to unfold. The Linfield partisans took their traditional place at the Donegall Road end, the Celtic fans theirs in the home end by the Falls Road at the ground known as 'Paradise'.

The shipyard of Harland and Wolff was by some measure the largest employer in the city of Belfast during the early part of the twentieth century, infamous for having built the ship which met a fateful end one April night. But it was two things that occurred five months after the RMS *Titanic* had sunk in the North Atlantic

Ocean that ensured 1912 would be a memorable year in the history of the municipality.

A certain amount of sectarian badinage – the flying of flags, the singing of songs – was seen to be the price of doing business. Indeed one newspaper primly observed that the language at such derbies 'would have shamed the denizens of Dante's Inferno' and we know that for the decade or so preceding the match, finding out which team a man supported was a fairly accurate barometer of his politics. Yet it was not by the Donegall Road, nor by the Falls Road at the Willowbank End but within the 'neutral' zone that the trouble began. Even then, it was not until forty-five minutes had been played and the half-time break had commenced that fistfights broke out. The score stood at a goal to nil in Linfield's favour.

When the Royal Irish Constabulary (RIC) made attempts to intervene, the situation escalated. Fans began throwing stones at both the police and each other. In the ensuing melee a shot rang out. The entire crowd turned to face where the gunfire had come from, spilling onto the pitch. A second shot was fired as stewards carried a man away from the scene, while angry Linfield fans tried to get to the section of the Celtic fans waving a *Sinn Féin* flag.

PARADISE WAS LOST

Each group of fans believed they were under attack from the other. Ten thousand Celtic fans versus eight thousand Linfield fans engaged in pitched tribal panic.

The referee remained oblivious to the precise nature of events occurring outside the confines of his dressing room as he sipped his half-time tea with the linesmen. That was until a rock smashed through the window. Being from the mainland – Stockport, to be precise – he was bemused to discover that both sets of players wanted to continue with the match as soon as the fighting had subsided.

He was not used to such incidents. They were. The match did not continue; further gunfire was heard, then rocks and other improvised ammunition from the shipyards consisting of nuts, bolt and rivets known as 'Belfast confetti' were exchanged. Celtic Park was in the process of being built and there was a plentiful supply of construction materials around which could be repurposed as missiles.

The *Irish Times* reported that during the break a 'party of Celtic supporters in the unreserved area; carrying the club colours - a green and white striped flag - marched through the crowd in the direction of the Linfield supporters, who carried aloft a Union Jack.' The nationalist newspaper lamented 'the large numbers of revolvers now in the possession of more or less irresponsible youth of both parties in Belfast is one of the most appalling facts...it is laden with the most dangerous possibilities.' Eventually the Linfield fans were pushed out of the ground by the RIC onto the Donegall Road where they proceeded to wreck trams and assault bystanders, with reports of brawls in the loyalist enclave in west Belfast now known as The Village.

UNION MAN

Edward Carson was the leader of Ulster's Unionists and a figure who more than likely facilitated the whipping up of certain elements of the crowd, in order to prove that he could make the place ungovernable in the event that Home Rule came to pass. He knew that the stakes had been raised. Most importantly for his cause, so did everyone else.

Believe we dare not boast,
Believe we dare not fear:
We stand to pay the cost
In all that men hold dear.
What answer from the North?
One Law, One Land, One Throne!
If England drives us forth
We shall not fall alone.
'Ulster 1912', Rudyard Kipling

Many newspapers who would not usually have made great bedfellows, including the *Daily Express*, the *Irish News*, the *Irish Weekly* and the *Ulster Examiner*, blamed Carson for the violence. The suggestion was made that he had stoked up the situation for political ends, and the *Irish News* editorialised that 'Sir Edward Carson and the gospel of hatred so zealously expounded in the Belfast Unionist Clubs have so far affected the minds of their dupes that even the area of sport is not considered sacred from mob violence.' Another paper with nationalist sentiments posited that 'with the memory of Sir Edward Carson's incitements...the Unionist clubmen planned, organised and carried into effect last Saturday's indefensible "scene" at the Celtic Football Grounds.'

The same writer went on to suggest that Carson welcomed the disorder, which 'no doubt, brought pride to the statesman.' As Barry Flynn's *Political Football* makes us aware, Philip Gibbs of *The Graphic,* a London-based magazine, described Carson as 'Ulster's Dictator' adding, 'He has put a spell on them. They have a kind of worship for him as a demi-god, a superman, master of their fate, a champion of their rights.' The *Daily Mail*, on the other hand, was full of praise for the unionists in the Linfield crowd, happily declaring that 'the rioters on Saturday did succeed where the *great leaders* failed.'

Sixty casualties of the afternoon's events were admitted to the Mater and Royal Victoria hospitals in the hours that followed. Five of them were suffering from gunshot wounds and one sixteen year old's skull had been fractured. The unionist *Belfast News Letter* blamed Celtic fans for what had occurred, seeing provocation in the flourishing of a green and white flag. Linfield fans had reciprocated with an Orange Order bannerette and a Union flag, though the conservative *Sport* paper pointed the finger at 'officialism', suggesting the police were bound by red tape and would or could not act with the force required. Another source saw Linfield fans as the culprits, 'carrying a purple and Orange coloured flag, and singing party songs, and cursing the pope.'

The *Gaelic Athlete* opined that the phrase 'Red rag to a bull' could now be amended to 'Green flag to a Soccerite', seeing not sectarianism but the entire sport as being at fault. The reality is that the whole thing had very little to do with football, owing a lot more to the communities of the Pound Loney (the present day Falls Road area) and the Sandy Row, home to some of Belfast's most hardline unionists and the Orange Hall where Linfield held their general meetings. This simmering inter-neighbourhood feud had existed for at least half a century, before either club had even been established, but they went on to draw the bulk of their support from these adjacent districts, even when Linfield had moved nearly a mile away to Windsor Park. *The Times* 'Special Correspondent' wrote that 'the sensation that Belfast had been waiting for so long occurred yesterday in totally unexpected fashion', exclaiming that 'in no city has the hooligan no better opportunities and better accommodation than in Belfast.'

The anonymous reporter foresaw further disturbances on the horizon in the city, writing 'It is certain, however, that the Roman Catholic mob will now be boasting of a glorious revenge for its discomfiture on Queen's Island Belfast shipyard last July. Therefore it is scarcely possible to doubt that the Protestant mob will not be satisfied until it has in turn carried out successful measures of reprisal.' The government even saw fit to send troops into the shipyards the Monday after the abandoned fixture at Celtic Park, in order to quell any trouble that might arise, stationing the King's Own Scottish Border Regiment and members of Royal Army Medical Corps around the premises.

In the event, no physical violence occurred at the Harland and Wolff yard but at Workman, Clark & Company, a young Catholic was severely beaten by masked men. The situation was such that many Catholics did not go back to work after lunch that day, having been 'chalked' in the morning by a hand casually placed on their back. Often this was done by someone they trusted with the intention of marking them out for attack when they were alone or in smaller groups later in the day. Philip Gibbs of *The Graphic* was becoming fearful about the fate of nationalists and Catholics in the city:

> “Already there is a reign of terror in the Catholic quarters of Belfast. Hardly a day passes but some man or lad is brought home battered or bloodied to his wife or mother, For many weeks now hundreds of sturdy men have abandoned work or wages because they are afraid of coming back in the same condition. And before them lies the constant terror of a day when the Protestant majority will get out of hand and when the sound of their drums will be a warning of death to the Catholic minority.

Celtic's 'Paradise' ground had taken on an even greater significance in the life of both clubs, when Winston Churchill had spoken at a pro-Home Rule rally there early in 1912. Its use had been secured by Joseph Devlin, the Nationalist MP for the West Belfast constituency and Celtic shareholder, after unionists had effectively blocked Churchill from speaking at the Ulster Hall by securing its hire the previous evening, pledging that they would refuse to leave. A week before his speech *The Times* had reported:

> Celtic Park is, of course, situated close to a Protestant district, but unless there is provocation everything should pass off peacefully without any collision between the parties. A very large force of police will be on duty around the park and a small force of military may also be employed.

Extraordinarily, it was Churchill's own father, Sir Randolph, who had stoked the unionist fire some twenty five years earlier when the First Home Rule Bill was before parliament, declaring 'Ulster will fight, and Ulster will be right' and that 'Home Rule is Rome Rule.' He had fulminated 'Mr Gladstone asks for time before he plunges the knife into the heart of the British Empire...But now may be the time to show whether all those ceremonies and forms which are practised in your Orange Lodges are really living symbols or idle and meaningless shibboleths.'

The younger Churchill's appearance provided another excuse - as if one were needed - to air dirty sectarian laundry in a footballing venue. It also produced a headache for the Irish Football League who, in the days after the game, produced a document stating that 'under no circumstances will any banners, flags, or other emblems of any kind be permitted inside our respective grounds at football matches...', adding that if a revolver was fired at a game again it would be abandoned. In a similar vein, the Irish Football Association held an emergency meeting on the 18 September, announcing it was determined that the match should be replayed at a neutral ground and drawing up a 'Manifesto to the Football Public'.

STRENGTH IN NUMBERS

On 28 September, 237,368 men signed Ulster's Solemn League and Covenant, while 234,046 women signed a corresponding declaration pledging 'uncompromising opposition' to the Home Rule Bill before parliament. Their objection was to the Bill's provision for a limited form of self government for the entire island of Ireland. The majority-Protestant Ulster was anxious that Home Rule would really be Rome Rule; a Catholic tyranny; their campaign energised by the Catholic church's *Ne Temere* Decree in 1908 which meant all children of mixed marriages should be baptised and raised as Catholics. Then, in 1910 a man had - along with their children - walked out on his Protestant wife, saying a Catholic priest had told him to do so.

It was decreed that all but one of the matches scheduled for Ulster Day would be postponed, with the exception of the Distillery v Celtic fixture. The rationale was that this would draw nationalist crowds away from trouble elsewhere, acting as a distraction. Indeed, the match was played in front of a capacity crowd at Distillery's Grosvenor Park in the Falls and, in the absence of a serious rivalry between the clubs, there were only a few skirmishes with no serious disorder occurring during Celtic's 2-0 win. It was only after the game that a huge police presence was required to keep Celtic fans away from the Protestant Roden Street area.

A month later Celtic and Linfield would meet again to fulfil their abandoned fixture. Distillery's Grosvenor Park was chosen as a neutral venue and, this time, the match passed without any significant crowd trouble, relatively speaking, anyway although revolvers were still discharged into the sky. This was less remarkable than it might seem, as it was becoming commonplace for the sound of 'revolver music' to be heard at football matches in Ulster. The echo of shots being fired had been heard at Linfield's match against Cliftonville and Ireland's fixture against England in Belfast. The sectarian divide in Irish football was crystallising rapidly; Glentoran's fans had arranged themselves into s Union Jack at their Oval ground, just as Celtic Park was increasingly being used for pro-Home Rule rallies and drills by the National Irish Volunteers, a nationalist rival to the UVF.

ORIGINS

Belfast Celtic had been formed out of a cricket team named Sentinel, whose members lived around the Falls Road. Its footballing offshoot modelled itself on the nascent Celtic club that was ruffling Scottish footballing feathers in Glasgow, and the team was established in meetings at the home of James Henry, 88 Falls Road, and the Beehive Public House at 193 Falls Road in August 1891. The streets around the Falls were said to be 'alive with excited fans', and within a few years supporters were filling trains leaving Great Victoria Street to travel to away games. The largest concentration of Catholics in Belfast's rapidly growing population was in the Pound Loney district at the foot of Falls Road, so it seemed only natural that this should have formed the home for Belfast's foremost nationalist association football team of the next sixty years.

Milltown, Millvale and Clondara had been junior teams (meaning the level of football they played rather than their ages) in the Falls Road area. Amalgamating these sides meant that a more competitive outfit could take on Belfast's established teams and with the help of a sizeable sum of money from their Scottish namesake, a new club was born.

Just as Belfast Celtic took their first few steps, the Second Home Rule Bill was working its way through parliament. The leader of the Orange Order was a Dr Rutledge Jane, who promised his fellow Orangemen that he would 'die' should the Bill pass, calling it a 'bastard combination' of Irish and English government, continuing:

> “Brethren and Friends: We are face to face with a stupendous crisis. If we had lost a thousand Boynes, and surrendered at as many Derry's with halters round our necks, more disastrous or humiliating terms could be dictated by the conquerors than are contained in the Home Rule Bill. We have not, however, lost a single Boyne, not have we surrendered, and therefore we do not mean to accept any humiliating and disastrous terms.

That the Bill had got a second reading in the Houses of Parliament was seen as a small victory for Nationalism, even though the Lords were sure to kill it on arrival in the other place. The celebrations by nationalists of this symbolic win served, of course, to rile unionists and fighting broke out between groups from the Falls and Shankill districts. Barrels of tar were set alight, as well as widespread burning and looting. Later in the year, the Lords duly voted the Bill down 419-41.

A PLACE TO CALL HOME

Belfast Celtic's first home was on a field at Broadway off the Falls Road and it was this pitch which witnessed their admittance to the Alliance Junior League. By 1894 they had won the coveted Robinson and Cleaver Junior Shield, going on to retain it for the next two seasons. Even in its infancy the club's reputation preceded it: the 1895 final against Glentoran Seconds was the scene of brawls and stone-throwing. When the final whistle was blown, a pitch invasion ensued during which the Glens players and staff were attacked, some requiring hospitalisation for their injuries.

Though they had already become known as a club associated with Irish nationalist politics, Celtic were making waves on the pitch too: despite still being a 'junior' side they won the 'senior' County Antrim Shield in 1895, beating Distillery in the final. Contemporaneous reports tell of how the 'Falls Road turned out to a man' to witness it, as Celtic ran out 3-1 victors. Their victory in the final of the Robinson and Cleaver Senior Trophy in 1896 (against none other than Linfield Swifts, the second team of the Windsor Park outfit) meant they had a strong case for entering the Irish League, which they did the following season.

Celtic's first season as one of the bigger boys was not as successful as had been anticipated: the field at their Broadway ground was not up to scratch so all of their 'home' games were hosted by their opponents. Their first match as a 'senior' team was against Cliftonville at their Solitude ground, where they fell to a 3-1 loss. On their way to finishing bottom of the Irish Football League in their inaugural season there was a visit to the Oval to play Glentoran, during which rioting broke out between fans. It was a day which also witnessed fighting between the Linfield and Cliftonville faithful.

The first time Celtic played Linfield as a senior side they managed a creditable 1-1 draw, but their second game was marred by the pitch invasions and crowd trouble, that were to become a frequent sight on Belfast's footballing landscape.

What must have been particularly galling for an Irish nationalist football team propping up the table, was the fact that the North Staffordshire Regiment - a military side! — had finished one place above them. Celtic's only victory that entire season had been by two goals to one versus Distillery. Another match against their neighbours in the County Antrim Shield was abandoned when Celtic fans pulled down the goals during a pitch incursion.

The club's second season saw an improvement in fortunes; they were able to find a more suitable pitch at Shaun's Park on the Whiterock Road, a site now known as MacRory Park and home to the Cardinal O'Donnell's Gaelic Athletic Club. Having a place to call home helped the Hoops finish a respectable fourth out of six clubs competing in the 1897/98 season, and by 1901 Belfast Celtic had become a limited company. Notable among the early investors is the fact that the largest proportion of shareholders gave their occupation as 'spirit merchant' and that the second most popular vocation was listed as that that of a Catholic priest.

Now on a professional footing, this entity acquired a ten acre site on Donegall Road for the construction of a ground, financed by selling 3000 shares at £1 each. This new abode is said to have been given the nickname 'Paradise' when a Scottish journalist said that it was like moving from 'a graveyard to paradise.' It bore at least one similarity with Linfield's Windsor Park: both were situated close to the Bog Meadows, necessitating the additional cost of an adequate drainage system.

WAR STOPS PLAY

When the Irish League was suspended at the end of the 1914/15 season, Celtic had just won their second title, consigning Glentoran to second place as Linfield trailed in third out of eight teams.

Beyond the pitch, UVF gun-runners had procured 25,000 weapons and three million rounds of ammunition from Germany on the shores at Larne, prepared for a war with anyone who would impose the hated Home Rule upon the unionist people of Ulster. The Third Home Rule Bill had been passed by parliament in late May 1914, and although amendments that included provision for the partition of the island of Ireland had been pushed through by Edward Carson and the Irish Unionist Party, the mood among his followers was fractious. There would almost certainly have been a unionist uprising, were it not for the fact that on 4 August 1914 Great Britain went to war with Germany, shelving the Irish question until the conclusion of the conflict. The Home Rule Act received royal assent on 18 September 1914 but its implementation was deferred, a turn of events the Liberal Prime Minister Herbert Asquith described as the greatest 'stroke of luck' of his career.

DREARY SPIRES

At the conclusion of the war, both unionists and nationalists thought they would be rewarded for their loyalty to the cause, and patience in holding off from pushing for their aims while the government was otherwise engaged. Winston Churchill wrote in 1918 that 'as the mists of battle cleared, there arose from them the dreary spires of Fermanagh and Tyrone.' For those not fluent in purple prose, Churchill's gist was that as one war ended, another one loomed on the horizon.

Much of the Irish nationalist populace no longer wanted 'Home Rule' as it had been constituted before the war, hoping for a purer form of independence. There were now two distinct camps: those that wanted Home Rule under the British Crown, and *Sinn Féin,* who wanted a total severance from Buckingham Palace. In the general election of 1918 the latter party won 73 of the 105 Irish seats represented at Westminster, to the six of the moderate Irish Parliamentary Party. Crucially, however, only three of these were in Ulster.

As they did not recognise British authority, *Sinn Féin* unilaterally established *Dáil Éireann* in Dublin on 21 January 1919, prompting the British government to declare both the Irish parliament and *Sinn Féin* illegal. That day the Irish War of Independence began in Soloheadbeg, County Tipperary.

PITCH BATTLE II - Belfast Celtic 0-2 Glentoran (match abandoned), 8 March 1919

This febrile atmosphere provided the setting for an Irish Cup semi-final match between Belfast Celtic and Glentoran on 8 March, to be played at Cliftonville's Solitude ground. Trams had whisked the Glenmen from

Ballymacarrett in east Belfast to the north of the city and the attendance was estimated at 18,000. Though Mickey Hamill and Fred Barrett were said to have stood out for Celtic, the match would not last a full ninety minutes; a second half pitch invasion meant the police had to intervene to confine fans to the cinder track on the perimeter, just as many others decided to leave early, sensing further trouble.

They were not wrong; *Amhrán na bhFiann* (The Soldier's Song) was sung by the Celtic faithful, as stones and wood were thrown at Glentoran players when they made to leave the pitch. Chairs which had been set out for injured war veterans to watch the match were instead used as battering rams, as the RIC attempted to move the crowds onto the adjacent Cliftonville Road. The *Belfast Telegraph's* 'Ralph The Rover' columnist (thought to be a former Linfield secretary by the name of John Gordon), described events as an 'orgy of rampant lawlessness...by an element so devoid of sense and decency,' stating that there was a section of fans who 'just cannot bear to see Celtic beaten.' But Celtic were beaten, albeit by fiat: the abandoned match was controversially awarded to Glentoran, who would lose in the final to Linfield.

PITCH BATTLE III - Belfast Celtic 0-0 Glentoran (match abandoned), 17 March 1920

A *Belfast Telegraph* editorial the following year was strident in its assertion of where the blame for this fresh outbreak of tumult at football grounds in Belfast. The author pointed the finger at the '*Sinn Féin* element, which has made itself conspicuous at Belfast football matches in the past year managed once again yesterday to disgrace the fair name of sport.' St Patrick's Day was the date of a head-to-head between east and west Belfast, squaring off once again at Solitude in the north of the city. The nationalist-leaning *Irish News* had chosen to pen an evocative editorial, drawing on the memory of the republican patriots of 1798, writing:

> Ireland has seen many St Patrick's Days within living memory when her hopes were high and the hearts of her children the world over were filled with the joyous confidence of an approaching and certain victory. Today we are back in 'Ninety-Eight, - so far as those who hold this country by armed force can control the national clock: but not in 1798, or in 1598, or at any stated period since 1169, was Ireland's determination to win back her freedom more resolute or truly unconquerable than it is at the present hour.

Given that the game was taking place on a public holiday, a large crowd was gathered at Solitude. The match itself was hard fought, as both teams set out their stall to attack. Incredibly, the opposing goalkeepers Bertie and John Mehaffey were brothers; their efforts ensuring the score remained 0-0 at half-time. It remained so until the eightieth minute, when Celtic's Fred Barrett tripped Joe Gowdy of Glentoran, causing the Celtic contingent in the stands to erupt, emitting what the *Belfast Telegraph* called a 'wild angry roar.'

Celtic partisans came over the railings and on to the field of play, resulting in the referee ordering the teams off the pitch. The Celtic fans quickly turned on the Glentoran supporters with bricks, bottles, nuts and rivets flying between the two sets of supporters. Some fans were engaged in hand to hand combat on the pitch, as a large

Sinn Féin flag was hoisted at the end designated for the Celtic fans.

By the time RIC reinforcements arrived, a man among the Celtic supporters had produced a revolver. He fired a bullet into the Glentoran end before disappearing back into the crowd until the police located him. The *Belfast Telegraph* denounced *Sinn Féin* as the aggressors, stating that 'the chief menace lay in a gang which had taken up position under the unreserved stand. For these the "Soldier's Song", "The Boys of Wexford", "A Nation Once Again" and other airs of an undoubtedly provocative character were chorused loudly during the game while one man was especially prominent with a large *Sinn Féin* flag which he waved defiantly amid cheers from his fellows.'

The Mater and Royal Victoria hospitals were busy again, treating a number of people for bullet wounds after the battle had spilled onto the surrounding streets. The game was left unfinished and scoreless, neither team making the final; Celtic were thrown out for the behaviour of their fans, Glentoran disqualified for fielding an ineligible player in John McIlveen. Shelbourne, a Dublin team, had beaten Glenavon in the other semi-final and won the cup by default.

The suspected shooter, a George Goodman of Pound Loney, appeared in court charged with attempted murder, reportedly wearing an Irish Volunteers badge when he was captured. The charge later was amended to firing a weapon 'with intent to cause grievous harm', as it was felt the attempted murder charge would be too hard to prove definitively, and Goodman was later found guilty and sentenced to eight years in prison.

THE IMPOSSIBLE YEARS

At the end of May 1920, Celtic had advised the IFA that they would not be returning to the league the following season, feeling that they had been unjustly punished with a severity that a unionist team would not have been. There was a pragmatic element to their decision too: if they had played on during the next few years, it would likely have resulted in the deaths of both players and fans. The situation on the island of Ireland was deteriorating by the day, and Edward Carson had told the British government: 'if you are unable to protect us from the machinations of *Sinn Féin* and you will not take our help, then we will take the matter into our own hands.'

July 1920 saw mass expulsions of Catholic workers from the yards of Harland and Wolff, as well as other smaller shipyards; a warning to them chalked on a wall near to both the Harland and Workman Clark yards. During an informal meeting, 5,000 unionist workers were called on to refuse to work alongside *Sinn Féin* members among their colleagues and that afternoon they — gently at first, then more firmly - informed their workmates to leave and not come back.

There were ten hospitalisations of Catholics, with cuts and broken bones, as some others swam in desperation across the Musgrave channel to safety. The focus had gone beyond suspected *Sinn Féin* members: all Catholics became targets, as the ejections spread beyond shipbuilders to smaller firms around Belfast. In the days that followed, a Jewish tabernacle on Townsend Street was burned down and an attempt to set St Matthews Catholic Church alight was made. The events of that Summer meant any chance of Celtic returning quickly had been extinguished and a correspondent in the *Irish News* reported that:

> Celtic were due to play Cliftonville this afternoon, but that is not coming off. Is this to be construed as the beginning of the end for this incoming season? I was always opposed to the Celts going out of football but could not blame them on this occasion. So long as thousands of people are compulsorily out of work, so long will matters be unsettled and not much chance of a normal time on the field for Celtic.

It would have been nearly impossible for a team associated with nationalism to travel to east Belfast, and when the delayed 1920/21 season started it was without Belfast Celtic.

The solution to the Irish question, proposed by David Lloyd George's Liberal government, was the partition of the island of Ireland, with both units being granted limited self-government. The Prime Minister saw this as the only feasible short-term solution, reflecting wearily:

> You had to ask the British to use force to put Ulster out of one combination in which she had been for generations into another combination which she professed to abhor and did abhor, whether for political or religious reasons. We could not do it. If we tried the instrument would have broken in our hands. Their case was "Let us remain with you". Our case was "Out you go or we fight you". We could not have done it. Mr Churchill and I warned our colleagues. Mr Gladstone and Mr Asquith discovered it. The first axiom is whatever happened we could not coerce Ulster.

Ulster had defeated him: six of its nine counties would form the new Northern Irish state, despite there being sizeable areas within its borders that were majority Catholic, especially in Fermanagh, Tyrone, parts of County Londonderry, south Armagh and, of course, west Belfast. It was a borderline that was never intended to be permanent, but became locked in once civil strife erupted. The Government of Ireland Act set up an All-Ireland Council above the two parliaments, in the naïve hope that it would be a forerunner to the reunification of Ireland. Instead, the North rejected the boundaries and the Free State objected to how the parliaments would work. The aim had been to placate all sides; the outcome was that nobody was happy.

When *Sinn Féin* called a vote on the Anglo-Irish treaty in the *Dáil,* it passed with 64-57 in favour, to the dismay of its leader Eamon de Valera and his faction within the party, who walked out in protest. Having been replaced by Arthur Griffith from the party's pro-treaty faction as the head of the *Dáil,* de Valera and his anti-treaty colleagues, and IRA members who believed likewise, refused to accept what they saw as a 'treacherous' document, seizing the Four Courts and other major buildings in Dublin. Those members of the IRA who did support the treaty were organised into the Irish Army, lead by Michael Collins and he ordered his forces to shell the Four Courts in June 1921, eventually succeeding in driving the IRA out of Dublin.

So began the Irish Civil War, lasting nearly a year. Though concentrated in Munster and Connaught, Ulster did not escape the frequent forays north, and for one week forty square miles in Fermanagh were held by anti-treaty forces. Many Protestants in Northern Ireland blamed local Catholics for the actions of IRA members, causing a rise in sectarian skirmishes.

In the midst of this warfare, the Northern Irish parliament met for the first time. Cardinal Logue, the leader of Catholic church in Ireland, refused to attend its formal opening or even recognise the new state despite an appeal by King George V for the two sides 'to stretch out the hand of forbearance and conciliation, to forgive and forget.' That was never likely to happen: by 1922, 455 people had been killed in Belfast, about 2,500 were injured and another 20,000 had fled their homes.

Ireland had been torn apart.

2

A NATION ONCE, BEFORE

What is widely regarded as the first game of modern association football in Ireland took place on 24 October 1878, when Caledonians played Queens Park at the grounds of the Ulster Cricket Club in Belfast. John McCredy McAlery was manager of the Irish Tweed House gentleman's outfitters in Belfast, and the popular narrative has it that while on honeymoon in Scotland he witnessed a game of football, though unless his new wife had kicked him out of the bed and breakfast, it is probable he had some previous knowledge of the game in Scotland and had planned to attend the match.

McAlery invited the captain of Caledonians football club, J.A Allen, to bring a match to Belfast. This he did, coming over with Queens Park, who won 3-1 in front of what can have only been one thousand very curious locals. The latter team were a Glasgow-based outfit, who had been at the forefront of the development of Scottish football, even making a name for themselves in England as pioneers of the passing game. McAlery would likely have guaranteed the two clubs a certain income from the match, which would more than cover their costs, since Queens Park were not known for carrying out their missionary duties without a fee.

As well as his clothing business, McAlery was the treasurer of Cliftonville Cricket Club, and it was from this organisation that the first football club in Ireland was established. An article published in the 20 September edition of the *Belfast News Letter* in 1879, asked for 'gentlemen desirous of becoming members' of Cliftonville Association Football Club to turn up for a practice the day after. Those who did would play a team of rugby players, from a team by the name of Quidnuncs on the twenty-ninth day of the same month.

Cliftonville's first year saw them play 14 matches, winning eight, drawing two and losing just four times. The team's season end report notes that 'considerable difficulty was at first experienced in obtaining a sufficient number of players to engage in the practice matches', and their meeting with Banbridge Academy more closely resembled a tuition than a competitive tie, as none of the Academicals had ever seen a game of football, let alone played in one. One draw was played out against Ardee of Scotland who — as well as Caledonians, Ayr and Portland (from Kilmarnock) - were frequently crossing the Irish Sea or hosting a Belfast side at their place.

Back on the westerly shore, the growth of football paralleled the expansion of a relatively secure industrial working class along Ulster's east coast. Whereas rugby required a certain amount of space and equipment in the form of posts that the ball could be kicked over, football could take the form of a street game with improvised materials, able to more fluidly adapt to spatial limitations. Workers in Belfast's York Street Mill were said to have played with a ball made of waste yarn, and it is possible

Distillery went on to compete in white because their shirts were made of disused flour bags.

A meeting was convened at Queens Hotel in Belfast on 18 November 1880 to discuss the formation of an Irish Football Association. This first get together drew up rules for the Irish Cup, a high stakes knock-out competition, seen as the best way to propagate a new sport as quickly as possible. Four clubs had been playing matches on a regular basis; Cliftonville and Knock in Belfast, Moyola in the Castledawson area of County Londonderry, and Banbridge Academy in County Down, with Avoniel (formed by Scottish construction workers), Distillery, Oldpark (a team of Scottish printworkers) and Alexander FC of Limavady making up the eight founders of the new association.

Among those original clubs, Knock had their origins as a Lacrosse club before its members took up the new game with the same John McAlery an influence in their origins. The Moyola Park club had even grander origins, formed under the patronage of Major Chichester, who provided funds and land; his paternalism allowing the local aristocracy to feel good about themselves.

The first trophy, designed by William Gibson & Co., was won by Chichester's club, eking out a 1-0 victory over Cliftonville. Ten years after the cup's inception Distillery had appeared in five finals and won it on four of those occasions, which made them early heavyweights when the Irish League was inaugurated in 1890 as Major Spencer Chichester became the IFA's first President. Clearly there was something in the family ties; thirty-one years later his grandson (and Glentoran shareholder) James Craig would become Northern Ireland's first Prime Minister.

Though clubs from Dublin were included in cup draws from the earliest days of the Irish Cup, a Belfast side would appear in every final until 1906, reflecting the balance of footballing power on the island. When Linfield defeated Bohemians 10-1 in the 1896 final, it was their sixth consecutive time as one of the last two, though Bohemians eventual triumph in the 1902 final earned them a place in the Irish League when they became the first team outside of Ulster to be admitted. In the 1904/05 season another Dublin team, Shelbourne, had joined them, and the 1906/07 season witnessed the first all-Dublin Irish Cup Final, which Bohemians won after a replay.

Irish football's original booster John McAlery's contribution to the game was not limited to the club game, serving as he did as captain in Ireland's first 'international' fixture in February 1882. Billed as a match between Ulster - playing in a Saint Patrick's blue jersey with a shamrock crest, as IFA sides did until 1931 - and England in front of a crowd of 2,500 at Bloomfield Park, it pitted a nation with twenty years of experience against players who had been competing for just two.

It showed: McAlery is said to have wept at the 13-0 scoreline, although things improved marginally when he took the team to Wrexham the following week, escaping with a 7-1 thrashing. It's not known whether further tears were shed but McAlery would have to wait another five years before Ireland would experience the thrill of their first victory.

LATE BLOSSOMING

Football had taken off relatively late in Ireland compared to its progress across the water. England had created its Football Association in 1863, Queens Park made Glasgow one of the focal points of the British game from 1867, before Scotland formed its own FA six years later. Even the Welsh had got in on the act by 1877.

In the mid-1870s, rising incomes and more free time for some of Ireland's working population, meant leisure pursuits like football were increasingly an option: wages to individual farm labourers more than doubled between 1850 and 1900 (rising 80 per cent in real terms), and the Factory and Workshop Acts meant that some industrial workers did not have to toil as many hours. Those positive effects of the Acts were felt most in Ulster and especially in Belfast, where the linen industry supported a large workforce.

A mere hamlet when it was acquired by Sir Arthur Chichester in 1603, Belfast had by now firmly supplanted Carrickfergus as the significant settlement in Ulster. The proportion of the Irish population living in communities of more than two thousand persons nearly doubled between 1841 and 1891, and Belfast's own population - 19,000 in 1801 - had mushroomed to 256,000 ninety years later. More people residing in towns meant more opportunities to organise football teams and more spectators too.

Nevertheless, the growth of football across the island was wildly uneven: though Ulster's strong links to the rest of the UK facilitated rapid economic change, figures from the five decades after 1861 show that the GDP of Ireland as a whole was consistently lower than that of any of the other nations ruled from Westminster. It was a provision of the 1874 Factory Act that meant the situation in the north-east of the island was more conducive to sporting growth; now many working men in Belfast had Saturday afternoons off, as well as the six half-day holidays a year that were required by the legislation. Workers could arrange these to cover some Saturday mornings, meaning at least six times a year they would have a full Saturday off.

In Dublin, the situation was quite different. Less than a quarter of workforce were employed in manufacturing by 1881, and fewer people benefitted from the laws, which did not apply to the sectors which dominated employment in Ireland's capital. Thus there were far less opportunities to participate in leisure activities taking place on a Saturday in Leinster and the circumstances in Cork were even less conducive to the everyday man being able to get involved in sporting activity.

ON THE RIGHT TRACK

The impact of the rapidly growing railway network on the leisure time of the everyday man and woman was substantial: Ireland had 2,285 miles of railway track by 1879, carrying a cumulative 16 million passengers each year. Teams and spectators were able to travel to games further away than ever before, creating an economy of scale: the Clogher Valley Railway Cup was donated by owners of the eponymous railway company in 1903, with sporting assistance from Clogher FC, becoming an annual competition which was open to all affiliated clubs in the area served by said railway between Caledon and Maguiresbridge. By 1905 there were nine participants including clubs from Monaghan, Tyrone and Fermanagh.

In certain areas, tramways also fulfilled the purpose of allowing people to get to new venues that were springing up into the town or city centre from the suburbs. In Belfast the lines were not electrified until 1906, when they were brought into public ownership although the networks had been widely used in the decades beforehand. The 1890s also saw at least a dozen sports newspapers spring up in Ireland, albeit some with more longevity than others. These helped spread the popularity of football and other sports in their own way, by familiarising punters with the names of players and some of the finer points of the rules.

Ten years after the formation of the Irish Football Association and the establishment of the Irish Cup, things had progressed such that a league competition was a viable proposition. The inaugural season of the Irish League contained seven teams from Belfast and one from Milford in County Armagh. Linfield came out on top with 25 points from 14 games (at two points for a win, of course) losing and drawing only once. At the other end of the table, Milford finished bottom, their record: played 14, lost 14. For: 10, Against: 62. Perhaps wisely, they resigned from the league.

OUT OF THE BLUE

Linfield's reputation as the originators of the passing game in Ireland dates from this time: a dribbling based approach had been the norm until around 1890, when Nick Ross, a veteran of Preston North End, became their coach. The new style took hold around Ulster but even a decade on the kick and rush game was still prevalent in Dublin.

The Belfast club had been formed in the mid-1880s by workers at the Ulster Spinning Company's Linfield Mill in the Sandy Row - 'where the Fenians never go' — though the initial ideal of an employees only team was jettisoned:

> “Permission has been obtained from the management, who promised to give every support. Originally it was intended to confine membership to the Linfield workers, but this was later altered to ensure the strongest possible side being put in the field. In fact, there were six "outsiders" in that first eleven.

Nevertheless, they benefited from encouragement and material assistance from their employers: their first ground was on property owned by the company, with the canteen used as changing room.

The Blues distinguished themselves in an early incarnation of the English FA Cup, in which Irish sides participated until the outbreak of the Great War. Although the Irish were mostly seen as physical players who were not particularly skilful, the Blues nevertheless beat Nottingham Forest in the first round of the competition just two years after they had been established, winning 3-1 in Belfast. Sadly they would make it no further, the costs of travelling to play their second round game in Kent proving prohibitive and in any case it transpired they had fielded an ineligible player against Forest.

The Distillery club was birthed in similar circumstances, formed as Genoa FC (after a nearby street) in 1880 as an offshoot of the V.R Distillery Cricket Club. They had turned to football in late when a member decided to form a football club for something to do in the Winter months and were given a pitch at a nominal rent by their benefactors, the Dunville & Co. whiskey producers, constructing a facility behind the premises when the company filled in a pond. The Gallaher's cigarette manufacturer fulfilled a similar purpose for the Park Drive club, constituted of employees at their factory, the owners generously providing complimentary cigarettes at club functions.

These were all teams who had several Scotsmen in their membership, men who had been playing in Glasgow where the game was already established. A wave of skilled Scots emigrating — it's just twelve miles from the Mull of Kintyre to the Antrim coast - to work in Belfast's burgeoning industries meant the city became a hotbed of footballing activity. The influence of Scotsmen on the Irish game was not confined to a supply of early recruits to its fledgling teams, however; the IFA adopted the Scottish FA rules wholesale, and the Scottish association donated the sum of £5 to fund the purchase of the first Irish Cup trophy.

FIT AND PROPER PERSONS

Victorian beliefs around the moral benefits of increased physical prowess meant the powers that be began to view sport as something to be encouraged: one speaker at the IFA AGM of 1887 volunteered that 'anything which develops the stamina and power of the people must ultimately be a good thing for the land.' In 1891, a proponent of more public pitches in Belfast argued for their increase on the basis that they would be a place 'where the sons of artizans can exercise their frames and enable them to grow up strong, hardy men, with a constitution to enable them to labour, and become a credit to the city, and an ornament to the state.'

Opinion was divided on the efficacy of football as a way to curb drunkenness, however; on the one hand it was a 'great temperance reformer by providing amusement for young men during the two hours on a Saturday when they are most assailed by the temptation of the public house', though another school of thought suggested the fact that pubs in Belfast displayed signs saying 'Football results received here' meant the same young men were encouraged to the pub later in the day.

One of today's foremost Irish League clubs, Crusaders, were formed after raising funds in a pub on York Road, though Temperance societies such as the Catch-My-Pal organisation also formed teams to keep wayward drunks busy. Churches founded teams too, including the Central Presbyterian Association in Belfast, and a Catholic Reading Room was the instigator of a new club in Armagh.

A SIGN OF THE TIMES

In an event that portended the future of Irish football matches the Spring of 1899 saw the first significant crowd trouble during an Irish Cup semi final between Belfast Celtic and Glentoran, formed in 1882 and moving to the Oval in Ballymacarrett a decade later. This marked the start of what one commentator called the 'curse of party bigotry' in the football arena, 'threatening to destroy not only the reputation of footballers, but the peace of the community.'

There had been a genuine — if misguided - hope in upper class Ulster society at the end of the nineteenth century, that football could be a vehicle through which men were 'brought together in equality, free from the friction of everyday life' and that this would foster a 'congenial halo of civil and religious liberty.' Yet by 1902 fans of both Linfield and Belfast Celtic were chased down the Donegall Road by the constabulary for exchanging 'party tunes'.

Back then — as now - football was not the only game in town. Rugby was also popular in Ireland, especially among well-to-do Protestants, but it was Gaelic football which provided the toughest competition for the affections of Catholics and nationalists. Proponents of the ancient Irish game were keen to portray association football as a 'garrison' game, an imperialist import by British soldiers who would play this alien sport in and around their army bases. When McAlery had brought Queens Park and Caledonians over for that first game, the *Athletic News* carried reports of the association game being discussed as 'the noxious Scotch weed'.

Douglas Hyde, who went on to become the first President of Ireland, had penned *The necessity of de-Anglicizing Ireland* in 1894, writing 'The GAA has done more for Ireland in the past five years than all the speeches of politicians', though somewhat ironically he would be dethroned as patron of the Gaelic Athletic Association (GAA) decades later when he attended the Republic of Ireland's football match against Poland. Sentiments like Hyde's ran deep within nationalist circles. In 1896 Michael Cusack, a founder of the GAA and committed nationalist, remarked that association football players in Dublin came to 'learn their game by fagging the ball for soldiers in the Park.' On another occasion he had launched a broadside against British football as 'a denationalising plague, carrying on through the winter the work of ruin that cricket was doing through the summer.' Cusack saw it as a deliberate anti-Irish tool, designed to sap the morale of a nation, 'The conspiracy was not merely intended to extend the sway of English cultural imperialism, it was being purposefully directed to encompass the degradation of individual Irishmen by inveigling them into varieties of sporting competition in which they might readily be defeated.'

There *is* evidence of English and Scottish soldiers furnishing recruits to teams that were springing up and in Dublin regimental sides served as opposition to clubs that were struggling to find teams to compete against. It is however possible to overstate the influence of the military in the propagation of the game. No military team had affiliated itself to the IFA by 1888 and although the following decade did see a brief spell of participation from military teams the Boer war ended that: The Royal Scots regiment withdrew from the Irish League and the King's Own Scottish Border from the Irish Cup semi-final in 1900.

The military sphere of footballing influence was strongest in areas where the game had not caught on, as it had in Ulster; the Army Cup provided a demonstration of the new sport for locals in Leinster, who went on to acknowledge the Irish Army Association as having 'proved of the greatest service in introducing the game into the South of Ireland.' In a similar vein it is thought that the first game played in Munster occurred between the 14th Irish Hussars and a local side on Boxing Day 1896.

To say there were no tensions surrounding the participation of military sides would be equally false, however; though at least one of these gripes was of a footballing nature: military teams had more time to train, their own gymnasiums, and were able to consistently field strong sides as their men were not waylaid by work commitments. Military men had resentments of their own too; being stationed in Ireland was seen as a boring assignment, with apparently little else to do 'but get noisy in a pub or try to lure a girl under a hedge.'

GROWING PAINS

On the international front, such as it was since the 'home' nations only ever competed against one another, Ireland's record by the turn of the nineteenth century was played 57, won 6 (all against Wales), drawn 5 and lost 46. The for and against column also looked much like that of a hungover pub side, 17 goals scored to 273 conceded. This included two impressive 13-0 drubbings by England, an 11-0 loss to Wales and a 10 goal concession against Scotland in Belfast.

Sectarianism and shocking score-lines aside, the thorniest issue during this period of Irish football was that of professionalism, eschewed for a long time after it had been introduced in England. The paying of players was seen as essentially vulgar by many; Cliftonville Football Club retained their amateur status until 1970, and the GAA famously remains amateur to this day.

Despite this, it is clear that at least one club had implemented professionalism in all but name, as evidenced by an 1890 advertisement in the *Belfast Evening Telegraph* offering work to '5 whitewashers, 2 tarspreaders and 4 handymen.' Linfield had officially objected to professionalism but at the same time were quite clearly practicing it: applicants were required to be 'expert players' and list their age, weight, last club and wages expected. Indeed it was from Linfield that the first Irish professional to be transferred to England originated, John Peden forging the pathway to Newton Heath (latterly Manchester United) that many of his countrymen have later followed.

By 1899, five years after the remuneration of players had grudgingly been permitted in Irish association football, eleven clubs had registered professional players. We know that around this time fourteen Roman Catholic players were plying their trade as professionals, nine of them at Belfast Celtic. Records unearthed by Neal Garnham in *Association Football and Society in Pre-partition Ireland* show professionals employed at Windsor Park in 1900 consisted of three Church of Ireland men, another three were Presbyterians, with one Congregationalist and a Jewish player making up the eight pros on the Blues books. You will have noticed the absence of any Catholics, though Belfast Celtic had at least one identifiably Protestant player named Isaac Docherty.

Though professionalism had been adopted, this was no guarantee that players were being paid enough to survive solely on their football-related income, and most of those in question would have had another form of employment. The 1901 census provides us with the example of George McMaster of Glentoran who, in addition to turning out for the east Belfast club, also earned a wage as a carpenter in the shipyards.

Every single player who signed professional forms over the course of the next few years, were playing for teams in Ulster: fifteen in Belfast, eight in Lisburn, three in County Down, with one apiece in Tyrone and Armagh. Such was the ire of some onlookers that in 1907 a cultural nationalist in Dublin decried the 'money wasted at present on professionalism' by the 'unpatriotic Protestants in the North of Ireland.'

These words echoed the comments of the GAA's founding father Michael Cusack a year earlier. He had railed against 'the foreign faction, the Orange Catholics [and] the West Britons who played football at Phoenix Park in Dublin.' Even seven years later only one side fielding professionals existed outside of Ulster, that being Shelbourne - in Dublin, ironically enough — though it was really only in Belfast where sides paid more than a handful of players.

(Though not pertaining to the partisan participants of the sport, the new professional body representing match officials at the time was the Irish Referees Association, or the IRA.)

GREEN SHOOTS

At the dawn of the outbreak of the Great War, Ireland had finally emerged from beneath the shadows of the other 'home' nations, winning the British Championship for the first time in 1913 through victories over Wales in Wrexham, an easy triumph over England in Middlesbrough and even a draw with Scotland despite an injury-weakened lineup. The liberal unionist *Northern Whig* newspaper declared that 15 February 1913, the day a ten man

Ireland - reduced by an early injury to Frank Thompson after half an hour — beat England 2-1, would 'have a place of its own in football history.' The *Belfast News Letter* calling it the 'happy consummation of the long-cherished hopes of Irish footballers.' Even the nationalist *Irish News* said that 'Ireland was asserting not merely equality with, but superiority over, her powerful neighbours.' It was victory at the thirty-second attempt, the fixture hosted in Belfast for a second consecutive year in order to rectify the IFA's balance sheet after the breakaway of most of its clubs the previous year.

Two players who featured in that triumphant Triple Crown would go on to be pioneers for the game in their own respective paths; the first was the team's captain, Patrick O'Connell, the centre-half who became a manager in Spain and Catalunya and is recognised as one of the 'misters' who popularised the game beyond the shores of Britain and Ireland, credited with saving Barcelona from bankruptcy after the Spanish Civil War. It is the second, however, where we will briefly alight on this journey.

FIGHT HIM LIKE A MAN

Louis Bookman had arrived in Cork as a nine year old with his parents, Mathias and Jane, apparently having thought the ship's captain had shouted 'New York!' The first Jewish player to grace the English top-flight, Bookman had moved to Dublin and turned out for the Adelaide Road synagogue team. It was here that his family became the Bookmans, having arrived as the Buchalters from present-day Lithuania. That was a small concession to their new surroundings, though Jane and Mathias felt that their son had gone too far: by playing football on a Saturday he was not keeping the *shabbat* holy and his chosen path was not regarded as the ideal Jewish profession.

The young man whom football writer Anthony Clavane describes as a 'Lithuanian-Jewish-Irishman' in his insightful *Does Your Rabbi Know You're Here?*, made a conscious effort to play-up his Irishness and minimise his Jewishness. Nevertheless his teammates at Bradford nick-named the winger 'Abraham' when he arrived there via a spell at Belfast Celtic. The outbreak of war would deprive him of a more complete international career, though he did gain his fifth and final cap in 'Northern' Ireland's first game after partition, a fixture versus England in October 1921 which was drawn 1-1. He was one of only three non-Belfasters to do so alongside the Billy's Lacey and Gille-spie. Conversely, that year his very *Irishness* had been firmly established when walking the streets of Dublin: at the butt of a Black and Tan's revolver he had been asked if he was an Irishman, and when he answered in the affir-mative the soldier had relieved him of his possessions.

FISSURES

By 1910 there were 420 clubs affiliated to the IFA. Even a brief schism that saw all but two senior clubs briefly secede and form the 'new Football Association' had not derailed the progress of the game. The split had lasted for a three month period, during which all but two teams temporarily seceded from its auspices, the renegade asso-ciation emerging primarily due to the IFA's intransigence, particularly over matters of finance.

The Leinster FA, a regional association second to Ulster in its strength, had been instrumental in this albeit short-lived separation, believing the Ulster FA to be a dictatorial presence within the IFA. Ulster's many dele-gates made sure its own players got international call-ups and secured the lion's share of any investment for the already privileged clubs within its jurisdiction. A Leinster Nomads delegate remarked after a heavy defeat by England that 'all this has come upon us because of the prejudice of five men who select the teams, preventing anyone outside the Belfast area being chosen to represent his country.'

It was often alleged and probably true that certain Belfast clubs — principally Linfield and Cliftonville - would invent fictitious 'junior' teams to pack out the Ulster delegation, when it came to key votes, amid concerns in certain quarters that the IFA was far more concerned about Protestantism than fair play. This bias appeared to manifest itself in the length of time it took for Belfast Celtic to be admitted to the League, and the perceived harsher punishments meted down to them when infringements occurred. There were disagreements over Sunday play too, resulting in Celtic being censured by the IFA for allowing their ground to be used for another sports meeting on a Sunday. Truthfully, Celtic wanted to be able to play matches on Sundays themselves, a wish shared by the Leinster FA. In Dublin it was thought ridiculous that games could not take place on the Sabbath but the IFA's rules stated that to even play football on a pitch on a Saturday which was also used for another sport on a Sunday was strictly forbidden.

CRACKING UP

The fault lines that would eventually break Irish football in two were already evident in Derry, a handful of miles from what would become the border which separates Ireland and Northern Ireland to this day. Though a Unionist mayor of the city had remarked that 'there was something beautiful...composed of men representing different religious persuasions and different lines of politics', by 1912 football had become just another site of sectarian strife.

On 3 December 1912, the IFA had received a letter from one of its constituent members, the North West FA, grumpily enquiring as to why it had granted permission for the formation of a Junior Alliance competition in Derry. It had, the letter explained, been 'formed out of spite' and 'to produce political feeling.' The IFA, for its part, replied there was little it could do other than outline the responsibilities of clubs within its purview.

The source of the discord was a charity match which took place in May 1912 between the Institute and Derry Guild clubs. Institute took its name from the Presbyterian Working Mens Institute in the city, the latter club deriving its nomenclature from the Derry Catholic Young Men's Society. The unionist *Londonderry Sentinel* reported that, after a foul against a Guilds' player a fight broke out between two players from either side, spreading to the large crowd which had gathered to watch the match. According to the *Sentinel,* Institute's players were trapped in their changing rooms by a crowd singing nationalist songs.

The nationalist *Derry Journal*'s account of events accepted that a fight on the pitch was the flashpoint for the incident, but countered that it was Institute's refusal to continue the game which had caused matters to spiral further. According to the newspaper, the crowd around the Institute dressing room had not been indulging in nationalist chanting and intimidation, but 'chaff and horse-play.' The political aspect of the exchanges had only come later, it was said, when a loyalist mob from the Fountain area arrived chanting anti-Home Rule slogans and throwing stones.

The *Sentinel,* on the other hand, spoke of a team of

Presbyterian men 'besieged for two hours by a howling mob', and accused a group of Catholic children of cheering the funeral cortege of an Institute player's wife. By September a new league of Protestant teams sympathetic to Institute had been created and formed a breakaway from the existing competition. The *Journal* began referring to this as the 'City of Derry and District (Protestant) Alliance', and joked about 'the holy sectarian alliance.' By New Year's Eve 1912, the IFA had no choice but to become involved, sending a delegation to Derry to hear how the Protestant clubs had in effect caused the collapse of the original league, by taking most of the teams out of it and refusing to allow a Catholic club to join their new formation. The breakaway clubs denied this was true but the damage had been done.

BREAKING UP

The advent of war brought enforced changes to Irish football. The creation of the Belfast and District League was the only way that sporting activity could realistically continue. Glenavon, some 25 miles from Belfast, were incorporated into the fold for the duration of the conflict, as well as a new side - Belfast United - lead by former Belfast Celtic manager Jimmy McGowan. Celtic themselves were temporarily absent from the fixture list because, it is said, so many of their players and fans signed up to the war effort; apparently more than all the other Belfast clubs combined.

Glenavon, however, reputedly furnished recruits to the war effort in greater numbers than any other club in the league and it was — officially, at least - for this reason that at the war's end the IFA saw fit to grant them £100 to put the club back on a stable footing. It was something that would go on to be seen as proof of the governing body's bias towards certain members, especially when less avowedly unionist sides in similar circumstances were not beneficiaries of similar financial assistance.

The Irish Cup continued to be contested on a nationwide basis, even after league football had been regionalised and when in 1921 Glenavon's semi-final fixture versus Shelbourne went to a replay the IFA decreed that it would take place in Belfast (where the first match had been played) and not Dublin as the rules indicated. Glenavon had been reticent about travelling to Leinster, their fears stemming from the fractious nature of affairs in Dublin where a curfew was in place (although an identical one existed in Belfast) and the fact that the execution of six republican prisoners was scheduled to take place just two days before the replay. Shelbourne made the understandable decision to withdraw from the cup, forfeiting the fixture.

DECREE NISI

The Football Association of Ireland was born two weeks later, when the Leinster FA began acting independently of the IFA. Though harsh treatment by the IFA was a factor in the splintering of the unified Irish game, the beginning of the end can be found in the rubble of the Irish Civil War, when travelling any great distance to play a match was simply not feasible.

In reality, the creation of the FAI was the culmination of ructions that had been stirring within the IFA for a decade or more. The league had been divided into geographic clusters since the outbreak of the Great War in 1914, and several Dublin clubs – Bohemians, St. James' Gate, and Shelbourne – had actually withdrawn from the IFA-controlled competition at the start of the 1921/22 season but continued to participate in the Irish Cup until their situation became untenable.

When it did, a meeting was convened at Molesworth Hall, Dublin and the *Cumann Peile na hÉireann* (Football Association of Ireland) was formed. If each association had seen its jurisdiction as being confined by the boundaries of their respective states, things may have been simpler. Instead, the two associations saw themselves in competition with the other across the whole island of Ireland. Some teams in Belfast played in FAI tournaments and for a while it looked as though Shelbourne and Bohemians may rejoin the IFA. It was a chaotic situation.

The virginal FAI had reason to be suspicious of the IFA: James Wilton, chairman of the Northern body, was a member of the UVF, serving as secretary of its Londonderry Division, and Thomas Moles, a member of the IFA's Emergency Committee, had been involved in loyalist gun running at Larne.

Though this was all a matter of record and despite Wilton's UVF connections, he went on to be a councillor in Derry's North Ward, elected unopposed in 1923 as a 'British Legion candidate'. He gained unanimous support of the council when he stood as mayor in 1935, and upon his death in 1946 a eulogy in the nationalist press said 'there was not a Nationalist or Catholic who knew him who had other than the kindliest word for Jemmy Wilton.' The IFA were keen to stress that they curbed the worst excesses of certain individuals, and marginalised Thomas Moles when his indiscretions became apparent. Despite its leaders links with the paramilitaries, the IFA did not want to become an official sporting wing of armed loyalism, and rejected pleas from the UVF to establish a sporting division.

CUSTODY BATTLE

Anyone who has been through a breakup can attest that these things are rarely clean, and this one could definitely be filed in the column marked 'messy'. The FAI was officially ratified on 2 September 1921, the League of Ireland having been established a few days earlier on 30 August.

Dundalk, who had opposed the split, immediately tried to rejoin IFA, and their hopeful missive was sent to the Mid-Ulster section of the IFA with a recommendation to accept. Mirroring this scenario, the Falls and District League actually *did* join the FAI and a match was organised between Shelbourne and a representative team from the Falls, with a return fixture the following month. The Falls and District League counted 23 clubs as members including Alton United, which absorbed a lot of Belfast Celtic players, while the club remained absent from the game.

After the dust had settled, the Irish Football League was left with only six senior teams: Linfield, Glentoran, Distillery, Glenavon, Queen's Island and Cliftonville. Entrance fees to matches were reduced in an attempt to provide the ailing league a stimulus, yet the IFA remained steadfast in their refusal to recognise the new body, and denied Queen's University Belfast permission to play Trinity College Dublin in the Collingwood Cup, a competition which still exists today.

The future of the League of Ireland meanwhile, was looking bright (if not Orange), mustering eight senior teams. When the cup finals came around, the FAI event boasted 15,000 attendees compared to a rather meagre 5,000 for its IFA equivalent. The outlook was not rosy for the Belfast institution, whose membership had fallen from 387 affiliated clubs in 1921 to a rather worrying 282 the following year.

Though the early indications were positive for the FAI, its pathway would not be without obstacles. Not least among these was the attitude of the Irish Free State government, which was extremely anti-soccer. Within its newly constituted army and police force, *An Garda Síochána,* Gaelic games were to be the only permitted activities for recruits. Indeed, the first commissioner of the *Garda* was unwavering in his opposition to the association game, fuming:

> “The game of the British Garrison, the atmosphere surrounding it is anglicised, and no one can contradict me when I say that the enemies of Irish freedom patronise and finance it. Ireland asks her sons to play and support our National games; the friends of the Empire ask you to play and support soccer — make your choice and for goodness sake do it at once, We welcome every Irishman to our fold who has pride in the ancient traditions of our race and who, to preserve our individuality, is prepared to cast aside everything which means to make us slaves to the mannerisms of an alien race.

It was not only in words but deeds that the Free State government made their allegiances clear, later imposing an Entertainment Tax on sports not deemed to be of Gaelic origin. Even so, the sport cast as the scourge of true Irishmen remained popular, especially in the border counties.

Post split, the Dublin clubs who had wanted to organise friendlies with teams from France, where football was and is routinely played on Sundays, were now free to do so. Football, though not alone in being split across two associations in Ireland, is at least an outlier. Rugby union continues to be competed on an All-Ireland basis to this day and cricket actually unified its Irish bodies in the 1930s. What differentiates football from these pastimes is that it was headquartered in Belfast; whereas sports with a Dublin-based governing body could continue more or less as normal.

Almost as quickly had football in Ireland been ripped apart came talks aimed at reunification. James Wilton relented from his previous hardline position, and allowed Queen's University Belfast to play University College Dublin as a gesture of his willingness to compromise. He even gave the wink to Belfast Celtic, that they could permit their ground to be used by Alton United FC to play Shelbourne in an FAI cup match, though in what must have been a bit of a morale-sapper for the infant FAI, Alton went on to win the Free State Cup final 1-0 against Fordson FC of Cork on St Patrick's Day 1923.

That Summer, Shelbourne, Bohemians and a number of other FAI-affiliated clubs thought about re-affiliating to the IFA, because their parent body's lack of international recognition meant that trying to arrange friendlies or tours outside of the twenty-six counties was almost impossible. However, the threat of departure diminished significantly once the campaign to get international recognition seemed to be gathering pace: FIFA's reluctance to do anything that would upset the English FA - despite it no longer being a member of the world organisation — had caused one observer to remark that it was 'like slicing water with a knife.' The FAI could claim with some credibility that they had clubs in all four of Ireland's provinces, while the entirety of the IFA's membership was contained in just one.

DECREE ABSOLUTE

Clarity as to the governance of the game in Ireland - or at least a semblance of it — was imposed by FIFA in 1923. The Dublin-based FA had first applied to join football's world governing body in 1922, but its initial application was rejected. After reunification talks with the Northern body were unable to reach a compromise, it was accepted into the world game as the Football Association of the Irish Free State (FAIFS). This was on the condition that it was responsible only for the twenty-six counties, while the IFA retained control of the game in the other six. The Falls League in west Belfast (under the patronage of Belfast Celtic) could no longer be affiliated with the thegoverning body down south, but the matter of who would organise football internally in each nation had been solved for now. The international game was another matter. Despite finally achieving international status, the FAIFS still felt it was being ill-treated. Their 1926/27 season end report decried 'the stupid policy of labelling the small Northern Province as Ireland continues to be favoured by England, Scotland and Wales so that the Northern Association has no incentive to come to an agreement.' Much of this annoyance stemmed from the fact that gate receipts from a single match against the English at Dublin's Dalymount Park, would have funded their operations for an entire year, yet progress remained elusive.

Another persistent irritation was the IFA continuing to select players without reference to the border, a practice they would not cease until 1950. This meant there were a handful of players at any given time over those thirty years who were competing for both the Irish Free State and Northern Ireland, often in the course of the same week because, as Con Martin explained, 'With a fixed wage ceiling in operation, there wasn't huge money to be made in football, so when the chance came to play for Northern Ireland, I didn't need a second invitation to accept.' Aston Villa's chairman, Fred Normansell, had friends in Dublin, and told Martin that he would make up any money Martin would lose out on by turning his back on the North. Johnny Carey was another such individual, playing against England twice in three days on 28 and 30 September 1946. Among those who opted out early were Tom Farquharson, a goalkeeper who eventually put his principles before cash, having won seven caps for Northern Ireland between 1923–25. By then, strong republican beliefs had been instilled within him by Sean Lemass, who served as *Taoiseach* from 1959 until 1966, and with whom he had pulled down British Army posters, for which they were arrested.

THE GLORY YEARS

When the Falls League fell, Belfast Celtic returned to the IFA fold for the commencement of the 1924 season, its players having lost their alternative competition. The sectarian situation in Belfast was looking marginally better than it had a few years previously, too. Celtic had removed themselves from the playing field in 1919, threatening legal action against the IFA, when the governing body suggested that money would be deducted from the club's gate receipts to pay for damage sustained during *that* fixture against Glentoran.

Ultimately the Hoops were successful in forcing a climbdown by the Irish FA, but decided not to field a team the next season (or indeed the 3 after that). The feeling was that it was too dangerous to do so, especially between 1920 and 1922, during which Belfast and the surrounding area witnessed the killing of 450 and the wounding of 1,100 more. In 1920 around 11,000 Catholic workers had been expelled from their jobs in the shipyards, a sequence of events more than one observer saw fit to describe as a pogrom.

It was in February 1924 that Celtic agreed to re-enter for the league the following campaign. In their opening fixture that Summer they played Glenavon and those who made the trip saw Celtic win 3-1, with Sammy Mahood scoring a brace to help them on their way to victory. The club's first game back at Celtic Park was witnessed by 22,000, a match against Linfield that passed off with little trouble. Celtic would finish third that season, winning the league the following year. Their great rivals Linfield were in the midst of a crisis, slumping to seventh place at the end of the 1926/27 season.

The situation on the island of Ireland had de-escalated from its peak in the early 1920s, but there was still some crowd trouble at Irish Football League games, albeit at a relatively low level. An uptick in disorder was not seen again until the 1930s: early in the new decade the Ulster Protestant League had been formed, encouraging Protestant employers and landowners to hire only workers who were their co-religionists.

This effort was given high profile support by Basil Brooke, a future Prime Minister of Northern Ireland, who was then serving as Minister of Agriculture. He gave a speech explaining, 'I recommend to those people who are loyalists not to employ Roman Catholics, ninety-nine per cent of whom are disloyal', boasting that on his country estate in Fermanagh he employed not one Catholic. On 12 July the previous year he had made similar remarks at an Orange rally, 'Many in this audience employ Catholics, but I have not one about my place. Catholics are out to destroy Ulster with all their might...I would appeal to loyalists therefore, whenever possible, to employ good

Protestant lads and lasses.' The serving Prime Minister uttered similar remarks, telling an audience, 'I have always said I am an Orangeman first and a politician and member of this Parliament afterwards...They still boast of Southern Ireland being a Catholic state. All I boast is that we are a Protestant Parliament and a Protestant State.'

Unemployment was high among Protestants and higher still for Catholics; Belfast's shipbuilding industry was on the wane after several strong decades, and in 1933 no ships were launched onto the River Lagan from its slipway. The Wall Street crash had affected the city more than those with more diverse employment bases, and the Workman and Clark yard closed in the teeth of financial ruin in 1935.

Upon its folding, a curtain was drawn across fifty-five years of east Belfast history; the 'wee yard' had been the brainchild of Frank Workman and George Clarke - both of whom had served pupillages at the 'big yard' of Harland and Wolff - and just six years after its founding boasted 3,500 employees. When its assets were acquired by its larger rival following its winding up it had launched 530 ships of its own. That same year violence erupted before Belfast Celtic's contest with Linfield that year when a Catholic pipe band was attacked while playing at half-time; and again later in the season during the Hoops cup game against Crusaders, a team from the staunchly loyalist Shore Road district in north Belfast.

By January 1937, the constabulary had become so concerned about violence at football matches that the houses of several Celtic supporters were raided in search of weapons, though the most notable incident was at a Derry City v Linfield fixture, after which the pitch was invaded as fans attempted to gain access to the pavilion. It was another eventful year: the Irish Free State declared its constitution, setting alarm bells ringing in the North due to its claiming the 'national territory is the whole island of Ireland.' Furthermore, Article 44 acknowledged the special position of the Catholic church in the new Republic, and Article 8 specified Irish as its official language..

Just as some twenty-five years previously it was war, first on a European and then a global scale, which turned attentions away from domestic matters. The Irish Football League completed the 1939/40 season, at which point it was suspended with Belfast Celtic as reigning champions, beating Linfield on their way by five goals to nil. The war years would see them compete in a six-team regional mini-league, centred around Belfast, and when the full league resumed for the 1947/48 season the standards between the teams competing had become wildly variable: Linfield had beaten Coleraine 10-5 in one particularly exciting fixture.

PITCH BATTLE IV - Linfield 1 - 1 Belfast Celtic, Windsor Park, 27 December 1948

> *'When we had nothing, we had Belfast Celtic;*
> *When we had Belfast Celtic, we had everything.'*
> Popular saying in west Belfast during the 1930s

For having the temerity to play for Belfast Celtic, a twenty year old Jimmy Jones had his leg broken by a small group of Linfield fans, intent on causing deliberate injury to a man they saw as a legitimate target. Legitimate, in their eyes, because he was a traitor: a Protestant playing for Belfast's foremost Catholic team in the late forties. His cousin Jack was a former Linfield player, so why was he playing for the enemy? Tensions between unionists and nationalists were rising once more after the

Second World War, during which the southern state had remained neutral, to the chagrin of the British government and Orangemen in the North. In the coming months, John Costello would declare Ireland a republic, secede from the Commonwealth and announce himself *Taoiseach* of all of Ireland 'no matter what the Irish in the North say.' Counteractively, the British government would pass the Ireland Act which stated that, 'in no event will Northern Ireland or any part thereof cease to be part of His Majesty's dominions and of the United Kingdom without the consent of the Parliament of Northern Ireland.' Everything was at stake once again. The story of Belfast Celtic spans fifty-eight years and includes periods of dominance over their bitter rivals from across the way, yet the afternoon of 27 December 1948 is a violently accurate summary of their time as members of the Irish League. Being one of the best supported clubs in Ulster, the fact that they were a club formed by Irish nationalists with a predominantly Catholic fanbase, made them a lightning-rod for retribution from unionists with a grievance about matters not strictly pertaining to football. Their spectacular clashes with Linfield in 1912 and again thirty-six years later, are the best known, but these were snapshots among a litany of others, often against rivals less bitter than Linfield or Glentoran. Sometimes the blame could be apportioned a little more towards the Hoops, at others it lay at the feet of their opponents. Pieced together, they help to explain Celtic's eventual permanent cessation of fixtures in 1949.

Both teams had played on the day before. Celtic had travelled to Ballymena, beating them easily. Linfield had faced off against Glentoran, whom they brushed off with a couple of goals to spare. Their home grounds just half a mile apart, the biggest game was the next day: the Falls versus the Shankill, a crowd of 27,000 present hoping that their boys would give them a belated Christmas gift when the game kicked off at 2.15pm

Already on twenty-six goals half-way through the season, Jimmy Jones was a gifted player. This inevitably brought more attention than might otherwise have been given to him. Then there was the incident in the first-half of the game when an unfortunate collision with Bob Bryson broke the Linfield man's ankle. Crucially, the Blues club secretary, Joe Mackey, announced over the tannoy that Bryson's *leg* had been broken, identifying Jones as the opponent responsible. Add to this the fact that he was playing for the *wrong* team and you would expect a spirited atmosphere in any football match, anywhere in the world. But this was not anywhere, this was Belfast.

Even with so much of the season left, it was already looking like this game would be a league decider. If the stakes were not already high enough, it was played out against the backdrop of an impending Northern Irish election, called to reaffirm the case for partition in light of Ireland's new found independence from the commonwealth. Basil Brooke told the electorate 'We are fighting for our very existence.'

When Norman Boal had blown the half-time whistle, Linfield had only nine men left on the field, after Alex Russell had joined Bryson on the injury list. Two more were to depart the field before the end of play; Celtic's left-footer, Paddy Bonnar, and Albert Currie of Linfield, were both shown red cards for their sins. The game ended with the Blues counting eight men on the pitch, to the ten of their rivals in green and white.

As Jimmy Jones exited the field, the final score was 1-1 owing to Billy Simpson's late equaliser. Linfield fans spilled onto the pitch to relieve an outpouring of the tensions which had been fizzing in the unsegregated stands over the course of the tie. It had been a brutal affair but worse was to come. 'When I saw uniformed police throwing their caps in the air with delight [at Linfield's equaliser]' one Celtic player remarked, 'I realised that we were not going to have much protection at the end of the game.'

The Bluemen had easily crossed the inadequate barriers around the perimeter of the playing field, heading towards the Celtic players, of whom Jones was the furthest away from safety. Any trace of festive goodwill had vanished, as they began to hurl abuse at the striker they perceived to be 'fair game'. His mother and father could only look on as the verbal abuse turned physical; a sustained and entirely purposeful battering of the young man buried under a mass of assailants, many of whom were drunk on more than Christmas cheer.

Each time he tried to escape, he was pulled back into the fray, thirty or so men unleashing an unremitting beating on the prone youngster until he was rescued by the arrival of a gaggle of Royal Ulster Constabulary (RUC) officers and a friend, Sean McGann. His life was saved when he reached the Musgrave and Clark clinic but the same could barely be said of his leg.

Jones remarked in the days after the game 'I tried to get up but the leg just hung limply.' He was officially a minor in the eyes of the law at the time, so it was required that his father lodge an appeal for compensation from the Belfast Corporation, the body ultimately responsible for the safety at football grounds in the city. He won, receiving £4,361 in damages — or about £143,000 in today's money – a calculation equating to ten years of potential earnings. Mercifully, he kept his leg, too. The assault on him was described by the esteemed Northern Irish football journalist Malcolm Brodie as 'probably the most vicious assault on any player in the history of British football.' Kevin McAlinden and Robin Lawler, two of

Jones' teammates, were also attacked by the Linfield mob and required lengthy hospital treatment.

The surgeon would have amputated the leg were he not a sportsman, although one — it's not reported which – was noticeably shorter than the other. The leg had to be re-set four times, with the young man spending seven weeks in hospital. Happily, Jones went on to have a football career despite the judgement of the Belfast court, spending eleven years playing for Glenavon before rising to the position of manager.

For Celtic, the match was the last straw. They limped on until the end of the 1948/49 season, rattling ten past Distillery in their next game, but things would never be the same again. Their directors saw Linfield FC and the RUC as responsible for allowing the situation to spiral out of control, with particular scrutiny on the role of the police, as the club's statement in the hours after the game makes clear:

> During the whole of this concerted attack the protection afforded to the unfortunate players may be fairly described as quite inadequate. In the circumstances the directors wish to make the strongest possible protest against the conduct of those responsible for the protection of the players in failing to take measures either to prevent the brutal attack or to deal with it with any degree of effectiveness after it developed.

The unionist establishment did not concur with this view. Harry Midgeley, Linfield chairman and an Ulster Unionist member of the Northern Irish parliament at Stormont, issued a statement expressing his disgust and condemnation, concluding that 'no incident on the field could justify conduct so alien to the high Linfield tradition.' The RUC, for their part, conceded no arrests had been made in relation to events of that afternoon.

In the local press, a letter writer to the *Belfast Telegraph* made criticism of the referee, going on to say that Linfield would 'do well to recognise that sport should not be prostituted with politics or religion.' Another letter writer 'Ashamed Bluesman', suggested that 'some of the missionaries who leave these shores should stay at home', while yet another, 'Lisburn Road', said that he and eighteen others would boycott Linfield until the hooligan element was brought under control.

Within nationalist circles it was whispered that Celtic should attempt to join the League of Ireland, especially when Linfield appeared to be dealt with very leniently by the IFA. They were banned from Windsor Park for just one month, or two home games which were to be played at Solitude instead, allowing them to collect the full gate receipts and pay Cliftonville a small fee to use their ground.

Harry Diamond, a Republican Socialist member of parliament for the Falls, including Celtic Park, fumed that 'this million pound force [the RUC] brought shame to the city!' He inferred that the police had gone easy on the Linfield fans by not readily drawing their batons, as they would have against nationalists, adding 'It was current in the city that there was going to be trouble at this match. The name of a right honourable member of this House was associated with the promotion of that trouble.'

For this rather tame outburst, his language was ruled out of order by the Speaker. Neither did Midgeley take too kindly to the remarks of which he was the target, angrily responding that 'all they want is that members of the community, including the ill-mannered and badly conducted people whom Mr Diamond represents, respect the law.' Later, he would add the qualifier 'some of' the people.'

Diamond further accused Midgeley of leading the singing of 'bitter sectarian songs which were an incitement to the players', during private events at which Linfield players were in attendance. Midgeley pushed back against the charge on behalf of 'the illustrious, honourable and high-traditioned club', of which he was chairman, recalling a similar incidence of disorder in 1920, where Belfast Celtic fans had produced revolvers, for which 'Paradise' was closed as punishment.

Arguing that he could not control every section of his club's supporters, as no club could, he went on to allege that Diamond was trying to discredit the Northern Irish state by dragging down its foremost football club. Regarding Diamond's primary accusation he retorted 'what we do at our private functions is a matter entirely for ourselves and for those who control our club. If we choose to sing Christmas carols...and to follow that with [singing] "The Sash My Father Wore", we are perfectly entitled to do so. The Belfast Celtic club have their favourite types of songs which they have a right to sing if they wish to do so.'

A week later Eddie McAteer, a Nationalist MP, would again raise the matter, asking why the police had not been able to step in more quickly. The Ulster Unionist Minister of Home affairs, Edmond Warnock, said Nationalists were making hay out of the events for 'political purposes' in order to 'blacken the name of the RUC', which in any case was 'impartial.' It was a state of affairs reflective of the contempt which each side of the sectarian divide held the other in.

FIRE SALE

Soon after that infamous afternoon, the Celtic board began to offload their best players to English clubs, with everything pointing to a club who were winding up their affairs. Whether they wanted to drop out of the game forever (or not) is unclear, but their Summer tour to the USA (which Jimmy Jones was devastated to miss out on) had all the hallmarks of a farewell to the game. It was during this trip across the Atlantic that the team was lead around a stadium by someone carrying an Irish flag, a moment fraught with tension for their half-dozen Protestant players with unionist families back home, including their captain Harry Walker.

When they returned, Celtic did not re-enter the League and on 29 May 1949, Crusaders of north Belfast were co-opted to take their place. There was no way back for them in the short term and although the club remained affiliated to the IFA for many years after their last game, this option was never taken. In their lifetime, Belfast Celtic had won fourteen league championships and eight Irish Cups, a record only bettered by their fiercest of rivals from Windsor Park.

The original Belfast Big Two rivalry was no more. Linfield had won the league by five points in Celtic's final season, and while it's scarcely imaginable that such fixtures could have been played when the Troubles began to rage a couple of decades later, the Celtic directors can hardly be blamed for refusing to put the players at increased risk. Austin Donnelly, the club's chairman, is said to have told his players, 'we can't let you boys put up with the likes of that.'

As renowned Derry football journalist Frank Curran concluded many years later: 'They knew that it wasn't a football problem, and that there was nothing they as a football club could do to end it. So they got out.' Still, their disappearance from the landscape surely left the Irish League a poorer place and deprived one part of Belfast of a senior team to call its own for many years.

Former player Jimmy Donnelly concurred, 'With the demise of Celtic, west Belfast lost a facet of life that was part of the social fabric of the area.' Speaking decades later, one Celtic fan described it as 'like a black cloud coming down, as if there was nothing to live for or look forward to on a Saturday. It's a grief which never went away.'

3

PLAYING AT HOME

In 1858, Edward James Harland acquired a small shipyard on Queen's Island from his employer Robert Hickson for £4,900. He could scarcely have known his investment would come to be woven into the fabric of the city. Back then, just one hundred men counted on the yard for their paycheque, and Belfast was a mere town among towns. That was all about to change.

Harland took on his distant cousin Gustav Wolff, first as a designer and later as a full partner in the firm. It was Wolff's uncle, Gustav Schwabe, who had provided the finance required to fund the purchase of the yard. As well as supplying a loan, Schwabe lined up potential customers for his young relatives; his own involvement in Liverpool's Bibby Line meant welcome first entries into the order book of the new company: construction of the *Venetian*, the *Sicilian* and the *Syrian*.

By 1888, Belfast's population eclipsed that of Dublin for the first time. Construction of homes in the 1890s was running at a rate of 2,000 new dwellings every year: it was a city with a purpose. As the nineteenth century rolled into the twentieth, Harland and Wolff were employing thousands of men in a wide variety of roles including welders, riveters, platers, plumbers, painters, carpenters, designers and naval architects.

Straddling the River Lagan, Belfast was the very model of a company town; in 1899 the shipyards of Harland and Wolff began operating on a twenty-four hour basis, employing nearly 10,000 men, working eight hour shifts throughout the day and night. In the eight years from 1901 to 1909, the Harland yard, alongside Workman and Clark's 'wee yard' were responsible for a combined 1.2 million tons of shipping, 50 per cent more than the Swan Hunter company on the Tyne. In the three that followed, the total tonnage of output from Workman and Clark, specialists in cargo ships and with a workforce of 9,000 workers, would surpass that of the 'big yard'.

Many of the men who supplied this were coming from the banks of the River Clyde in Glasgow, and the Wear in Sunderland, two other great shipbuilding cities as well as hotbeds of the burgeoning working class pastime of association football. Some of them were even half-decent, and they helped the north east corner of Ireland become the nation's hub of footballing activity, as older pros who had plied their best years in the English game came over in the hope of finding a club to see out their final years as footballers.

The cost of housing in Belfast was relatively low, compared to elsewhere in Britain and Ireland and because it was easier for women to find work, their real incomes were potentially higher than almost any other corner of Edwardian society. It was into this world that many young men, footballers themselves and the fathers and grandfathers of some of Northern Ireland's future legends, came in search of work.

Derek Dougan was the scion of one such economic

migrant, albeit an internal one: his grandfather began his new life as a boilermaker at Harland and Wolff and retired from his time there as a foreman. He was a skilful enough footballer to have attracted the interest of a couple of Scottish clubs, thought to be Hibs and Hearts, but Dougan Senior's penchant for pigeon racing prevented him from following that path, as he could not take his prized specimen over the Irish sea with him.

Indeed, so keen a pigeon fancier was Sandy Dougan, that shortly after Derek was born in 1938, his parents Jackie and Josie moved into a house on Avon Street in east Belfast next door to Sandy's. The two properties were chosen because together they shared a large pigeon loft. Dougan's sister remembers it well, telling his biographer David Tossell in his book *In Sunshine or In Shadow*: 'it was two up two down and you had your outside loo. You came out the house at the back and that was where the pigeon shed was. Once the pigeons were there that was the big thing for my daddy. You couldn't go out the back if there was a race on, oh my God, no. He raced them every weekend and he was good, but going out there was a no-no because he was clapping them in.'

Derek would go on to captain the Northern Ireland team that beat England 1-0 at Wembley in 1972 but was to remain in Belfast until football took him away to Portsmouth. He honed his craft on the playground, finding a footballing home at Mersey Street School when he was nine. 'East Belfast was a place of its own and Mersey Street School was an important part of it,' Dougan wrote in *The Sash He Never Wore*, looking back on his time there. The 'east' aspect of his recollection cannot be overstated. 'All the men and boys were one hundred per cent Protestant. Within our area, which was a couple of miles square, there wasn't a single Catholic living,' he recalled some years later, perhaps striking a more ominous tone than had been intended.

The young Dougan would not knowingly meet a Catholic individual until he had been in education for several years: 'The first time I came across a Catholic would have been when I was eleven years old, and I was playing centre-half for Mersey Street School. We were drawn in the Belfast Schools' Cup and played a team from Ardoyne - a Catholic School.' To anyone living outside of Ulster this might sound remarkable, but for a young boy growing up in post-war Belfast it was perfectly normal, even mundane.

He would eventually go on to play for Cregagh Boys Club at inside-left. That club's most famous graduate would emerge onto the scene just a few years later but Dougan, ever the pragmatist, had chosen Cregagh because he believed it offered him a better chance of game time than would have been the case if he had joined the Boyland Boys Club. It was while on the road with a Boys Clubs' of Belfast team that he became aware of life outside Northern Ireland, travelling to Dublin aged fourteen or fifteen to play representative team from the southern city, the young man's first foray into the Republic.

Like most young schoolboys of a footballing persuasion, there was always time for a kickabout. Dougan and his friends chose to play theirs on a patch of barren wasteland which they nicknamed 'The Meadow'. These matches would take place on weekday evenings after school until the light faded, reconvening for an all day session on Sundays. Players dipped in and out as and when their presence was required elsewhere, the scoreline moving into the thirties and forties as the day wore on. 'It was rough stuff, a hurly burly. But I learned how to avoid crunching tackles and how to use my initiative.'

Continuing his education at Belfast Technical High

School meant Dougan could prolong his spell in the Irish Schools International team, and he reflected in his autobiography: 'two or three of the players were Catholic - but those of us who weren't had a respect for their football and that was a good enough reason for thinking other things unimportant.' Dougan had fond memories of his time at 'Tech', describing it as a 'marvellous experience in itself, because it educated me in the lay-out and character of the city. I had to catch a bus that went over the Queen's Bridge, round by the docks, and right through the city centre itself. I got off at the City Hall, and walked past the Athletic Stores and arrived at the school.'

That same school had seen Billy Bingham and Danny Blanchflower pass through its hallways just a few years earlier. Bingham, in particular, was a hero to Dougan, seven years his junior. The older man was a regular for Glentoran until he was sold to Sunderland in 1950, and by the end of the decade he and Dougan would be turning out for Northern Ireland together.

The period after the Second World War (during which the infant Dougan had been evacuated to his maternal grandparents home in Bangor), saw tensions in Belfast and beyond ratchet up once again — as if they had ever gone away - and both men evidently regarded football as a means of injecting a bit of fun into a society plagued not only by sectarianism but post-war austerity and, for Protestants at least, a fiercely puritanical civil society. Bingham explained, 'Playing football as a schoolboy was what you did just after [the] war and if you were good enough you got picked to play for your country. Then you might have a choice of Linfield or Glentoran or, if you were a Catholic, Belfast Celtic. But things just tended to happen; you were just stepping up to the next rung of the ladder without really thinking where it could lead — even though you knew that scouts would be there watching your games.'

In his 1972 autobiography, Dougan recounted very much yearned to climb those rungs as quickly as possible, casting his mind back to his days as a teenager in the early fifties. 'Football was my only outlet, my only means. What did I want to get away from? I'm not sure that it had taken any kind of definite shape in my mind.' Football was to be his escape from the land with which he had such a conflicted relationship but he did not know it yet. After leaving education and getting a job at Triang, a factory which manufactured toys, Dougan began training with Linfield two nights a week on Tuesdays and Thursdays while continuing to play for Cregagh in the Boys Club League which ran from September to May. His grandfather — he of the pigeon fancying - had been on the fringes of the Linfield team as a half-back in his day, and Dougan would surely have been happy to follow in those footsteps.

It was not to be. He could not break into the team, which is perhaps not surprising given that he was fourteen. Neither were Glentoran convinced of his abilities when he was scouted by them, indicating that he probably would not even make it into their fourth team. This was a team he would have loved to have turned out for: he had fond memories of going to the Oval as an eight year-old in 1946 to, in Belfast parlance, catch 'smicks', which — before you ask - are tadpoles.

Dougan's memories of Saturday nights in the family home paint a picture of a closely held rivalry between those two great bastions of Belfast football. His grandfather, the former Blueman, was of course a Windsor Park devotee, yet his aunt and uncle were staunch Glentoran fans and 'even if the wee Glens beat Linfield decisively, three or four nil, he would give no credit to them.'

It was further across the city at Distillery where Dougan got his first chance. When he joined the Whites in 1953 at the age of 15 it was not the first time he had played at their Grosvenor Park ground, having appeared there during his year at Belfast Technical High School in a schoolboy international against Scotland. It would take until 5 February 1955 however, until his debut in an Irish Cup match against Glenavon: the match ended goalless, before Distillery lost the replay four days later.

It was a start. Preston North End had sent a scout, although the *Belfast Telegraph* report must have made for grim reading, noting 'seldom did he see the ball, let alone gain possession.' Over the next year or so, the seventeen year-old Dougan bounced between the first and reserve teams, learning his footballing trade and some life lessons too. Grosvenor Park was located in west Belfast and the team had a history of fielding Scottish players of both faiths.

It is almost certain that this aspect of Dougan's routine brought him into regular contact with Catholics, more than anything else that was going on in his life at the time. Reminiscing on the start of his career he explained, 'Those teams I played for in the middle fifties were mixed sides of Protestant and Catholic players. We also had two or three Scots over, and even they were mixed - Scottish Protestant and Scottish Catholic.' Indeed, a year before Dougan's death in July 2007, he spoke with immense warmth of his time there, telling the BBC in his typically robust style that playing for Distillery 'was the happiest period of my entire footballing career and that was brought about by the camaraderie of the players. If you believe people who should know better there is a terrible conflict between Protestants and Catholics. I genuinely don't believe there is. I played on a team that was six Protestants and five Catholics.'

The Distillery club seems to have been a place of relative peace in the pre-Troubles era, which gives a poignancy to the club's exile from its home and eventual departure from Belfast, after Grosvenor Park was firebombed in 1972. Norman Uprichard played in goal for Distillery before being transferred to Arsenal in 1948 and described it as a 'nice, friendly place' in his book *Norman 'Black Jake' Uprichard,* co-authored with Chris Westcott, adding that he 'would finish work about five and on Tuesdays and Thursdays I'd get up to Grosvenor Park. We would train between 5.30pm and 7pm and then have a bath or a shower. The terraces would be packed when we played one of the big clubs, Glentoran or Linfield and really it was up to you if you progressed or not. If you did well you would be noticed.'

Uprichard had agreed to join Distillery because they would pay his expenses for every home and away trip he was involved in. When he left his previous employ as an apprentice textile fitter under a cloud, the Distillery reserve team trainer, Dick Meek, got him a new job with a sprinkler company called Mather and Platt, which also brought a significant pay rise. The company was based on Belfast's Bedford Street and brought him into close contact with Charlie Tully and Jimmy Jones - both of Uprichard's favourite boyhood club, Belfast Celtic - who also worked there. Indeed, Uprichard regularly travelled to work on the back of Jones' motorbike.

Then, as now, the Irish League operated on a semi-professional basis. Most players are paid a very modest amount by their clubs, but it is not a full-time living for all but a handful of players. In the early fifties playing for an English First or Second Division side would definitely pay the bills, though most players would need a career to fall back on once their playing days were over and some would take on additional jobs before they were signed as professionals, or during the off-season.

The long and short of it is that during Dougan's time at Distillery, he needed another job and it seems Derek barely had any input in his own employment, describing in his autobiography how, 'As my grandfather worked in the shipyard, and my father worked in the shipyard, my mother decided that my future lay in the shipyard as well, and I was never asked about it. They decided I should be an electrician.' So it was. Here was Dougan following in the footsteps of his father, two uncles and a grandfather, noting in his comically overblown fashion 'We had our traditions to follow, just as they do in England. There a man goes to school at Eton and his sons will go there. He goes to Oxford, or Cambridge, and his sons consequently do likewise.'

It was more than just a family thing. He was also treading the path of his hero William 'Billy' Laurie Bingham. Born in August 1931, in a two-up, two-down terraced house on Woodstock Road in east Belfast under the shadow of the Harland and Wolff yard, Bingham left school at sixteen to become an apprentice electrical engineer in that very shipyard. 'I used to get out of the shipyard and do early training before the others arrived. I reckoned I was getting better and I wanted to be fitter than the other guys,' he recalled of that time, as reported in *Billy: A Biography of Billy Bingham*. Billy signed as an amateur for Glentoran's third team, 'Co-op Rec', aged sixteen in 1947, playing in the Northern Ireland Amateur League. He was risking his job by ducking out of work early so often, so he must have had some self-confidence but his trajectory was good: just as he turned seventeen, Bingham became a part-time pro, earning £6 a week in footballing wages.

Six months after he had made his senior debut in

March 1949 in a 1-1 draw with Ballymena United, he was on his way to Sunderland; a migration in the opposite direction to so many of his compatriots in the shipyards a few decades earlier. Just eighteen when he made the move, he carried on with his apprenticeship at Doxford's on Wearside. His tremendous belief had paid off, but this was not the moneyed football of the Premier League era, even if he had joined the club that were known as the 'Bank of England' during the early fifties. A man needed a safety net: if he could not get a job in football after his playing days were over, how would he provide for himself and his family?

Bingham had been raised in the Bloomfield district of Belfast between the Beersbridge and Upper Newtonards Road by 'thrifty Presbyterian' parents, growing up in the street adjoining that of his future Northern Ireland team-mates Jackie and Danny Blanch flower. His father, also called William, earned his living as driller at Harland and Wolff; while his mother brought in extra money as a spinner at the linen mill when there was enough work about. Young Billy had finessed his skills on the streets of Dunraven and Orangefield Park (immortalised in song by Van Morrison), attending Elmgrove Elementary School on the Beersbridge Road. 'As a lad I'd go throwing stones at Catholic lads from the Short Strand which was just across the road. It was nothing personal. We didn't understand the larger picture,' he told journalist and broadcaster Eamon Dunphy on the eve of his retirement as a football manager in 1993. After Elmgrove, it was a scholarship to Belfast Tech, which meant he could stay on in education past the age of fourteen. He would go from playing for his school to playing for his country in just four years.

Later, Dougan got his own transfer to England, and it was suggested to him by Portsmouth manager Eddie Lever that he should complete his apprenticeship in the dockyard there, as Bingham had done in Sunderland. After initially telling Lever and his father that he would do so, Derek changed his mind: it would be another two years before it would be complete, and he decided he was going to England to become a full-time professional 'or nothing at all.'

On the Monday following his agreeing a deal with Portsmouth, he went to the shipyard 'delighted' to let them know he would no longer be on their payroll; they already knew though, as it had been in the Belfast papers that weekend. He would later write scathingly of his time in the Belfast shipyards, and the 6.30am starts that working there often entailed: 'I always found it an effort to go down there every day. Men went there because there was nowhere else to go to work,' adding that, 'ritual meant that you ended up there whether you like it or not; that is, if you came from the class and district I was brought up in, Dee Street and Avon Street told you which way you should go in more ways than one.'

'Working in a shipyard, or working in a factory, if you are not cut out for it, is like a jail sentence,' he wrote. After all, he had only gone into the shipyard in the first place as he knew it would make his mother happy: 'I simply couldn't look forward to half a century of going down to the same mundane and repetitive job every day when I knew in my heart and in my mind that I had a special skill. This could involve me in a profession I loved. Football was really the only thing I wanted to do.'

Happily for the young Dougan most of the electricians he worked with were football fans, either of Linfield or Glentoran. Once the work for the day was done, he was allowed by his colleagues to leave early and do some extra training at Grosvenor Park. 'When I was able to sneak away for two or three hours the electricians I was working with would kindly check in my board for me —

which was against the rule,' he explained, noting that in the year before his departure to England's south coast he was not exactly a model employee. Being a minor local celebrity granted him some leeway at the shipyard, though, and he was even allowed ten days off to play a youth international tournament in the 1954/55 season.

DANNY AS A BOY

Billy Bingham's near-neighbour Robert Dennis 'Danny' Blanchflower was born on 10 February 1926. The first-born, his parents John and Selina went on to have another two boys and two girls whom they brought up on Grace Avenue in the Dunraven Park district. It was his mother who was the footballing pioneer of the family, playing for a women's team in Belfast by the name of Roebucks as an inside-forward. His father was a craftsman as well as a keen jazz musician and Jackie Blanchflower recalled hearing how dad had played in bands at the 'curfew dances', which had sprung up in Belfast in the aftermath of partition, so called because the disturbances that were commonplace at the time meant that Belfast (and Dublin, for that matter) were under a military curfew that ran from 10pm to 6am. To get round this, dances would start just before the 10pm deadline and end when it was lifted the following morning.

His schooling at Ravenscroft Elementary and Belfast Tech complete, Danny was approached by Glentoran just shy of his sixteenth birthday in 1942. He had come to their attention playing for Bloomfield United, a team he had set up and run himself. Such was his youthful resourcefulness, that he had acquired some shirts for ten shillings and set about putting a team comprised of his friends and acquaintances together to play in the East Belfast Summer League. The great Peter Doherty was playing for Glentoran and the young Danny eagerly signed amateur forms for a team that allowed him to be within the same orbit as a man who he held in such high regard. Yet he was young and small; unable to break into the team; he became disillusioned, drifting back to Bloomfield United where he would at least be guaranteed a regular game.

Soon he would be whisked away from Northern Ireland in the ranks of the RAF, despite the absence of conscription in Northern Ireland during the Second World War. This historical curiosity can be comprehended when one considers the delicate domestic situation of the time. Northern Ireland had an avowedly Unionist government at Stormont, keen to demonstrate its willingness in the war effort. Indeed the Prime Minister of Northern Ireland, Lord Craigavon, told the House of Commons in Westminster on 4 September 1939 that 'We here today are in a state of war and we are prepared with the rest of the United Kingdom and Empire to face all the responsibilities that imposes on the Ulster people.' Yet the British government came to the conclusion by 1941 that introducing conscription in Northern Ireland would, as the minutes from a cabinet meeting noted, be 'more trouble than it was worth.'

There had been fierce opposition from the Irish nationalist community, as well as trade unionists. Furthermore, the governments in Ireland, the United States, Canada and Australia had advised the British that they believed it would be an unwise move. Knowing that if they pressed ahead with it, there would be mass demonstrations on nationalist streets across the country, the decision was made that Northern Ireland's contribution to the British forces would be on a voluntary basis, as it had been in the First World War.

Before Danny's basic training in Canada was complete, the war was over. He had joined up voluntarily as 31,000 of his fellow countrymen had done. Indeed, although their service was of a different nature to that of their male counterparts, 7,000 women had also volunteered. Even with its larger population, it is perhaps surprising that a further 43,000 volunteers had enlisted from the Republic of Ireland, which would leave the Commonwealth by 1949.

Though victory for the Allies had been won, Danny remained stationed at Kings Lynn in Norfolk where the actor Richard Burton was also posted. With no war left to fight the men were allowed to do pretty much as they pleased, and Danny and his comrades played a lot of football. It was while home on leave during the Christmas of 1945 that he was again invited to turn out for Glentoran. This time he got a shot in the reserves and the old concerns about his physical strength had been dispelled, toughened up through his military exertions of the previous few years. He must have played well since he was called up to the first team's next match against the Belfast Celtic. Glentoran's fortunes were not great: the Oval had been heavily bombed during the Blitz, forcing the team into playing their home games at Distillery's Grosvenor Park.

Blanchflower's plan had been to stay in the RAF and progress through the ranks but his Yuletide interlude with Glentoran had reignited in him the desire to give his football career another go. Offered £50 as a signing on fee and £3 a game, he committed himself until the end of the season. It was only a few weeks later that he realised that the contract he had signed (without reading it) paid him a lot less than his colleagues, some of whom had received £500 to sign on and £10 every time they played.

Back in the RAF Danny was assigned to a base near Plymouth but because he was a volunteer from Northern Ireland his exit from the air force would be straightforward. He played in Swindon's reserves a few times but by April 1946 he was back in Belfast and playing for Glentoran again. On his return, Blanchflower resumed his apprenticeship as an electrician at Gallaher's; a position which his uncle had secured for him and when he eventually left the cigarette manufacturer, his brother Jackie recalled in *Danny Blanchflower: A Biography* that he 'got a medal for good attendance, though I don't know how because he was hardly ever there!'

The following season Glentoran made an administrative error, neglecting to ask their young recruit to re-sign. Because of this oversight, he could have gone elsewhere, but waited to see if they would come back for him, in part because he so idolised Peter Doherty - 'Peter The Great'. The precocious Danny apparently took on a lot of Doherty's habits and mannerisms, including always eating ice cream before a game. When the club did get round to offering Blanchflower a deal, they proposed paying him £3 a game, rather than per week. Con Martin had been signed in the close season, so Blanchflower was switched from inside-right to right-half which actually better suited his skilful, if slow, style of play.

Still, he remained irritated that the coaches at Glentoran - as was commonplace in Britain at the time — often held training sessions without the ball with the thinking being that the players would be more hungry for it on a match day if they had not had the opportunity to touch it during the week. There was another point of conflict, too: Danny still believed Glentoran were not paying him enough, so the club found him some extra work in the shipyards in the afternoons, in order that he could earn an extra £3 a week while keeping his mornings free for his personal training regime. He did not last long at his new employer, finding the work pointless and still not granting him the professionalism he desired.

The headstrong young man jacked it in and took a job at the Falls Road bus depot instead, exercising before work to keep his fitness levels up. He had become bitter towards the club, believing they had been less than straight with him, as Dave Bowler discovered in his biography of the man: 'I was quickly losing my respect for them. All their glad talk in previous years about wishing they could pay me more if league rules permitted was now meaningless.' Nevertheless, Danny would be a regular for Glentoran (the biggest post-war exporters of players to Britain) until he was transferred to Barnsley in April 1949.

STRAIGHT-LACED

'I'm the product of a mixed marriage,' Billy Bingham had joked in his conversation with Eamon Dunphy. 'Yes, my dad was a Presbyterian, my mother Church of Ireland.' Presbyterianism, for good and ill, has shaped the character of Protestant Ulster and the footballers it has spawned. A look at the religious denominations of players who were deemed professionals in the Irish League around 1900, uncovered in Neal Garnham's book on football before the partition of Ireland, shows that Presbyterians were wildly over-represented as footballers, compared to the number of Presbyterians in Belfast as a whole: of fifty-five professionals, twenty-four, or forty-four per cent were Presbyterian when their co-denominationalists made up a rather more modest thirty-four per cent of the city's population. A year earlier the Central Presbyterian Association in Belfast had begun fielding its own amateur team, seeing it as a route by which evangelism could be carried out. Back then it was a denomination that skewed working class, whereas the Church of Ireland - like its English cousin —

provided a rather more genteel experience of the Almighty.

'Our family were Protestant, Free Presbyterians to be exact,' George Best recounts in his second autobiography, *Blessed*. 'We always went to church on Sunday morning or evening. My mum's dad, George, was the one that made us do it.' This was a Northern Ireland - as it remains today — far more religious, and far less compromising in its religiosity, than England, Scotland or Wales.

Dougan, a sometime roommate of Best's on international duty, had observed in his own book how the 'the Protestant community of the Newtonards Road dressed up in their best clothes and going to Bible class … ' and bemoaned the 'dullness of the Belfast Sunday, with no cinemas or dance halls open. Well, that isn't quite true. The dance halls *were* in the Catholic area. Some Sundays I used to forsake the Puritan ways of our part of the city and go to Catholic dances.'

Puritan. Puritanical. The opposite of what George's life in England was to become; a life lived in a bleary eyed fog of vice: liquor, women, gambling, *a prison sentence*. He was *El Beatle*, the first football celebrity; everything to excess. Back then, before he got on that ferry across the Irish sea, George's biggest rebellion had been watching the television on a Sunday, despite the fact his granddad explicitly forbade it, as he tells in *Blessed*, 'When he went upstairs for his afternoon siesta, all the kids would crowd round the set. We had to take it in turns to keep watch at the bottom of the stairway. When we heard him get up, the telly went straight off.'

Not long after George was born at the Royal Maternity Hospital in Belfast, his parents Dickie and Ann moved the family to 16 Burren Way in Cregagh. Theirs was the first house on a new estate, located about a mile south of the streets where Bingham had spent his own earliest days.

Ann would continue living there until her death from alcoholism at fifty-four, a woman who had been teetotal until little over a decade before that. Dickie, George's dad, still called the place home until he passed away in April 2008, outliving his son by two and a half years.

It was on Saturday, 3 December 2005 that George's body left the family home, the cortege travelling the four or so miles to Stormont, seat of the Northern Ireland Assembly. Police estimates put up to 250,000 people along the route paying their respects that day, the largest ever turnout at a funeral in that part of the world. A further 300,000 had watched the procession on the BBC. Billy Bingham, Peter McParland, Derek Dougan, Harry Gregg and Gerry Armstrong were among the coffin bearers; three Protestants and two Catholics. Inside the Grand Hall at Stormont were 300 invited guests, outside in the grounds were another 25,000 mourners. George, our George, Bestie; Northern Ireland's most famous non-Troubles export.

Well, almost Troubles-free. There had been that time in 1971 when someone had threatened to shoot him if he took to the field against Newcastle. Or that other time in the mid-eighties, when some loyalist paramilitaries wrote to George offering to spring him out of the prison in which he was serving a sentence for drink driving, assaulting a police officer, and refusing to answer bail. Except it was an open prison, and if George had wanted to walk out he could have done so at any time. What had happened to his life? It had all looked so rosy forty years previous.

Dickie Best was twenty-seven when George was born, working alternating day and night shifts at an iron turner's lathe at Harland and Wolff and playing football on Saturdays when his shift finished just after noon. Ann worked on the production line at Gallaher's tobacco factory, and George spent a lot of his boyhood with his Granny Withers on Donard Street, recalling his days there with great affection in his autobiography, co-written with Roy Collins: 'Family life always seemed to centre around my grandparents. Even after we moved to Burren Way, my primary school was near Donard Street, and I was in and out of there every day.'

Football was central to family life and Dickie told Joe Lovejoy in *Bestie: Portrait Of A Legend,* of taking a young George to his first match: 'He was only five when we took him to matches at Wilgar Park.' Wilgar Park is home to Dundela, currently playing in the NIFL Premier Intermediate League, the third tier of Northern Irish football. The family had links to Glentoran, too. One of George's grandfathers, James 'Scottie' Best was a fan, as George himself remembered: 'He lived right by Glentoran's ground, The Oval, and he used to take me there sometimes. If there was anyone who really fuelled my interest, it was him.'

Mind you, George's recollections of Glentoran seem to have been clouded by the passage of time, substance (or both) because he tells readers of his 2002 autobiography 'If you were a Protestant you automatically supported Linfield and if you were a Catholic you supported Glentoran, or the Glens as we called them.' Ask any Northern Irish Catholic how they would feel about going to The Oval and you will understand how plainly wrong this assertion is. The difference is somewhere closer to this: Linfield has zero Catholic fans, and Glentoran likely has one.

Best had practiced his art during kick-arounds on the fields near Bell's Bridge in Cregagh, a few hundred yards from his home, or if there were no other boys to play with he would go down to the garages at the bottom of Burren Way, 'on my own and kick a tennis ball against the garage doors for hour after hour. It used to drive the neighbours nuts.' Until he joined Cregagh Boys Club, Best had played in what we would recognise as trainers, known this part of the world as 'gutties'. Proper boots were too expensive.

Passing the eleven-plus exam meant entry to a grammar school, Grosvenor High. Back there and back then this meant going to a school where rugby, and only rugby, was the sporting option during the school day, as Best bemoaned in his account of that time 'I was always getting into trouble, always being kept behind in detention to do my lines, and when I came out of school, on my own, I had to walk through this Catholic area with my Protestant uniform on, and it was like running the gauntlet most afternoons. But that wasn't the reason I left. It was a combination of the fact that I couldn't play football there, and that most of my pals were at the secondary school.'

George stuck it out for a year and did a passable impression of a competent fly-half, although he was often 'mitching'; playing truant from the place that denied him the opportunity to excel at the thing he most wanted to do. Dickie picks up the story again in Lovejoy's biography, 'I think the journey to and from the grammar school bothered George more than he lets on. He had to get a bus through a Catholic area, and you know what kids are like. He'd go through with his badge clearly visible, and they'd throw stones and call him names.'

He was much happier when he made the move to Lisnaharragh, since demolished, which was also the alma mater of the infamous Protestant paramilitary Michael Stone. It was closer for one thing, he could play football again and most of his friends were there. He got into the football team almost immediately; his trips to and from his old school being good for one thing at least, as *Blessed* informs us, 'They used to wait for me and call me a Proddy bastard and try to steal my scarf or cap so that in the end I would wait down the road from the bus stop and time my run to perfection so that I could reach the bus and jump on to the platform just as it was taking off. It wasn't very nice but it turned out to be good sprint training.'

Best had ample company amongst Northern Irish Protestant footballers, who had to weigh up the academic versus sporting merits of their secondary education. Harry Gregg, who would go on be a teammate of Best's at Manchester United, was put forward by his parents for Coleraine Academical Institution, but it would seem he almost certainly failed the exam on purpose, knowing that to go there would have deprived him of sufficient football. Instead, he went to Coleraine Technical College and was chosen to captain Ireland schoolboys versus Wales a year later.

A couple of other footballers often feted as the new Best were to confront a very similar choice. The first was Norman Whiteside, who talks of his fears of a non-footballing future in the mid-seventies in *Determined*: 'When I got to the age for secondary school, my two brothers - Ken and Hugh both went to the Boys Model school. But I was always worried because I knew the Boys Model was a rugby school so I went to Cairnmartin because they played football in first year.' Such was Whiteside's footballing ability that he had become 'Shankill famous' by the age of eleven, when it was time to leave Edenbrooke Primary School, meaning he had the pick of whichever Protestant school he wanted to attend.

Keith Gillespie was unable to dodge the grammar school as his United predecessors had managed, attending Bangor Grammar School for his secondary education. It even had its own song in Latin, should its upper-middle class credentials be in any doubt. 'They hated football,' he wrote in his 2013 autobiography, claiming they went out of their way to make it harder for him to become a footballer: 'Rugby was king.' The walls of the school were decorated with celebrated rugby men, and David Feherty, the golfer. The only footballer who got a passing reference was Terry Neill. 'What they didn't mention was that he only lasted six weeks in the Grammar, and I can understand why. The hostility towards my passion was remarkable.'

There was no football option at Bangor Grammar: you had to play rugby, and as Gillespie wrote 'The rules were a mystery so I stood on the wing and just ran with the ball when I got it, and used my pace.' He did well and was picked for the team, which clashed with football fixtures for the Saturday boys side Gillespie was enrolled with, 'I always chose football, but it landed me in constant trouble.'

He was not any luckier in his second year, when he chose hockey. Unfortunately for the young Gillespie, the pick up point for their Saturday morning fixtures was across the road from where he was to catch the train to Belfast to play football, hiding away under his jacket, 'My parents spent so much time down the school complaining, that the other kids started to think they were teachers,' he recalled, explaining in his book that eventually his mum gave the headmaster short shrift, telling them they should cease giving him Saturday morning detentions because he would not be turning up for them.

Gillespie's formative football exploits were, however, helped on by a cornerstone of Northern Irish life: the Boys Brigade. So closely does he associate the unapologetically unionist institution with his country, that he likens it to a Northern Irish version of the Boy Scouts, although it counts 50,000 members throughout the UK and ten times that worldwide. Gillespie was far from the first footballer to have come through the ranks of the organisation. It established a presence in Belfast in 1888 and seven years later sent a representative team to play one from Dublin where it was also strong; so much so, in fact, that the Leinster FA bestowed honorary affiliation upon it. Danny Blanchflower had gone before Gillespie, describing in his typically enthusiastic style, in comments found in Dave Bowler's biography on him, how he remembered 'playing three games on some Saturdays - for the school in the morning, the Boys Brigade in the afternoon and for the local team in the evening.'

Norman Whiteside was another who gained his first experience of football in the 72nd Belfast Battalion in a church on the Crumlin Road. The building backed onto the Whiteside's yard behind their house on the Shankill Road, and the young Norman became an 'anchor boy' within the Brigade. Like Gillespie, who wrote that the organisation 'only offered one thing [he] was interested in', Whiteside mainly went on Sundays in order to get the attendance stamp required to take part in the Saturday football matches, though he realises it was a 'godsend' to his parents because it meant he and his brothers could go out without being too far from home in the Shankill.

Another former United man in the form of Jimmy Nicholl, whose time there had the briefest of overlaps with that of Whiteside, also came through the Boys Brigade. Indeed, it was during one Saturday game that he was scouted by the Old Trafford club in the early seventies, writing in *Determined* of how 'Bob Bishop was there, he was looking at someone else and I shouldn't even have been playing, but somebody got injured and I took their place.'

BOB WHO?

Probably the most important name in Northern Irish football that you have never heard of. First in the highlight reel of his finds would, of course, be George Best: the original *Galactico,* a man who would put thousands on the gate, could beat three or four men for fun and yet probably never even reached the peak of his potential.

Norman Whiteside once proclaimed, 'The only thing I have in common with George Best is that we come from the same place, play for the same club and were discovered by the same man.' Bishop had first cast his eye over the Shankill boy wonder when he played in the Northern Irish Schools Cup Final for Cairnmartin, not yet into his teens. Northern Irish football may have had a very different trajectory had Bishop not had an eye for precocious footballing talent. Described by Best as 'teak tough', Bishop had worked in the Harland and Wolff shipyard for more than thirty years - of course he had, where else - and felt most at home amongst working class, footballing people.

His role in the yard had rendered him almost entirely deaf due to the incessant ear-shattering noises from the riveting and caulking machines, meaning he would shout at boys stood mere inches away from him. In addition to his role at the Boyland Youth Club on Lomond Avenue, he was appointed Manchester United's chief scout in Northern Ireland in 1950, at the urging of United backroom stalwart Jimmy Murphy. It was a position he held until he retired aged 86 in 1987.

The man described as having a Woodbine permanently gripped to his lips knew his stuff. His most famous commendation was immortalised in the telegram he sent to Sir Matt Busby in 1961: 'Boss, I've found you a genius.' This was the man who launched Britain and Ireland's - if not the world's — most renowned superstar. Where Glentoran had seen in Best a boy who was not physically strong enough to make the grade in the Irish League, Bishop saw potential. Busby recounted how 'Bob Bishop ... wrote to us to say that he had seen a young boy with an enormous ration of football gifts, though he had hesitated because the lad was so small and skinny. "Send him over and let us have a look at him" we said.'

Best said of this pivotal time in his young life that 'the advice was I was too thin, too frail, too scraggy even for the part-timed, half-paced Irish League. That was the unanimous verdict. Hugh McFarland, who was second team trainer with Glentoran refused to accept it. He got in touch with Bob Bishop, the leader of our biggest boys' club rivals, Boyland Boys' Club who also happened to be Manchester United's Scout in NI. Unknown to me the pair of them arranged a friendly for the single purpose of giving Mr Bishop the chance to have a good look at me. I was nearly 15 and the rest of the players were around the 17 mark. We won 4-1 and inside right George Best - all 6 1/2 stone of him — scored two of the goals.'

Bishop would eventually receive a bonus of £8 net for spotting the nascent Best, a cheque for £100 not arriving until 1970. 'Ninety-two pounds went on tax,' Bishop said, though he was not complaining, it was not in his nature. Reflecting on the short time George was at the top of his profession, Bishop told the BBC, 'It was a real tragedy. It was a real tragedy because George, to my mind, had six or seven more good seasons football in him if he had have behaved himself, but he's living his own life and…I don't blame him to a certain extent, because no matter where George went he would get crashed and he couldn't take it. I think if his Mother and Father would have went over with him, it would have been a different story, because Mr and Mrs McIlroy went over with Sammy, no trouble; Mr and Mrs Nicholl went over with Jimmy, no trouble.'

So many years on, it's all speculation. What is without question is the skill of this man, already in his early fifties when he took on the job of scout, as a young Norman Whiteside found out when travelling from Belfast International with Bishop. Each of them had to enter his year of birth on a form that was part of an anti-terrorism effort at the time, and the Shankill boy recalled in his own autobiography, 'Before my first trip to Manchester in August 1978, I have never forgotten that Bob entered his year of birth as 1899. Never mind my grandad, he was old enough to be my great-grandfather, but he had such a sparkle and a gift for communicating with young footballers that it never felt as if you were dealing with an old man.'

When 'The Bishop', as he was to affectionately become known, knocked on the Whiteside's front door at 10 Danube Street it was seventeen years after he had sat in Dickie Best's kitchen. An Ipswich scout, a certain Jim Rodgers, had been in their living room a year earlier but Bobby Robson had felt that twelve was perhaps too young for a lad to come over to England for a trial. It could all have been very different but for the eye of the diminutive Ulsterman.

Former Irish schoolboy manager, Jake Gallagher, testified at the time as to how 'Bob can spot potential long before anyone else. He sees past faults which would put others off.' Sammy McIlroy, barely ten years old when Bishop noticed him playing the park, also spoke effusively of the man who set him on course for an eleven year stint at Old Trafford, during which he would score 57 times in 342 games, 'I owe everything to him. He guided me in those vital, formative years. He was like a father figure to me. I suppose I also owe him a few bob, because it was Bob who bought me my first pair of modern football boots.' McIlroy, whose father had played for Linfield, was brought up close to the Glentoran's Oval ground, telling Teddy Jamieson in *Whose Side Are You On?* 'In them days it was out playing till the light went, playing in the gables, playing football till you were shouted in. At school I never really did anything at all. I got on well with the teachers at school because of football, not because of any work. I got made a prefect in the secondary school because of football.'

Though Pat Jennings is not a name associated with Manchester United, his career path could have been very different, as Bishop once let slip, 'I told United about Pat Jennings when he was playing for Newry Town. They could have had him for £3,000 but when the chief scout and his aides came over they went to watch the wrong match, and Pat ended up signing for Watford instead of United.'

Whiteside picks up the story again in *Determined*, 'If all he had done was spot George it would have been more than enough to justify forty years employment, but he had such an eye for talent and such an extensive knowledge of the relatively small Northern Ireland pool that he came up trumps time and again.' That's just how the unassuming Bishop was; happy to blend into the scenery and not seek the limelight. 'Twenty players of mine made it out of hundreds,' he said, without acknowledging just what an incredible return on investment that was and remains to this day.

It seems fitting that we return to Best's musings in *Blessed* for the final word on Bob Bishop, who died in 1990. 'Take the usual image of the club scout — big man, heavy overcoat, trilby and insight eyes - and Bob is just the opposite. He is a short fellow, straight out of the shipyards. Football is his porridge, roast beef and night-cap. I came home from school — to find Bob sitting at home in my dad's chair. "How would you like to join Manchester United?" That was his greeting and my parents just stood there waiting for some reaction from me. I thought they were all having me on…'

COMPETING CODES

Though there were undoubtedly challenges for young Protestant footballers in Northern Ireland, their Catholic counterparts had one more hurdle to jump: most of their routes towards professional football presented challenges unique to twentieth century Ireland. Want to play football? Sure. Oh, you mean soccer? Well, no. Such was the life of many adolescent Catholic boys.

The Gaelic Athletic Association, *Cumann Lúthchleas Gael,* had come into being in 1884, organised partly in response to the formation of the Irish Football Association in 1880: the late nineteenth century witnessed a number of activities that had been organised informally for a number of years, seek to codify their rules and set up recognisably competitive structures to better spread and promote participation in their sports.

In the case of the GAA, this meant a ban on 'foreign' games existing for most of the next 85 years. Rule 27 of the GAA code prohibited hockey, rugby, cricket and 'soccer', but not tennis, basketball, American football or boxing. In reality the ban on foreign games was a ban on English team games, seen as tools of an imperial power, an assertion that was not entirely without merit.

Until 1971, when the Ban was finally repealed, the reality was that any boy, girl, man or woman who was a member of a GAA club could face being banned from competitive hurling, handball, camogie or Gaelic football, if they were found to be playing one of the proscribed

English pastimes. But that was not the extent of it: even if they went to a stadium and *watched* a sporting event that they should not have been, their name could be struck off the membership rolls at their GAA club, for a period of time to be decided by the administrators.

Pat Jennings is one who knew this only too well: 'Soccer was banned at my school,' he remembered in *Pat Jennings: An Autobiography*. Born in 1945, the keeper went to a Christian Brothers school where Gaelic was the only footballing code allowed, though he credits his time as a midfielder in the Irish game as teaching him to catch the ball one-handed. What ardent proponents of Gaelic football must have made of his description of the ancient Irish game as 'a cross between rugby and football', in his autobiography, is another matter. It was when the big man was on the fringes of the County Down Minor side that his turn to the infernal English activity effectively ended his dual sporting participation.

Even years after the Ban had lapsed, there was still fierce opposition to association football amongst educators and certain ecclesiastical figures. Neil Lennon describes his time at St Michael's Grammar School in *Neil Lennon: Man and Bhoy*, where a Sister Mary St Anne became something of a nemesis for the Lurgan native: the problem was that although he enjoyed Gaelic football for *Clan Na Gael* and St Paul's, 'soccer' was his first love. Unfortunately, St Michael's played its Gaelic matches against other schools on a Saturday morning at just the time he should have been turning out for Lurgan United. According to Lennon, for Sister Mary St Anne it was 'Gaelic football or no football at all' being, as she was 'determined to uphold the school's traditions.'

Young Neil thought this meant the end of his 'soccer' career, which was progressing so well that several scouts had already expressed interest in the fourteen year-old.

Threatened with expulsion if he did not toe the line, his sister Orla got involved, confronting the Sister about her sporting decree, and alerting their parents to the mistreatment being meted out to her brother. Eventually a compromise was found: Lennon would be allowed to play for Lurgan during the soccer season provided that he did his bit for the school's Gaelic side when he could.

The flame haired Ulsterman's future manager at Celtic, Martin O'Neill, would have been able to empathise. His father Leo - a barber by trade — had helped set up a Gaelic Athletic Club in Kilrea, County Londonderry, where Martin was born, named after the first black American saint Martin De Porres. The younger O'Neill recalled going to an All-Ireland final aged six to watch his older brother play, in comments reported in Simon Moss' *Martin the Magnificent*: 'I loved Gaelic. My older brothers ended up playing for County Derry and I spent a lot of time with my father supporting them greatly.' When O'Neill was sixteen his father needed to find alternative work and they moved to Belfast. Martin transferred to St. Malachy's college, getting a place on the Gaelic team as well as joining a local soccer team, Rosario, which was one of the biggest youth teams in Belfast, located on the Ormeau Road.

It would not be long before O'Neill was turning out for Distillery, who allowed him to juggle his sporting commitments and still turn out for St Malachy's. Sadly, the local Gaelic club were not so accommodating, ruling that due to his transgression, the GAA semi final between O'Neill's side and St Mary's College should not be played at Casement Park in Belfast but instead at an alternative venue in County Tyrone. According to Moss, O'Neill would later tell the *Irish News* that he 'found it perturbing; it left a real taste. I could not believe it, My father, who had been a major supporter of the GAA was desperately disappointed. I think there was a culture change in him. He felt let down and I certainly did...Perhaps for a second I started to reflect on my own identity.'

One of the most remarkable stories of dual GAA and soccer loyalties takes us to Wellington Street back in Lurgan. Norman Uprichard had moved there with his mother Henrietta when he was thirteen years-old, 'I was a Protestant and most of the people in the street were Catholic,' he recalled in his autobiography. The young man had a barber by the name of Bobby Carville who organised street soccer teams and founded a league in which Uprichard played for Wellington Rovers.

In 1943 Bobby asked him if he wanted to join St Peter's Gaelic Football Minor team, which he had founded and managed. Uprichard told him he had Sunday school on the Sabbath and that, in any case, he was a Protestant. Since there was no organised schools football at the time Bobby said this would not matter. Uprichard had reasoned with himself that he could 'walk up Church Walk and come back down North Street, and nobody would see me...my mother, fortunately, didn't find out for years.' The most unlikely of Gaelic football careers was born.

Uprichard's father had died when his son was just six years old, four months after he had contracted Tuberculosis. It would be a further three years before his widow was able to pay off the medical bill. Had he lived, such a turn of events would have been unlikely to transpire, as Uprichard wrote of the staunch Orangeman who had been an avid Glenavon fan before his untimely death at 27 'I would never have dared play Gaelic football in the first place if he was alive.'

Norman's own Protestant and unionist credentials would not seem to be in any doubt, either. A few years later he would marry Elizabeth Gourley in 1949 at the

Richview Presbyterian Church on the Donegall Road in Belfast, followed by a reception at Sandy Row Orange Hall. Elizabeth had previously come over to London with him when he was signed by Arsenal and they had stayed in the same digs but separate rooms, of course.

It was his father's beloved Glenavon FC, a fiercely loyalist outpost within Lurgan, who had approached the younger Uprichard when he was sixteen. It did not take long for the local Gaelic club to get wind of this development, and he was banned from all Gaelic involvement on an indefinite basis. 'It was an unjust rule to my thinking because you should be able to play whatever sport you want,' he ruefully reflected in *Norman 'Black Jake' Uprichard*, published shortly after his death in 2011.

Uprichard was particularly upset because St Peter's had a big awards ceremony coming up, and he would have been awarded a medal there. Having never won anything before, this was enough to bring him to tears as a young man, but there is a hopeful coda to this tale: in 2004 Uprichard received a letter from St Peter's, inviting him over to Lurgan to receive that medal he should have been able to hang round his neck all those years ago.

He was going home to make things right.

4
PLAYING AWAY

Harry Gregg can take credit for alerting Bertie Peacock to the talents of his Manchester United teammate, George Best, in 1964. According to a conversation with Teddy Jamieson in *Whose Side Are You On?*, he had called up the Northern Ireland manager, telling him 'Bertie, there's a bloody kid here, he's incredible. He's a bloody genius.' Best had the audacity to put the ball through Gregg's legs twice in training. 'You do that again,' he had told the winger, 'and I'll bloody break your legs.' He remembered their first encounter well in a book by Chris Moore, *United Irishmen*, 'I thought about the game as a player, even when I was a young man. Very few people caught me in a one-on-one situation. See George Best, he is the only c—t to have done me, through one-to-one with a goalkeeper.'

After an initial truncated trip to Manchester with Eric McMordie - both young men had become homesick and returned home just two days into a two week trial - Best was persuaded by his father Dickie to go back and try again on his own. This time there would be no turning back, and George settled into a new home with his landlady Mrs Fullaway by night, and by day at the Cliff, United's training ground. Yet he would wonder if he had made the right decision.

The Scottish and Irish Football Associations had complained bitterly of their young talent being whisked from the clutches of their clubs by the comparatively rich English clubs, and there had been a decree by the English FA to placate their fears. The end result was that young men from those nations could not be signed as apprentices by English club sides, so George joined with United as an amateur. Practically speaking, this meant he had to have a job and was officially only able to train with the other amateur players on Tuesday and Thursday nights. In some ways it would have been better to have stayed in Belfast for a few more years, as he now had to deal with the tedium of being an errand boy on the Manchester Ship Canal, far away from the familiarities of home.

When young George had put pen to paper Matt Busby had sent £150 to Cregagh Boys Club as a goodwill gesture but Dickie and Ann were not forgotten. Gregg explained in his own autobiography, *Harry's Game*, 'the club's contract [with Best] was £5 per week for 40 weeks, with £200 to his parents in lieu of what George would have received had he been an apprentice at the Harland & Wolff shipyard.'

The man who would famously claim that he had 'spent a lot of money on booze, birds, and fast cars and the rest I just squandered', could not have foreseen as a fifteen year old that he would become bankrupt a few short decades later through wine, women and song. In those earliest days he recounted in *Blessed*, 'even embarrassed to speak to the conductor on the buses because everyone had trouble understanding my accent and people were always asking me to repeat myself. So I tried to make sure I had the exact money, threepence or fourpence or whatever it was, so that I wouldn't have to ask for a particular destination.'

While George's star was ascending, Dickie continued his work at the shipyard. In the days before cheap and convenient air travel he would make an arduous thirty-six hour pilgrimage to watch his boy when he could. 'Once George had made the grade, I used to try to get over to watch him play maybe six or seven times a season. It wasn't easy. I used to go over on the boat overnight on a Friday and come back the same way on Saturday night.' He continued, telling Best biographer Joe Lovejoy in *Bestie*, 'When I was on the nightshift, we worked four and a half nights.

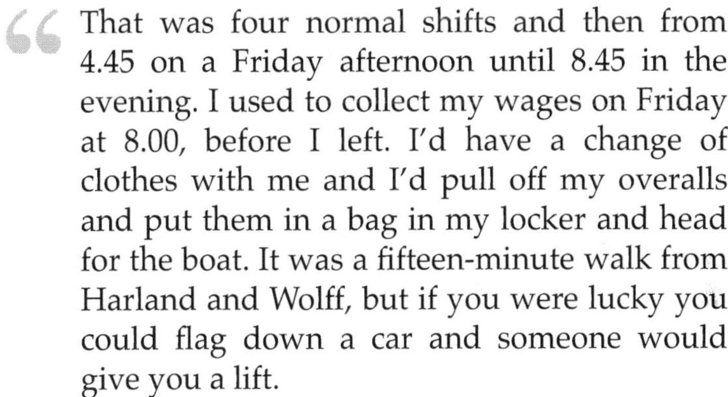

> That was four normal shifts and then from 4.45 on a Friday afternoon until 8.45 in the evening. I used to collect my wages on Friday at 8.00, before I left. I'd have a change of clothes with me and I'd pull off my overalls and put them in a bag in my locker and head for the boat. It was a fifteen-minute walk from Harland and Wolff, but if you were lucky you could flag down a car and someone would give you a lift.

While Dickie was making this unglamorous trip as and when, he remained firmly rooted in east Belfast, just as his son became cut adrift from the deteriorating situation in the land of his birth. Many years later, Best would sound naïve — if we are being generous, and myopic if we are not - when describing where he came from, declaring in his autobiography 'The Troubles, as we know them now, hadn't started then. Our troubles amounted to name calling, no more than that. The street my dad has lived on for forty-nine years is totally mixed. The next-door neighbours I knew are still there, and they are Catholic. The woman there, Melda, was my mum's best friend. A couple of doors away there is another Catholic family, living happily next to a Protestant one. Everyone gets on so well that my dad can still leave his front door open, like he used to when he was a kid.'

Dickie spoke frankly in the early nineties, asserting that his son has been gone too long if he thought anyone in Belfast could still leave their doors open, adding that he actually kept a piece of wood by the door and another under his bed. Pat Crerand, a contemporary of Best's at United and not unfamiliar with sectarianism as a Scottish Catholic, wrote perceptively on the subject, telling Teddy Jamieson in *Whose Side Are You On?* 'I think sometimes if you bring people out of their environment and they're away from it, it can change their whole outlook. George came to Manchester when he was 15 before the Troubles had really started. He had a different outlook.'

Indeed George would remark in his own writing that the 'only time the Troubles came close to me personally was when I was in Ford Open prison and some lunatics wrote to me, saying they were going to spring me. They wouldn't have needed to do much springing since Ford was like a holiday camp and if I had really wanted to get out, I could have simply walked through the open gate!'

Perhaps memories of a death threat at St James' Park - of which more later — had eluded him. Nevertheless it speaks of a man detached from his former reality in a way that was not possible for other players of an ever so slightly later era.

OVER THE WATER

As Conor Curran's research *Irish-born players in England's Football Leagues, 1945-2010* expounds, 417 players born in Northern Ireland played professional league football in England. One of those names is spoken more than any other, yet there are plenty more stories which tell of a difficult transition from the often insular, closed society of Northern Ireland. Their journeys took them to a mainland which was breaking free from its own constrictive post-war chains and, by the 1960s, beginning to feel much more at ease with itself.

In the decade after the Second World War, it was to Burnley that the largest number of players gravitated from across the Irish Sea. Curran's article informs us that six were transferred in this direction by 1955, seemingly because the Clarets had a scout by the name of Tommy Coulter in the Belfast area during this time. Jimmy McIlroy was one of the more notable of these signings, making the journey to Turf Moor after spending a year in the Glentoran first team. He stayed twelve years there before falling out with the club's chairman Bob Lord and being sold to Stoke.

When rumours of a rift between McIlroy and Lord had emerged in 1962, Danny Blanchflower had contacted his former international teammate in a journalistic capacity to ascertain him what the cause of the falling out might be, asking Jimmy if it was possible he had been 'messing about' with one or more of Lord's daughters. McIlroy's response was firmly negative, and according to Ronnie Hanna's account of Northern Ireland's time at the 1958 World Cup in Sweden, *The World at Their Feet*, he had enquired of his friend, 'Have you seen them?'

Blanchflower had been transplanted from Glentoran to England a year before his compatriot. The plan had always been that Danny, the senior of the two footballing Blanchflower brothers, would achieve a move to England and then send for his brother. Yet it was Jackie who was signed as a youth by Matt Busby's Manchester United just as Danny was putting pen to paper for Second Division Barnsley. He had been due a percentage of the transfer fee from Glentoran as part of an earlier deal with them but once more they were frustrating him by their refusal to honour their promise. Eventually he decided he would have to drop it and, summoned to the Grand Hotel, he sealed his move across the water.

From Yorkshire he would move to Aston Villa and eventually to Tottenham, where he is best remembered for a ten year spell, which saw 337 appearances and two Football Writers Association Footballer of the Year awards in 1958 and again in 1961. Evidence from his time at White Hart Lane detailed in Bowler's biography of Blanchflower illuminates a man who remembers where he came from; arranging a tour of White Hart Lane for the Lower Shankill Boys' Club after the 1958 World Cup and taking the time to have a photo with each one. Later there was another trip of forty boys from Dunlambert in Belfast's northernmost reaches, his pride at having home-town folk as his guests at White Hart Lane seemingly undeniable.

Though there were aspects of the wheelings and dealings of early fifties football which infuriated Blanchflower, he seems to have adapted to life outside of Northern Ireland very quickly. This was no doubt because of his service in the RAF which had seen him travel to Dundee, Plymouth, Canada and Norfolk. Yet many of his contemporaries did not fare so well, at least at first: Harry Gregg was signed by Peter Doherty for Doncaster in 1952, leaving his home town of Coleraine at the age of twenty-one, 'Moving to working-class Yorkshire might not sound like much of a transition to make, but, believe me, this was a whole new world,' he would remark of the impact it had on his young life in *Harry's Game*, determined to take advantage of this opportunity. Gregg was the child of a mixed marriage: a loyalist father who had been a soldier in the British Army and a Catholic mother whose family disowned her for the rest of their lives upon her nuptials.

'Before joining Doncaster, I had sworn never to return to Ireland a failure,' he wrote in his autobiography. The man between the sticks would go on to make 210 appearances for Manchester United, crowned FIFA World Cup Best Goalkeeper in 1958, having been on that fateful plane in Munich only months earlier, before returning to the blazing aircraft to save the lives of Vera and Vesna Lukic. When Gregg returned to Ireland, he was far from a failure.

Remaining at Old Trafford, a generation later we find Jimmy Nicholl, whose fears about Ireland were of a different nature: how the conflict back home in the mid-seventies was affecting his family. It was Tommy Doherty who sorted things out for him, if not for the whole Northern Ireland, telling Chris Moore in *United Irishmen*:

He was the one who got my ma and da a house in Manchester, and got them out of Rathcoole. I was only 16 when he helped get them out. I got the message from home about how things were beginning to cut up rough. I used to go home every month and got the message, don't come back for a wee while. After a game at Preston I went back to the Doc and said if I didn't go back now I will be going back for funerals. Things were starting to creep into Rathcoole. I told them I was away and went off back home. The club told

> me to bring my ma and da back with me because the club had a house for them in Sale, a three-bedroom detached house in a cul-de-sac with a garage.

It was a similar story to that of Sammy McIlroy, who had left Belfast in 1969 and told Moore:

> “The Troubles were just kicking off when I left and I was very, very worried about my family. I decided to bring them over in the seventies. When I went back home during 1969 and 1970 the Troubles were well under way with people marching the streets at night and my dad, who was no spring chicken, was having his door knocked on at night by men who were calling on him to go on vigilante duty. I was worried sick and thought this was not for me. So I asked them if they would come over and they said yes, they'd come over.

They did, living in a house just behind the Stretford End. It was during McIlroy's time that the whispers 'back home' about United began to intensify. Under Busby's stewardship the club had a noticeably Catholic ethos, the manager himself being devout in the faith. This emphasis was especially strong in the fifties, when Busby and the scout Joe Armstrong promised the parents of kids they took onto their books that they would continue to go to Mass. This, as Teddy Jamieson notes, was all quite well known and little remarked upon until things in Northern Ireland began to spiral out of control, and the chatter took on a sharper edge.

McIlroy had escaped a part of the earth that seemed intent on destroying itself, just before things really kicked off. In *Whose Side Are You On?*, he told Jamieson, 'My mum and dad lived in Severin Street, just off the Newtownards Road and there was a lot of tension around the place. Oh, I was so homesick, but my dad said, "Listen, the way things are going here we don't want you anywhere near this. Don't worry about me and your mum. You go over there and try to be a footballer. And it'll be a fantastic achievement if you do".'

When a few years later the Shankill skinhead Norman Whiteside found himself at Old Trafford, the talk surfaced again. In *Determined,* Whiteside recalls how his parents were told by fellow loyalists, '"He's married a Roman Catholic, he's friends with McGrath and Moran, United are a Catholic club."' There was even a jibe about United having a chapel in the tunnel at Old Trafford.

Wee Norman's introduction to life at United had been something of a whirlwind of new experiences, as he explained to Jamieson, 'I went to Old Trafford on the Monday. I'd never been on an aeroplane before. I did really well and I had to go back home on the Friday because my school was going over to America to play in a schools tournament on the Saturday. That Monday we were in the Oval Office with President Jimmy Carter. So one Monday I'm at Old Trafford, the biggest club in the world. Next Monday I'm in the Oval Office. And when I came out of the Oval Office one of the teachers called me and said, "Your parents have been on the phone. Man United want to sign you."'

Carter's term in office would be similar in length to that of Whiteside's United club boss Ron Atkinson, yet the peanut-farming President being referenced by Whiteside tell us that the Ulsterman is not the lumbering oaf of the footballing, or indeed loyalist stereotype. His reflections on the Troubles in *Determined* reveal a thoughtful man at once connected with his Shankill heritage and aware of how it is perceived: 'Some English people I know have the idea that what happened in Northern Ireland when I was a boy happened to all the people equally and we were all used to it. But it was not like that at all, so when your family was affected it was just as horrifying as it would have been for any family in other parts of Britain.'

Those people who had been telling Big Norman and Aileen Whiteside that their son had married a Catholic were not wrong. He had, albeit an English one. Writing about the situation, the younger Whiteside describes his first words to her as an 'embarrassing remnant of the mentality I'd been used to in Belfast.' He had spotted her one day in Manchester's Arndale Centre (later bombed by the IRA) following training and after three weeks of biding his time he made his move, asking her what her name was. She replied that it was Julie - in Northern Ireland a first name can give away a lot about someone — but her reply was no help to the teenage Whiteside, who blurted out, 'Are you Protestant or Catholic?'

'The need to know was part of the cultural baggage I'd brought from the Shankill,' he wrote of his mindset back then. She told him that she was a Catholic and as it turned out, he did not care. They were together for the next twenty years. Not that every moment of that was without difficulty. His mum and dad were worried about the real danger this marriage posed for their son, and at one point suggested he break it off for fear of a corrective action from their 'own' side.

A CITY DIVIDED

Six years later another young man from the 'other' side in Ulster would join the 'other' Manchester club. Neil Lennon joined Manchester City as a trainee in 1987. There had been a brief spell earlier that year on the books of Motherwell, which he describes as disastrous; it surely could not have helped that, as told in *Man and Bhoy*, an unnamed senior professional grabbed a broom that the apprentice Lennon was using and 'demonstrated' how to sweep up, telling him, 'There, that's a bit more Protestant-like.'

He returned to Northern Ireland where he played a couple of games for Glenavon, scoring on his debut. It was then that the Maine Road outfit made their second approach and he headed south of the border, staying put this time. City life in north of England seems to have been a big shock to the sixteen year-old's system. It was a ten hour ferry ride from Larne to Liverpool, but fortunately a friendly face in the form of Gerry Taggart would be waiting for him at the end of it.

Even so, life in Lurgan had been a very caucasian affair and there were a few surprises, as Lennon wrote in his autobiography:

> “As I set out for the ground my first thought was that I had somehow woken up in the wrong country. I had seen maybe only a few brown — or black-skinned people in my life, and here was I now in the Asian quarter of Manchester. I think I probably stared goggle-eyed at women in saris and men in turbans with big long beards — sights I had only seen on television before. As I walked along the road to Moss Side, which is the Afro-Caribbean area of the city, I really did begin to wonder where the white people had gone.

Although this was a new experience for the teenager, it would appear to be one he relished, expanding his horizons beyond the shores of Lough Neagh: 'It shows you how naïve I was when I arrived in Manchester, and it was to be the first of many culture shocks that I would experience over the next few weeks and months. It was a whole new world to me, yet I never found it intimidating. On the contrary, it was exciting to find new cultures on my doorstep, and I thoroughly enjoyed exploring Manchester.'

Manchester can boast of being the destination for more Northern Irish - and indeed Irish in general — players than any other city. Why should this be? There are a few explanations worth looking at: it is accepted that relative to the population numbers, there are more professional clubs in the English north than the south of the country. Then, if we take the example of the historic county of Lancashire, we see that football clubs of the mid to late 1800s helped foster a local and regional identity and its obvious proximity to Ireland, through the port of Liverpool, saw the city and its environs develop a distinctly Irish feel.

Manchester United, as documented in Conor Curran's detailed study, recruited more Northern Irish born players than any other club during the sixty-five year period to 2010, nearly seven per cent of the total who braved the Irish Sea for pastures new. Yet City were no slouches either; in the period between 1986 both they and United brought over four players each from north of the border. Between 1966 and 1976 a staggering eight players had made the leap over the Isle of Man to Oldham and in the years between 1996 and 2005, a further four found a home at Blackburn's Ewood Park. Even the four year window between 2006 to the end of the decade saw two apiece to Everton and, of course, to United.

When you remember Burnley's penchant for an Ulsterman just after the war you see the emergence of a pattern; even now when it's as easy — if not easier - to travel to the airport-strewn capital of England, the historic link between Lancashire and Ireland persists into the twenty-first century. This suggests firstly that clubs in that region have deep and well-cultivated scouting networks on Ireland's east coast, which they have taken time to develop and finesse. On some level Lancashire, with all its Irish tentacles, is one of the more comfortable places to land for a young Irishman torn from the familiarities of home.

BEYOND LANCASHIRE...AND BACK

'The contrast between it and Belfast was so great that it was like living in a new world,' wrote Derek Dougan in *The Sash He Never Wore* following his move to Portsmouth. Although recognising the cities shared certain characteristics, he was evidently glad to be free from the strait-laced aspect of east Belfast culture: 'The two had something in common because each had a shipyard, but Portsmouth thankfully was a good deal less "religious".'

On the footballing side, he was surprised to learn that, in his opinion, the training methods were not as good as those at Distillery. He was nevertheless delighted that fellow Grosvenor Park old boy and Ulsterman Norman Uprichard was already at the club. While still at Distillery, Uprichard had played in a friendly against Charlton, at the end of which his opposite number Sam Bartram had, according to Uprichard's autobiography, run the length of the pitch to tell him 'Norman, you'll make it.' The shot stopper from Lurgan had been at work all day, and had only gone to the game to watch from the stands when he put into the team at the last minute, so this was a great encouragement.

He did make it: after a year at Arsenal without playing

a game and realising his lowly ranking in the pecking order, the keeper moved on to Swindon where he made 73 appearances before becoming Eddie Lavery's first signing for Portsmouth. He would make the Hampshire town his home, living there with Lily and his mother who had come over to join them from Lurgan. Uprichard had particularly strong memories of games against Everton, who used to have a large contingent of fans from Dublin attend their games, 'they knew I was from the north and, being a Protestant, would give me stick,' he recalled in his book, adding that when he made a good save he would turn round and stick two fingers up to them.

Five years after his own arrival at the club, his friend Dougan turned up believing he was looked upon as an 'Irish upstart', feeling fortunate that Uprichard was able to offer a slice of home away from home. He would later write of his friend that he 'was one of nature's noblemen, a gentle anarchist with a great sense of the ridiculous and a capacity for never being riled by adversity. He liked to deflate the hierarchy and he was no respecter of important persons ... But for him the frustrations of Fratton Park would have overwhelmed me.'

Dougan made his league debut for Portsmouth on 19 October 1957, a 3-0 win at home. After a few months across the water he made a trip home and remarks about how English his accent had already become were made: 'I suppose my friends were resentful that they couldn't get free from the Ulster situation,' he wrote dismissively. Dougan's playing career in England would span 546 games and an impressive tally of 222 goals.

Twenty-six of those were for Blackburn Rovers, an Irishman in Lancashire once again, where he played between 1959 and 1961, in a team that contained a number of Irish Catholics. Though he could often come out with bombastic pronouncements, here Dougan wrote incisively about the nature of North-South relations in Ireland in the context of that team:

> “We never fell out over religion, which goes to show that if you take Irishmen from north and south and put them together *outside* their own country, they can live happily, and in peace, in a different environment. The big problem over there is not the people themselves, whether north or south of the border; it is their whole environment.

He struggled to reproduce anything near the same level of performance for Northern Ireland, yet you get the sense that Derek knows how lucky he was. Especially when the alternative was what he saw as the dreaded monotony of Harland and Wolff, writing of how he ‘left home and have been a member of six football teams in England. They have given me a living I could not have enjoyed back in Belfast, or in Ulster.’ He was able to make the step up from Irish League to First Division with relative ease and speed, ‘In 1956 I played in the Irish Cup Final. Four years later I played in the English Cup Final.’

He had fulfilled not only his boyhood dreams but the hopes so many back home had placed in him; the first half of his career took place before George Best had even trod the hallowed Old Trafford turf. Best’s travelling trialist companion at United, Eric McMordie, who would go on to play 241 times over 11 years for Middlesbrough, was born eight years after Dougan but witnessed his rise, telling David Tossell in *In Sunshine Or In Shadow*:

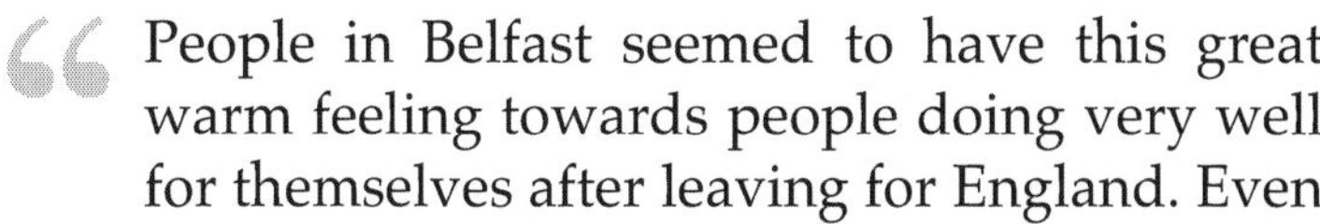

> “People in Belfast seemed to have this great warm feeling towards people doing very well for themselves after leaving for England. Even

> now, my own family speaks of people complimenting others for doing well. They really do look up to you. Everyone where we were brought up thought Derek was a real hero. And they still do.

Writing in 1972, Dougan summed up his story up to that point, having left Distillery in 1957: 'Fifteen years later I may say I am the local boy, from Avon Street, East Belfast, who in some way has made good.' In some ways, it would be hard to disagree.

5

PLAYING FOR PETER

In 1951 the Irish Football Association did something highly unusual: they appointed a manager. For anyone under the age of forty the name Peter Doherty will conjure up images of a floppy-haired wastrel mumbling something about Englishmen in baseball caps and burgling Carl Barât's flat.

To another generation, Peter Doherty was the man from Magherafelt who revolutionised Northern Irish football. Or Irish football. You see, the Republic of and Northern both lay claim to the name Ireland and it was not until 1952 that FIFA ordered them to identify themselves by more clearly defined terms. An incendiary document issued by the IFA continued to push back against this distinction, observing 'it is important at this stage to point out that association football is not recognised as their national game which is called "Gaelic" and is an amalgamation of association and rugby football.'

Northern Ireland had actually only desisted from selecting players born outside its borders two years previously; its last 'whole Ireland' side earning a 0-0 with

Wales on 8 March 1950, featuring 'outsiders' Bud Aherne, Con Martin, Reg Ryan and Davy Walsh. For Martin, it was the right time, as told in Malcolm Brodie's *100 Years of Irish Football*:

> 'It all came to a head prior to a match between Northern Ireland and Wales at Wrexham in the late Forties. On the morning of the game I received a call from a then prominent FAI official urging me not to turn out for Northern Ireland. I listened to his argument but turned out just the same. It would have been unfair to my team-mates to pull out at that late stage. We drew with the Welsh but when I returned to Villa Park I had made up my mind that was the end of playing for the North.'

Even so, the team from the North would continue referring to itself as Ireland well into the 1970s. It was a confusing time.

NOT A WASTER

Malcolm Brodie described Doherty as 'the father...of Northern Ireland international football second only to George Best. He was magnificent...Doherty came into it and he had the players there who could back him up. He made people feel tall.' Billy Bingham was equally delighted by his appointment as manager, gushing as if a teenage Libertines fan. In Evan Marshall's *Spirit of '58* he tells of how 'they brought in someone that I respected, and I listened to every word he said. And as a player, he was outstanding. I watched him play as a young boy at Windsor Park. He was my idol - I just looked up to him.'

Doherty was born in Magerhafelt, County Londonderry in 1913. Growing up he attended St Malachi's college in Coleraine where football was banned — not on cultural or class grounds - but because to play it on the asphalt playground was deemed too dangerous. His playing career began with local side Station United, able to play owing to an inventive ruse related to his day job as a bus conductor. As the vehicle followed its route between Coleraine and Portstewart, the young man would disembark near the team's ground, play the match, then hop back on and continue his afternoon's work with a complicit driver collecting the few fares who boarded.

Just a few years later, he helped Glentoran to a 3-1 Irish Cup final replay win, aged twenty, as scorer one of the Glens goals against Distillery. This brought him to the attention of Blackpool, who signed him shortly afterwards. The medal he earned that day remained once of his most prized possessions despite the metal being of inferior quality to the one he won in England with Manchester City. Yet strangely his appearances for the Northern Irish side were limited to 16 in 15 years, apparently ignored by the selectors. When Danny Blanchflower appeared on Michael Parkinson's chat show in 1977 he claimed, 'They didn't pick him in those days for the Northern Ireland team because he was too good for the others, that's what the selectors said.' The war interlude was another factor in his spotty international record, though seven of his appearances were as captain. Contemporary opinion has it that he should be recognised as one of the greats of that era, alongside Stanley Matthews.

His last game for Northern Ireland was in 1950 and a year later in September 1951 he became the team's first manager. The squad was still picked by selectors, as had been the practice up to this point, but Doherty was in charge of more or less everything else. It is evident now that Doherty was a footballing visionary, far ahead of his time. He believed, in remarks in Evans Marshall's book focusing on Northern Ireland's 1958 World Cup journey, that the reason for 'Ireland's mediocrity in international soccer circles is lack of coaching facilities. There is a love of football in the country which equals the enthusiasm for the game shown in England, Scotland and Wales. But, by itself, it has never been enough. Guidance and instruction have always been necessary before it could ever hope to become effective.'

Before being appointed Doherty had submitted a detailed plan to the IFA proposing centres of excellence to be located near to the grounds of Irish League clubs, rejected only because of the expense that it would have entailed. His 1948 instructional autobiography *Spotlight on Football* fleshes out his philosophy, explaining 'There are thousands of boys in Ireland who are as keen on the game as I was. From amongst them, a team could eventually be built which would make Ireland a power to be reckoned with in international soccer.'

Billy Drennan's appointment as secretary of the IFA, coupled with the new manager's arrival in the early fifties, finally had Blanchflower believing that the blazers at the IFA were finally thinking seriously about the national team, as comments found in Dave Bowler's biography testify, 'He was the best thing that ever happened to us. Peter's appointment was the beginning of the fairy tale. We had all respected him as a great player. He gave the team an identity. Now, we did not play for inefficiency and hypocrisy. We did not represent all those old men masquerading as important sporting figures. Doherty represented Ireland. It was an honour to play for the things he represented, his enthusiasm and adventure.'

Blanchflower became captain in 1953 during a tour of Canada, assistant manager in all but name. Together, he and Doherty pioneered new formations that went beyond the basic WM that had been prevalent in the British game before the war. None of this is to say that Doherty's was an overnight success, as Blanchflower is reported in Bowler's work, 'We didn't just go out and slay the world; but we quickly lowered the boom on those mammoth defeats.' The qualifying campaign for the World Cup of 1954 still took the form of the Home Championship, meaning that progression to the tournament itself would involve taking on the might of the English and Scottish teams. Qualification was already beyond reach by the time Doherty's charges played Wales at Vetch Field, so he used this as an opportunity to introduce some new faces to the team with one eye to the future: Harry Gregg, Bertie Peacock, Jackie Blanchflower and Peter McParland made their debuts that day and it was the Newry-born McParland who scored both goals in a 2-1 win.

Bertie Peacock saw this as a pivotal moment in the life of Doherty's Northern Ireland, as Bowler's Blanchflower biography notes 'It all started to come together that day in Wrexham in 1954.' Danny was predictably effusive in his praise of the new order, reported as saying 'It did my heart good to play in that team, and such a young side too, with an average age of twenty-three.'

Matches against teams beyond the British Isles were still a rarity in the mid-fifties, mainly due to the expense of travel for such a small FA in an era before the jet age. Nonetheless, Bertie Peacock, Jimmy McIlroy and Danny Blanchflower played in a Great Britain XI against a European XI in August 1955 to celebrate the 75th anniversary of the IFA's founding, the latter wearing the armband. Walter Winterbottom was the man in charge of the British XI that day and said of his captain, as Dave Bowler's book on his subject notes, 'Danny was so effervescent, so full of Irish mannerisms, cheerfully exaggerating everything, using "Irishisms" to explain defeats, always positive.'

Later that year Northern Ireland would make their own first appearance at Wembley: their matches before 1955 had not been deemed important enough to be held in England's centrepiece stadium. The Northern Irish players were reminded ahead of the November fixture what a privilege playing at Wembley was supposed to be but the team's trainer, Gerry Morgan, was having none of it, with an account in *Danny Blanchflower: A Biography of a Visionary* quoting him as saying 'Great honour be damned. Sure, the greyhounds have been running there for over twenty years!'

(Don't worry, there will be more of him later.)

NOW DOGS, NOW IRISH

Northern Ireland could now dare to tread where dogs had gone before them, their qualifying group for the 1958 World Cup, pitting them against Portugal and Italy presented a treacherous pathway to the tournament in Sweden. This was the first time that the 'home' nations would compete for a place in the finals without squaring off against one another for a single spot and the team from Northern Ireland had not played a team from outside the British Isles since a friendly against France in Paris in 1952. Though a qualifying group of 3 appears unbelievable to the modern eye, only fifty-three countries entered the pre-tournament pool. Unlike today, where more than two hundred nations vie to contend in FIFA's showpiece tournament, Northern Ireland was the least populous nation in the running.

The road to Halsmtad began in January 1957 at the *Estadio José Alvalade* in Lisbon. Peter Doherty travelled to the Portuguese capital with a squad of twelve, apparently reminding his players, as stated in Hanna's *The World At Their Feet* 'We go out to fight for the honour of Northern Ireland and for the glittering prize of a place in the World Cup final sixteen. Remember we are ambassadors for our country.' The Portuguese had planned to play the national anthem of the Republic, *Amhrán na bhFiann,* for their visitors, but were mercifully informed of their potential *faux pas* before the match and quickly substituted 'God Save The Queen' into the running order. Likely feeling an abundance of caution at this point, the cover of the match day programme was emblazoned with a Union Jack rather than the Red Hand of Ulster.

This was also a fixture which had the unusual distinction of being scheduled so late in the evening that it would begin one day and finish the next, though the Portuguese made one scheduling concession to the IFA: this would normally have been a match arranged for a Sunday afternoon, but their counterparts in Belfast would not countenance such an affront and the eventual timing of the tie meant it was the first match to take place under floodlights in Portugal. On the culinary front, no fripperies were permitted by the Northern Irish team doctor: a report in the *Belfast Telegraph* as revealed by Evan Marshall chronicles of events, stated 'Irish team are told to watch diet. British meals only until after game.'

Though clubs in England had come to an agreement with the English FA to release English players, they were not obligated to do the same for Northern Ireland and Harry Gregg was a notable absence in the team sheet. When the match got underway on 16 January, Billy Bingham wasted no time in putting his team in front, scoring after six minutes. A goal from Manuel Vasques in the thirty-fourth minute levelled the score, and this was how matters remained on 17 January when it ended.

Afterwards, Malcolm Brodie reports that Peter McParland described the game as 'the dirtiest in which I've played.'

A nil-nil draw with Wales in a British Championship matchup three months later was followed by the team's first qualification bout with Italy in Rome's *Stadio Olimpico*. It was an especially hot April day on the central Italian coast and the team's trainer-cum-physio Gerry Morgan had decided to fill a bucket with eau de Cologne and water, using it to wipe the players faces during breaks in play. Northern Ireland had conceded from Sergio Cervato after three minutes and battled for the rest of the match to level the score, managing to hit the woodwork no less than three times during the final ten minutes of play. The *Glasgow Herald* described Doherty's side as 'most unlucky to be beaten', though it was plain to even the most optimistic observer that the prize of a World Cup berth was already looking tenuous. The trip had not been entirely irredeemable, though: Alan Bairner and Graham Walker's paper *Football and Society in Northern Ireland* contains the interesting fact that the travelling party's only two known Catholics in Morgan and McParland were able to make a short pilgrimage to the Vatican.

McParland had attended a Christian Brothers school as a youngster, where he was only allowed to play Gaelic football, though this probably helped him to become as fearless and strong as he was. Eventually, he set up his own 'soccer' team upon leaving school at fourteen, helping to found the Shamrock Youth Club which competed in the Newry and District Summer League. From here he signed for nearby Dundalk, while also working as a barman and, additionally, in a timber yard.

It was not time for Peter and Gerry to discard the rosary just yet. The Irish case would be bolstered a week later when Portugal travelled to Belfast and were defeated 3-0, despite Doherty's side having not won a match for two years. Before Northern Ireland's decisive return fixture with the Italians at Windsor Park there would be two British Championship matches: a 1-1 draw with Scotland in Belfast and a 3-2 triumph over England. The travelling Irish contingent in the stands are said to have invaded the Wembley pitch and 'carried the Irish players to the dressing rooms, waving shamrocks and cheering what was undoubtedly a famous victory.' It was only the fifth time they had beaten the English and the first since 1927.

Peter McParland, in words captured in Bowler's book covering this time, would reflect that this was the game that gave them a new confidence in their abilities, 'That was a really great day and it was a stepping stone towards the World Cup. The greatest thing was we had an Irish team, we were all from Belfast, Derry, Newry, lads who'd grown up in Northern Ireland, which was very satisfying. We were a close bunch by then and beating England made us feel we could take on anyone.' The Italians seemed to take the renewed Northern Irish threat seriously, hastily arranging friendlies with Luton Town and Charlton Athletic to give themselves an indication of the 'British' type of football they should expect.

Derek Dougan was called up to the Irish squad to face an Italy squad which included former Charlton forward Eddie Firmani, now turning out for Sampdoria. This was a match Northern Ireland had to win, whereas a draw would be sufficient for the Italians to progress: the stage was set for a qualification showdown from which only one of them could emerge.

There was one problem: the referee, whose day job was as a stage manager at the Budapest Opera House, had a four-legged journey to Belfast, involving changes in Prague, Brussels and London. He only completed three of them, becoming stranded by fog in London. What was to be done? As Marshall and Hanna note in their respective books on the build up to the 1958 World Cup, the official waited in England hoping to catch the Ulster Flyer as hurried arrangements were made to source a replacement. The IFA contacted the English referee, Arthur Ellis, who was amenable but the Italians believed a British official could not be sufficiently impartial and rejected the idea. Given that this notion had been dismissed it was unsurprising that when IFA then sought the services of a local referee, this was also vetoed.

The game could not go ahead as planned, but to call it off would be to risk the fearsome wrath of the Windsor Park faithful, many of whom had taken a day off from the shipyard to attend this crucial encounter. A decision was made; the match would be demoted to a friendly with the qualifier to be rearranged for a later date. Tommy Mitchell, a Lurgan man, would officiate the match. Even so, the unwitting crowd were hardly likely to be overjoyed and it seems the players had not been kept in the loop either. As Dave Bowler's Blanchflowar-tinged telling of the story has it, Peter McParland set the scene in the Irish dressing room, 'Twenty minutes before kick-off we were up and ready for the game, raring to go, and Peter Doherty came in and said, "I've news for you. The referee hasn't turned up and the Italians won't accept the Irish referee."'

THE BATTLE OF BELFAST

The teams took to the field in front of 35,000 fractious fans who proceeded to drown out the Italian anthem with a chorus of jeers and boos. Though this sounds confrontational, it is probable that most of those present had never before heard the anthem: this was 1958 and a football match was still yet to be televised in Northern Ireland.

Neither had the team played a game outside of the British Isles before 1950 and even after that such ties had been limited to a mere handful. The cost of following the team to away games would have been prohibitive to all but the richest of fans, so it seems more likely a combination of a disgruntled crowd and an unfamiliar tune were to blame. The stage was set for what Bertie Peacock would, in Bowler's telling, called 'the battle of Belfast.'

He is not the only player who remembered it well. Billy Bingham recalled in Marshall's *Spirit of '58*, 'We were kicking the shit out of each other...I was getting whacked all the time. It was the unfriendliest friendly I played in.' He continued, 'They were all heroes in their own right. But they brought it on themselves unfortunately and they met a team that would have a go with the Irish temperament. Don't kick me or I'll kick you twice. We never let people away with kicking us at Windsor Park. No, you didn't get away with it. You were always going to get it back.'

When the game ended with the score at 2-2 the Irish crowd were still fired up, perhaps even more than they had been at kick-off. They had forsaken a day's pay in shipyards to watch what turned out to be nothing more than a friendly and their mood was far from genial. More than 2,000 of them invaded the pitch, charging in the direction of the departing Italian players who had to be given protection by their opposite numbers in the Irish side, who took responsibility for a man each.

It had been a bruising affair and they would have to do it all over again in January. Off the pitch, the government in the Republic of Ireland were quick to point out that it was the Northern Irish team and not theirs that had been involved in the dramatic events in Belfast. The foreign press had made some incorrect assumptions, forcing Dublin's Minister for External Affairs to send a hurried telegram to Irish embassies asking them to explain that Belfast was part of Ireland 'held by the British.' Per Marshall's record of events, the *Éire* legation in Rome issued statement explaining, 'Belfast has no political connection with us. It is the principal city of Northern Ireland which is part of Britain. The team which played against Italy represented only Northern Ireland, and not the Irish Republic.'

Nothing was left to chance in preparations for the Italians second visit to Belfast in the space of six weeks. Istvan Zsolt, intrepid Hungarian referee, arrived with his linesmen three days before kick-off while Peter Doherty took his charges to the cinema to watch a screening of their victory over England a few months earlier. There was also a more substantial police presence this time: two dozen RUC officers inside Windsor Park and more on standby outside. Perhaps most significantly for the men and women of Ulster lucky enough to own a television in 1958, the BBC were to televise the match, the first broadcast of a football match in Ireland. Well, most of it: the first ten minutes were not shown, schedulers deciding that something else — perhaps the news - was more important.

The Italians were on £500 a man to qualify but one of their number, Alcides Zhiggia, would not last the full ninety minutes. When he was dismissed in the sixty-sixth minute all three of the goals that would decide the tie had already been scored. Jimmy McIlroy had netted early for the Irish and Wilbur Cush made it two in the twenty-eighth minute. Though Dino Da Costa put the ball past Norman Uprichard (Harry Gregg having become another victim of fog), it would only be a consolation rather than the start of a comeback.

So impressive had Jimmy McIlroy's performance been that he was approached by Sampdoria with a package, including, according to Ronnie Hanna's *The World At Their Feet,* a villa overlooking the Mediterranean Sea and arrangements made for his children to attend an international school, as well as the promise of far higher wages than those on offer in England at the time. He put this to his wife, a Lancashire girl, who replied, 'Why would you want to leave Burnley?' Well, quite.

The players had done their bit, but there was a problem which many had not foreseen and those who had likely thought would never materialise: Northern Ireland were not allowed to play football on Sundays. This was fine when they were in a position to organise their own fixtures, as they had been in qualifying but when FIFA were in charge of scheduling there could be no such guarantees. The IFA's rules stated 'no match shall be played inside or outside of this area by this Association on a Sunday', as had been the case since its inception. There had been hope that the IFA AGM of May 1957 might have permitted a relaxation of the clause, but instead it was re-endorsed by an overwhelming majority, perhaps not surprising in an association where the Churches League had seventy-six affiliated clubs. The motion went down by 89 votes to 7.

In 1941 the four 'home' associations had agreed in principle not to play on Sundays but only the Northern Irish body had stuck to this on the international stage, although Scotland and Wales did not sanction domestic Sunday football at the time. While the dozen Irish League clubs were likely in favour of modifying the rule, the junior and church clubs remained opposed. A number of IFA bigwigs probably wanted the team to go too, yet were also keen to avoid becoming personally embroiled in a political storm. Instead they engaged themselves in some strategic fence sitting.

Sammy Walker, chairman of the IFA selection

committee and President of the Irish League, hoped that a compromise with FIFA could be found. In records brought to light by Ronnie Hanna, comments show Walker stating that 'It may be taken for granted that the Association [IFA] will go forward to the final stages. There are mid-week dates and should we be drawn to play on a Sunday there is nothing to prevent the match from being played another day.' In short, he wanted the rest of the world to bend to the will of Northern Ireland: 'There is nothing in the rules of the World Cup to say that any or certain games must be played on a Sunday. It is known that the Irish FA have a complete ban on Sunday football, and I am sure our wishes will be respected by the other associations.' IFA secretary Billy Drennan made an appeal to FIFA on these grounds, which was swiftly dismissed.

This was Northern Ireland in 1958: there was a real possibility that having gone to the hassle of qualifying, the team would have to withdraw because of their own statutes and an inability to alter them, though only Harry Gregg of the playing staff had any serious concerns about playing on a Sunday as most had played on Sundays during club tours of Europe with their English sides.

The controversy was regarded as faintly baffling, as McParland explained in Marshall's retelling of the saga:

> I remember getting a letter and it was from a Lord's Day Observant person and I think there was the name of a well-known politician on it but I didn't look at it enough. I rolled it up and threw it away. I wasn't for that. But as we were playing that season, going towards the World Cup, we were meeting each other, the players were playing against each other in England and that was the first conversation. The first thing they would say was look, this

> is a once in a lifetime situation, we're not standing any of this nonsense. We were in a situation whereby lots of people around the world didn't know where Northern Ireland was and we had a chance to go out there and put Northern Ireland on the map. So why should we lie down to people? The players had their own minds. Of all eleven, there wasn't one player in the group who said I'm not playing on a Sunday.

Bertie Peacock was of similar mind, stressing the pragmatism which informed his thinking on the matter, again in *Spirit of '58,* 'It was our work and if we had to play on a Sunday we just had to play on a Sunday. My minister said, "Bertie, you'll hardly go to the World Cup." I said, "Sir, if it's my work I'll be going," and he just laughed at me. He probably knew it was a chance in a lifetime. If you want to play in the World Cup you have to play on their terms.'

The IFA was the only association in the world which had a rule forbidding international matches being played on Sundays. Jimmy McIlroy reflected on the situation several decades later, 'Looking back now, I think what a silly decision. I suppose it wouldn't have happened in any other country except Northern Ireland.' In a book, *Right Inside Soccer,* published a couple of years after the tournament he had written that:

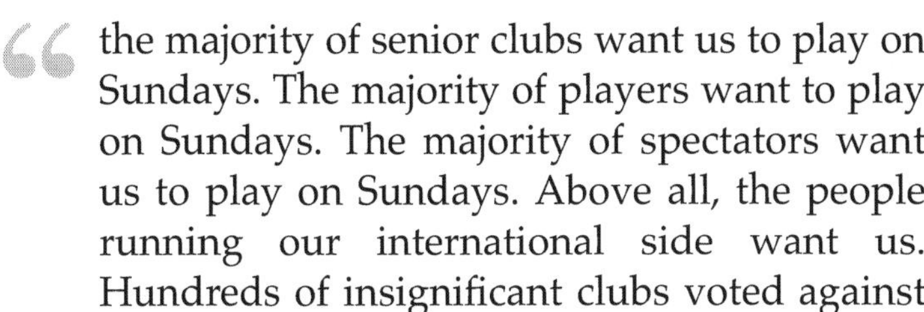

> the majority of senior clubs want us to play on Sundays. The majority of players want to play on Sundays. The majority of spectators want us to play on Sundays. Above all, the people running our international side want us. Hundreds of insignificant clubs voted against

> it. That is why...all major decisions ought to be taken by senior clubs. The opinions of the amateur leagues should be recorded...and ignored! Such men are millstones to Irish international prestige.

Harry Gregg's own misgivings were assuaged when Manchester United played Blackpool: he searched the telephone directory to find a clergyman and found the number of an Anglican vicar, who asked him whether he thought it was acceptable for a surgeon to operate on a Sunday, to which the answer was obvious. This apparently, if somewhat mystifyingly, reassured the goalkeeper that he — a footballer - was fine to play on a Sunday too. Gregg later explained in *Harry's Game* 'the decision to play in the 1958 World Cup was not one I took lightly. The fact that some matches were scheduled for a Sunday presented me with a very real dilemma. I'd been brought up to believe in the age-old tradition of strict Sunday observance.'

THE WISDOM OF CROWDS

Five days after the defeat of Italy, the Federation of Ulster Supporters Clubs met and reached the consensus that they were in favour of the team playing in Sweden. Delegates of the Belfast Minor Football League and the Irish Alliance League also came to the same conclusion, but a seventy-five per cent majority was needed to change the IFA rule and the strength of the Pharisaical voting bloc within the IFA was such that achieving it would be a minor miracle. The Belfast District Synod of the Methodist Church publicly urged the IFA not to compromise on the Sunday question, their fury not allayed by an IFA gesture allowing that players could decide for themselves whether they should play on a Sunday.

In early February, the FIFA organising committee had met and advised the interested parties that no dates would be changed to suit the IFA and that the matter was closed. Soon after, the draw was made and two of Northern Ireland's group matches, their first against Czechoslovakia and the last on 15 June against West Germany, were scheduled on Sundays. Further opinion was forthcoming, this time from the Methodist Council on Social Welfare, who, per Hanna's account, urged the Council of the IFA to 'abide by the spirit of its own rules and to advise members of the Irish team not to play on Sundays.'

Additionally, the Churches League was ready to seek an injunction to stop the team playing on a Sunday. Malcolm Brodie was downcast, writing 'If we have to withdraw let us hide our heads in shame, let us forget about being a world soccer power.'

On 16 February 1958, a meeting was convened (on a Sunday!) at the Assembly Hall in Belfast with representation from all the main Protestant denominations, presided over by The Very Reverend Dr AF Moody, who was a former moderator of the Presbyterian Church. As Evan Marshall's research shows, a statement was released stressing that this footballing liberalism was a 'retrograde step, bound to have a detrimental influence on the life of the community. This is bound to bring discredit upon the Province.'

In further examinations of contemporaneous reports in *Spirit of '58,* we learn that William Wilton, a vice president of the IFA, was also part of the platform and remarked 'Ireland will only play on Sundays over my dead body.' He knew a bit about dead bodies since in addition to his footballing duties, he was an undertaker. The Church of

Ireland's Canon Maguire had told those present that the idea of turning a blind eye to the rule in this instance would be the first step on a slippery slope to a widespread loosening up of protections on the Sabbath: soon people would want cinemas to be open on the day of rest too! Another delegate, Rupert Gibson, said that the IFA was not only in breach of its own laws but God's, while in Hanna's *The World At Their Feet* there is reference to a Revd Hubert Irvine, a Methodist from Dunmurry, who warned, 'I inform and warn the IFA council here and now that everything possible will be done to force them if need be to abide by the articles of association which forbids Sunday football inside or outside the area of their jurisdiction.'

This apparently included the sincere threat of legal action, which was hard to ignore, as was Irvine's letter mentioning 'further necessary steps.' Meanwhile, the Royal Black Institution - a sort of Orange Order/Freemason mashup on steroids — spoke of how they were 'profoundly disappointed that the Northern Ireland soccer legislators countenanced such an unprecedented and retrogressive step' and that if further Sunday football was put on the agenda it would 'meet with the strongest possible opposition from the Institution.'

Compromise would eventually be reached on 13 March, when representatives of the Churches League agreed to withdraw their opposition to the team going to the World Cup, on the condition that the IFA would commit to not entering any future competition that would require them to compete on a Sunday. In a mark of the small-mindedness of the affair, part of the deal involved the withdrawal of Northern Ireland's youth team from a tournament in Luxembourg at the beginning of April, organisers unable to guarantee that they would not be compelled to play on a Sunday. In Dave Bowler's coverage of events of the time, Danny Blanchflower is quoted as having proclaimed, 'A majority 75 per cent vote of the Irish FA decided we could not go to Sweden but, being Irish, we did.'

Peter's players would be going to the World Cup. Their passage to Sweden assured; there was a British Championship match with Wales to deal with first, though there would be no pre-tournament friendlies for fear that Doherty's paper thin squad would be weakened by injury. The Welsh would be going to Scandinavia too, following the collapse of the Afro-Asia qualifying group made up of Egypt, Indonesia and Sudan, meaning Israel had no opposition in the playoff. Having finished second in their own group, the Welsh won a lottery to contest the tie against Israel, whom they went on to beat.

Northern Ireland's own match with Wales was a closely fought 1-1 draw at Ninian Park, a fixture in which Peter McParland believed he had played so badly that he might not make the World Cup squad. He was quickly disabused of this notion by Willie Cunningham who, as recorded by Hanna, told him, 'What do you mean — we've only got sixteen players!' Malcolm Brodie's assessment of McParland's performance was scathing, writing that he had missed more chances 'than France has had post-war governments.'

Twenty-two players were permitted for each team going to the 1958 World Cup, though Doherty named just sixteen in the travelling party. The preliminary squad allowed up to forty men, a figure which provoked only laughter from the IFA offices, who told FIFA that there 'weren't forty men remotely under consideration!' Though the association was not a wealthy one and cost may have been another factor in the small squad, it is worth noting that England took just twenty and the reigning champions West Germany travelled with only eighteen players.

With Doncaster's post-season tour commitments demanding Doherty's attention, Danny Blanchflower lead the early training sessions in Belfast, before the team met up with the manager and those players with club commitments in London prior to their flight to Sweden. Understandably, Harry Gregg had his own arrangements, having been on the stricken plane which had crashed shortly after taking off from the Munich-Riem airport on 6 February 1958; a disaster which took the lives of twenty-three and the football career of Jackie Blanchflower.

Proof of just how divided the IFA still was on the issue of Sunday football is found in the actions of the selector who accompanied Gregg on his boat and train journey to Sweden, a man by the name of Joe Beckett: he returned home immediately by plane, not wanting any further part of a tournament in which Northern Ireland would be playing on the Sabbath.

Gregg had been struggling to sleep since the events of Munich and it was decided he would room with Gerry Morgan, the team's trainer, for the duration of the tournament. Given that Gerry was known for his daft antics one wonders how this helped Gregg's state of mind, perhaps other than to distract him from the tragedy that had unfolded only a few months earlier. Gregg wrote fondly of his roommate many years later in *Harry's Game,* 'Nerves....were easily dispelled when you had a man like Gerry Morgan around. Gerry, our trainer, was an amazing character. Hardly the epitome of health and fitness, he was bald. And Gerry didn't so much kiss the blarney stone as swallow the bloody thing whole.'

When the squad were in London readying themselves for the onward flight to Sweden, Morgan is said to have climbed on a soapbox at Speaker's Corner in Hyde Park, amusing the crowds with some comedic horse racing commentary. Charles de Gaulle had recently ushered in France's Fifth Republic and been elected its President and, in Marshall's recounting, a player had remarked within Gerry's earshot that all you ever heard about in the newspapers was 'de Gaulle, de Gaulle', to which Gerry replied that soon the team would have a new motto for their World Cup: 'de goal, de goal.'

ONE GERRY MORGAN

Francis Gerard Morgan had been born in Belfast in 1899, taking up a job as a linen-lapper in Linenhall Street aged fifteen after being educated by the Christian Brothers. He lasted for five days before joining the British Army where he saw service in Egypt with the Machine Gun Corps and, still in North Africa, played as a centre half against the Royal Engineers in the Egyptian Cup Final. On returning to Belfast he pulled on a Cliftonville shirt but joined Linfield after just three appearances, the latter subsequently fined 50 guineas for the 1920s equivalent of tapping up.

An unsung hero of Northern Irish football history, Gerry Morgan's career trajectory was extraordinary: a Roman Catholic who was part of the 1921/22 Linfield side which won all seven trophies it was competing in before signing for Nottingham Forest, spending seven seasons there before returning to end his career back home. He had been half-decent in his day, playing in the Northern Irish side that beat England at Windsor Park in 1927.

It was during his stint with Linfield that Morgan was handed a letter shortly after a game against Glentoran; a skull and crossbones drawn on it with a message for its recipient. According to Bairner and Walker's *Football and Society in Northern Ireland*, its message read 'If you, Gerry

Morgan, take the field to-day you are a dead man. Get that straight. We're talking business.' He played anyway but upon leaving Windsor Park in a taxi with some of his teammates, a man jumped alongside the vehicle and fired a shot. Mercifully, nobody was hurt. Was it a republican gunman? Who knows. It could just as easily have been a disgruntled loyalist. Nobody would have been very happy about a Catholic playing for Linfield.

During the era Morgan played for the Blues, he was not the only Catholic to take to the field on their behalf — others included Tommy Breen and Davy Walsh - but they came and went. In fact, the barbs directed at Breen came from across the Bog Meadows: his spell at Linfield followed a three year stint with Belfast Celtic, and as one historian of the latter club notes, 'had the grim prospect on more than one occasion of leading the Blues out at Celtic Park before his Falls Road neighbours, and on coming out of Mass on Sunday morning from St Paul's he would meet the usual banter with unfailing good humour.'

Gerry Morgan *was* the club, a Mr Linfield. After being forcibly retired from the game through injury he returned to Linfield once more, first as a trainer for Linfield Swifts, before graduating to the first team in 1939 while performing the same role for Northern Ireland. Billy Simpson played for both and remembered in Marshall's chronology how 'he wasn't much of a trainer, physically, to keep players fit, but he was good jokester!' In a similar vein Harry Gregg, once again in *Spirit of '58* reflected, 'I think they call them today sports psychologists and things like that. Gerry could have played tig with a fox. He was the most remarkable man. Peter, Danny and Gerry - to me, they made us what we were.'

Simpson and Gregg were far from alone in their high regard from the man the players called 'uncle'. Billy

Bingham described him, in Marshall's book, as 'amusing, amazing and inspirational and yet he was an ordinary man, he hadn't got big words or anything like that but somehow or other he got to you and I loved him.' In Hanna's pages, Jimmy McIlroy similarly saw the indispensability of Morgan, 'I honestly don't know how much he knew about injuries or how to treat them, but he certainly made up for it in maintaining team spirit in the side.' On the team bus he would often provide a running commentary of events on the other side of the window, joking 'we are now passing a large pub...Why?' On another occasion he asked, 'Have you seen the new ten pound notes? I haven't seen the old ones yet!'

Though there had been *that* incident during his playing career at Linfield in the early twenties, Gerry took an opportunity to lighten the mood of the day. His son, Dan, recalls in Marshall's work a game between Linfield and Glentoran, the Bluemen boasting in song about not having any Catholics on their team, the Glenmen asking in response; 'What about Gerry Morgan?' Morgan appeared on the touchline, waving his cap around Windsor Park to the amusement of the entire crowd. It was a ground so beloved to Gerry that during the Second World War he occasionally slept there, presumably with the intention of putting out any fires started by Nazi incendiary during the Belfast Blitz.

A decade later, during the celebration of the seventy-fifth year of the IFA, Gerry was on the sidelines as the trainer of the Great Britain team taking on the Rest of the World. Peter Sillett was playing right-back that day and according to Harry Gregg's account, Gerry shouted to a policeman on the side of the pitch. '"Officer!" "Gerry, what is it - Be quiet." "Officer! C'mere!" "Gerry, shut up." "C'mere." "What is it Gerry?" "Arrest your right back." "What are you talking about?" "For loitering."'

Later that year, Northern Ireland were preparing for a British Championship match with Scotland and Gerry learned it was going to be televised, quite a rarity in those days. He decided he wanted to be on TV and agreed with Peter McParland that the player would feign an injury towards the end of the match so that Gerry could have his fifteen-seconds of fame, unless - of course - someone had been genuinely injured before that point. Eighty-seven minutes had passed and McParland fell to the grass hurt. Morgan came on beaming and winking and when the referee asked him what was wrong with McParland he said, 'I think it must be old age.' McParland remembered to Hanna, 'I said, "I'll get you on Gerry"...I had a cramp in the second half and Gerry came on. He had a high step thing and he came running out to do the job. And they all thought I played that, but I didn't, I really had a cramp. I don't know if he was looking at the cameras or not but we said we'd get him on and I got him on.'

It's indisputable that Morgan - who, during the '58 World Cup would knock on the players doors at 7am with a can of Andrews Liver Salts and dish out a spoonful to each - was loved, but how did he survive at Linfield, whose boardroom was a who's who of Unionist politicians? We may observe the fact that he did not regularly attend Mass, as Bairner and Walker point out, as important in helping him run that gauntlet and it also seems that even the most ideological of football clubs was able to make an accommodation, when it was in their practical interest to do so.

Morgan was likely regarded as that jocular Irish stereotype: the harmless comedian; making wisecracks and supping on his pint of Guinness; a figure it was good to have around because he could do the odd jobs and make the lads laugh at the same time. What's true is that he was not seen as equal to a Protestant, and when he died the club was slow to give any benefit money to his widow, Annie. Neither, as Bairner and Walker note, did they take up his suggestion of a benefit match between Northern Ireland and the Republic, a match the team from the North would surely have won. All that having being said, the late 1950s in Northern Ireland was *relatively* calm. The Northern Irish Labour Party was at a high point; the welfare state had raised living standards and the IRA's border campaign of 1956-62 was not widely popular among nationalists. If a Catholic was going to make his home at Linfield better the late fifties than the late sixties.

According to evidence in Bairner and Walker's enlightening study, when Morgan died aged fifty-nine, in 1959, the club's president Sir Anthony Babington said of him:

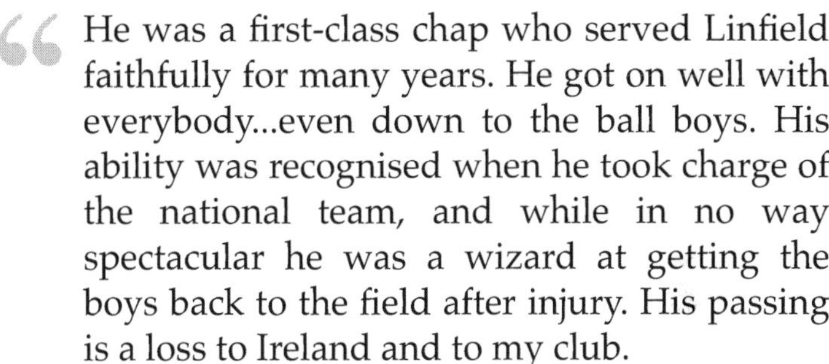

> He was a first-class chap who served Linfield faithfully for many years. He got on well with everybody...even down to the ball boys. His ability was recognised when he took charge of the national team, and while in no way spectacular he was a wizard at getting the boys back to the field after injury. His passing is a loss to Ireland and to my club.

Babington, it should be noted, was not noted for his warmth towards Catholics. He had previously been a Unionist MP at Stormont, as well as serving as Lord Justice of Appeal in Northern Ireland and a time as Attorney General.

Similarly, the same source informs us that Jackie Milburn, player-coach at Linfield at the time of Morgan's passing, had commented, 'What a shock his death is to me. He lived for Linfield. To work with him was such a pleasure. You knew that when Gerry was around everything would be all right. I have never had association with a more loyal colleague than Gerry. What a loss his death is to us at "the Park".'

Gerry's funeral took place on 5 March 1959, the procession travelling from St Patrick's Roman Catholic Church on Donegall Street to Milltown Cemetery on the Falls Road. Among those present were front and back room staff from Linfield, as well as some of the higher ups. At Milltown they were met by their opposite numbers from Glentoran to carry Gerry's coffin, from the hearse to the graveside.

SCORE JACKIE

Jackie Milburn, who went to the 1958 tournament as an opposition scout on Peter Doherty's behalf, had joined Linfield the previous Summer after fourteen years at Newcastle United. His five year contract at Windsor Park included the use of a four-bedroom detached house belonging to the club, and shortly after his arrival in Belfast he decided to go for a drive to appreciate his new surroundings. Though he was aware that he was a high profile signing, he had not expected crowds lining the streets to welcome him, as illustrated by comments attributed to him by his son in a subsequent book on his career, *A Man of Two Halves*, 'admittedly, I had heard plenty about their fine displays of hospitality, but this greeting simply took my breath away. And then someone pointed out that it was in fact the 12th of July.'

Though the flute bands were not in his honour, Linfield fans did come up with a song for Milburn, to the tune of the Geordie folk song *The Blaydon Races*:

I saw a smiling face today,
The face of Joe Mackey.

He said the greatest thing he ever did
Was signing Wor Jackie
First Wor Jackie wasn't used
To playing in strange places,
'Til Linfield bought a gramophone
And played the Blaydon Races

[Oh me lads, etc]

Up on the Spion Kop
The Blues supporters gathered;
Waving high the City Cup
Blended with the heather
The Glens were leading three to two
The Blues were none the wiser,
'Til Jackie Milburn got the ball
And scored the equaliser

As the verses testify, he was a popular figure on the terraces, said to put an extra five thousand on the gate during his time with Linfield. Yet there was an element that wanted him out of Windsor Park: Jackie began to receive hate mail signed by 'one of those who took care of Jimmy Jones.' At first he thought little of it, keeping it to himself and throwing the letters onto the fire. More letters came, Milburn continuing to ignore them until one arrived saying that if he continued to ignore its contents then acid would be thrown in his wife's face. The threat appeared to be serious, describing where she shopped and the school his children attended, instructing him to 'get rid of your Catholic hedge cutter or else.'

As his son's biographical account of his life discovers, 'Not only did it send shivers down my back but the whole situation seemed unreal…I didn't even have a clue what religion the hedge cutter was. It had never once crossed my mind to ask. Why should it?' Jackie Milburn's time at Linfield was over.

THE FAIRYTALE CONTINUES

Danny Blanchflower, as documented by his biographer, had penned a column for the *Observer* ahead of the World Cup, writing in his typically convoluted fashion that 'Northern Ireland is the Cinderella of the soccer world, and that we are here competing with the elite of international soccer is an Alice in Wonderland tale…'

Their arrival in Sweden may have seemed like the beginning of a fairytale, but soon began to feel like a fever dream when it became evident that the coach that had been sent to collect the team from the airport was flying the Irish tricolour rather than Ulster's Red Hand. The Swedish authorities were reprimanded by the IFA and allthough it was an easy mistake to make — particularly in the fifties - it was also a big deal, given that the Flags and Emblems Act of 1954 had actually banned the flying of the green, white and orange of the Irish standard in Northern Ireland, a law that was not repealed until 1987.

When diplomats from the Irish Republic had asked how they should reply when questioned about the team from the North, they were, according to Cormac Moore's *Irish Soccer Split*, told by Dublin they ought to, 'add a remark, regretting that the team is not representative of all Ireland as in the case of Rugby football.' A certain amount of confusion among foreign delegations was understandable when both associations were still insisting on being known as 'Ireland', despite FIFA insisting in 1952 that they should be known respectively as Northern Ireland and the Republic of Ireland.

It was not affairs of state which caused a delay in preparations for the team's first game of the tournament against Czechoslovakia, but a matter far more practical in nature. The IFA brass who had gone to Sweden for the *craic* had worn tracksuits intended for the squad on a fishing trip, and training could not get underway until their return. With physical preparations now satisfied thoughts turned to spirituality: the team attended a local church on the morning of their opening fixture, Evan Marshall's probing revealing that they sang the hymn 'Fight the Good Fight' and listened to a sermon entitled 'Faith Moving Mountains'. It was, Blanchflower says in the same pages, 'a well-aimed blow against the anti-Sunday-soccer brigade back home in Northern Ireland.'

Northern Ireland started the tournament as 33-1 outsiders, their Czechoslovakian opponents a mere 13-1 to go all the way. The team bus arrived at the stadium in Halmstad to the strains of 'When Irish Eyes Are Smiling', for a game in which Derek Dougan would make his international debut in front of 10,647 fans, witnessing a 1-0 win. Peter McParland was the originator of the sixteenth minute goal which separated the teams, playing a short corner to Jimmy McIlroy who made a precise cross on to the head of Wilbur Cush, placing it into the net.

Cush had started out with the 2nd Lurgan Boys Brigade before being signed by Glenavon, who he helped to become the first side to win the Irish League from outside Belfast in 1952. They won the Irish Cup that year too, and Cush's contribution was recognised when he was voted Ulster Footballer of the Year, which helped secure his eventual move to Leeds. Though he was often described as being too small to be a footballer his diminutive stature belied the fact that he was a hard man, evidenced by a match with Greece a few years later, during which he punched an opponent's jaw after the Hellenic player had spat on him. Cush had calmly walked away as Jimmy Nicholson went over to see what was going on and the latter was promptly sent off.

Having been to church that morning, the players spent a sanctioned evening in the Norre Kat NightClub in their adopted hometown of Halmstad. Issues of discipline on the pitch were one thing, but Doherty was keen to ensure his disciples kept to certain routines off the pitch during their Swedish adventure, imposing a 10pm curfew for the players for the duration of the tournament. As Ronnie Hanna recounts, one evening the man from Magherafelt checked with Gerry Morgan that all the players were in and was assured that this was the case, only to hear Norman Uprichard whistling 'The Sash' (deriving its tune from Carl T. Sprague's Red River Valley) somewhere outside the confines of the hotel. 'Gerry,' he said, 'I thought they were all in?' before turning to ask Uprichard, 'Where have you been?' Morgan answered, 'Aw...I missed that one' as Uprichard piped up, 'What are you looking at me for? McIlroy's down there with a bird.'

Gerry proceeded to moan for the rest of the evening that Uprichard - 'that stool pigeon' — had let him and McIlroy down. The latter, it would seem, had a bit of a reputation as a ladies man, 'Jimmy McIlroy? No, you mean Smoothie,' Harry Gregg later recalled in Marshall's work on the subject, although he went on to emphasise that his colleague had a footballing prowess too, 'What a charmer! Very strong on the ball. Once McIlroy turned to shield the ball from you, you never had any hope of getting it from him. McIlroy could have turned you inside out.'

The team's second group game pitted them against an Argentinean team who had had their own pre-tournament obstacles to overcome. Though the circumstance were of an entirely different nature, they had been another potential dropout; almost withdrawing from the finals due to the £30,000 it would cost them to travel and compete in Europe, incurring an almost certain financial loss regardless of how successful they were.

Many observers thought that Northern Ireland had fluked their win in the opening round of fixtures, and it looked as though their scepticism was justified when, after an early Peter McParland goal, the South American side put three past Harry Gregg at the other end. Everything now hinged on the last group game with West Germany, and it seemed that only a win against the reigning champions would be good enough to ensure Irish eyes continued to smile. Meanwhile, a draw would be sufficient for Sepp Herberger's men in Malmö. Yet even though the odds were against them, Jimmy McIlroy recalled to Marshall the quiet self-belief which coursed through Doherty's band of men, 'There was a great spirit in the Irish team in those days. People might say you sound conceited, but we had reached the stage where no matter who we were going out against we felt we had a chance or we would put on a good show.'

There was a phrase which appears to have first been spoken by Gerry Morgan but passed the lips of Danny Blanchflower on at least one occasion, becoming something of a motto for the Irish. It succinctly acknowledged their underdog status when they were speaking to journalists. This was reinforced when the players informed the press; 'We're going to equalise before the other team scores.' They knew that they did not possess the strongest eleven in the tournament and their squad was the thinnest of the sixteen teams competing but, as Malcolm Brodie explained, Peter Doherty 'had the gift of being able to talk moderate players into believing they possessed greater ability than they really had.'

Press reports estimate that 8,000 citizens of Halmstad followed their adopted team to Malmö for the fixture, which was also televised to an audience of hundreds of millions across the world. Things were tight: the Germans sat on three points, Northern Ireland and Argentina were in possession of two apiece, with Czechoslovakia still in the running with one. When sitting in church again on the morning of the game, a few players must surely have been begging for divine providence, playing on Sunday for the second time in the history of the IFA.

Ordained by the Almighty or not, Peter McParland wrought havoc upon the German defence and put the Irish ahead after eighteen minutes, though the Germans quickly equalised. It was McParland who scored again on the hour to restore the lead but with twelve minutes remaining the Germans equalised once more and the match ended that way: 2-2. Would it be good enough? Yes! The Czechoslovakian team had pulled off an unexpected win against the Argentine side, and an even more improbable score: 6-1.

A play-off would decide which team would progress alongside West Germany: so it was that on 17 June 1958, just two days after they had held the Germans in the *Stadion Malmö*, the Irish would need to rise to the occasion once more. An estimated 250,000 people in Northern Ireland had their ears pressed to the wireless, becoming irate when commentary was interrupted by the 9pm news.

Had the luck of the Irish been stretched beyond breaking point this time? It looked that way when in the seventeenth minute Zednek Zikan headed past Norman Uprichard, in for the injured Harry Gregg. Injury would soon befall Uprichard, who had no choice but to play on despite twisting his ankle and smashing his hand against the post. It was Peter McParland, once again the spearhead, who turned saviour when he equalised just before half-time. A goalless second half — and two bottles of

Irish Whiskey poured over Uprichard's ankle 'to try to keep the swelling down' - followed, before the clock ticked into extra time. Uprichard was sceptical about Morgan's medicinal methods, 'What a waste of good whiskey,' he would muse in Hanna's book afterwards, but ten unbearable minutes later McParland scored his fifth of the tournament: a right-footed volley which made it 2-1.

'What unrestrained joy when the referee called it a day,' Malcolm Brodie wrote in the *Belfast Telegraph*. Northern Ireland had made it to the quarter final. Politicians were as keen then as they are now to jump on the bandwagon of sporting success, as Harry Gregg recalled in *Spirit of '58*, 'People from the government were coming in to toast Northern Ireland when they found out somebody had drunk all the whiskey. I still laugh when I think of Gerry getting a bottle out of the skip and filling it up with black tea - it was black tea they were toasting with!' Of course, we know where all the good stuff had gone.

The dream was still alive, but for how long? The state of Uprichard's ankle meant that Harry Gregg would have to discard the walking stick he had been using. Referring to an east Belfast amateur side, one player is said to have observed that 'through injuries and tiredness, Dundela would have beaten us.' He was exaggerating, but not much: a small squad ravaged by the fixtures coming thick and fast went down 4-0 to France. Hanna's *The World...* details the story of a post-game a telegram from Northern Irish Prime Minister Basil Brooke to captain Danny Blanchflower, informing him 'Northern Ireland is proud of your magnificent performances in the World Cup. My heartiest congratulations on your fine sportsmanship in defeat as in victory.'

The tournament over, Harry Gregg - eventually voted second best 'personality' of the tournament behind Brazil's captain — was put on a British European Airways flight a day ahead of his team-mates. In fact, the airline even held the plane for him when his train from Norrköping to Stockholm was delayed. Accompanied this time by selectors Sammy Walker and Jack Gaw, he was pleased. Marshall explains that he liked Gaw, whose profession was a laxative salesman. As Gregg tells it, the brand he promoted was called Kest for Zest, and Gaw made speeches at functions prior to the World Cup where he quipped, 'My profession in life is I make laxatives. Billy Graham saves souls but Jack Gaw saves assholes.'

Though the words of England manager Walter Winterbottom found in David Bowler's text might seem patronising, he touched on something about the team spirit which made the team more than the sum of its parts:

> They were remarkable in Sweden, but that was the big joy of being a small country with so few players of truly international standard. You must stick with them, and that welds them together. If you have a wider choice, as we have in England, the committee always wanted to make changes. Playing for England became a reward for doing well for their club rather than trying to build a side to win matches or competitions...The Irish lads gave of their all because they were so tightly knit.

Their job done, the players had to give back their tracksuits as soon as the tournament was over, required for a youth international. No room for egos there.

IRELAND DISUNITED

> *You people of the Shankill Road, what's wrong*

> *with you? Number 425 Shankill Road - do you know who lives there? Pope's men, that's who! Fortes ice-cream shop, Italian Papists on the Shankill Road! How about 56 Aden Street? For 97 years a Protestant lived in that house and now there's a Papisher in it. Crimea Street, number 38! Twenty five years that house has been up, 24 years a Protestant lived there but there's a Papisher there now.*
>
> — THE REVD IAN PAISLEY, PERCY STREET, JUNE 1959

Having achieved their greatest triumph, it was clear that Doherty's libertines had peaked. 'A few of them were getting old even then,' McParland remembered in Bowler's biography of Danny Blanchflower, 'and they weren't going to get to the 1962 World Cup, especially when we drew the West Germans. It was asking a lot to get back to that peak again, because Danny was in his late thirties by then, as were a few of the other lads. It was time to rebuild.' Blanchflower's eventual swan-song came late in '62, as part of a 2-0 victory over Poland, 'I had captained Northern Ireland for almost ten years and I had been a player longer than that...if the selectors are intent, as they ought to be, on building a team for the future, then the sooner the better for replacing me.'

Relations between associations north and south had become increasingly conciliatory, to the extent that IFA bigwigs were invited to the Republic's fixture versus Poland in 1964. Of course, there were protests: the match was on a Sunday. Yet as Peter Byrne's *Green Is The Colour* explains, Donagh O'Malley had become Dublin's minister for education in 1966, rebuking the GAA for the 'Ban' and launching an attempt to break their grip on Irish school system:

> Equal opportunity of education for all our children should also give them an opportunity of playing games of their choice. I want to emphasise that there are people playing games beside those you support, who are quite entitled to call themselves just as good Irishmen. Or do you suggest that we should not cherish all our children equally but continue to create a feeling among our children that they are "Shoneens" because they play certain games?

The scale of O'Malley's mission was not insignificant. Years later Liam Brady was expelled from St Aidan's Christian Brothers in a north Dublin suburb, because he chose to captain an Irish schoolboys side instead of playing Gaelic for the school.

The sixties also saw a growing movement for political change off the field, in the corridors of power in the North, dominated as they were by the Orange Order with the Ulster Unionist Party as their proxy. Former Northern Irish Prime Minister, Basil Brooke, had famously said 'there is only room for one political party in Ulster', and for half a century Northern Ireland was ostensibly a one party state, verging on a dictatorship. Brooke was its figurehead for twenty of those until retiring in 1963: Protestant supremacy manifesting itself through discrimination in employment, housing, jobs and the action of the B-Specials, all enabled by quite blatant gerrymandering. Rond Duffy's excellent primer on this era, *Until The Trouble Started,* points to an article which appeared in the *Sunday Times* on 3 July 1966 described how in Derry:

> There are 14,325 Catholics on the local roll, and 9,235 Protestants, but the wards are so organised as to give Protestant majorities in enough of them to win control of the City Council. In employment the pattern is the same. In Londonderry the heads of all City Council departments are Protestant. Of 177 salaried employees, 145 - earning £124,424 — are Protestant, and only 32 - earning £20,420 - are Catholic.

The 1923 boundaries were drawn in such a way that it was only in areas where Catholics made up more than seventy-five per cent of the population that they could be certain of gaining control of a council. Wards were drawn in an extraordinary fashion, as the example of Omagh Urban District shows: its sixty-one per cent Catholic population somehow returned twelve Unionists and only nine non-Unionist councillors. In East Down the figures were equally stark: a fifty-six per cent Catholic populace was represented by nineteen Unionist Councillors and just five others while in Lurgan, forty-six per cent Catholic, there were zero non-Unionist councillors.

Though Northern Ireland as a whole had high levels of unemployment, Catholics were at the sharpest end. Duffy also cast his eye over Richard Rose's 1968 survey *Governing Without Consensus,* highlighting how Catholics made up a third of the working-age population but comprised two-thirds of the unemployed. In the ranks of the civil service administration, only six per cent of the workforce was Catholic. Elsewhere, a group of Catholic lawyers discovered in 1961 that since the formation of the

Northern Ireland government forty years previously, just two Catholic non-Unionists had been appointed to the High Court bench in the province.

Yet it was around the issue of social housing that civil rights marches and demonstrations were organised in the latter part of the decade. In the Summer of 1968 Nationalist MP Austin Currie and two local men occupied a vacant house in Caledon, County Tyrone. The property had been allocated to a nineteen year-old unmarried typist by Dungannon District Council, a woman who just happened to be the secretary of a Unionist politician in Armagh. That she was getting married later that year was all the justification the Unionist council required for awarding her the property despite the fact that Catholic families were living in condemned buildings not fit for habitation in the same district. They were made to sit on the waiting list for years on end instead while such patronage was given to working-class Protestants as a 'reward' for their loyalty to the Ulster Unionist party.

The IRA had waged a border campaign between 1956 and 1962, in the hope of sparking an uprising among the Catholic-nationalist people of the region. Over the course of those six years, half a dozen policemen were killed in attacks on their barracks, though eleven IRA operatives had also lost their lives. By the time the IRA drew this campaign to a close, even their own press release pointed to the 'attitude of the general public…' as reason for its cessation. The problem for the IRA was that although most Catholics in Northern Ireland were horribly discriminated against, they had a 'safety net' in the form of the UK welfare state and knew that as part of a 32-county Republic a comparable level of provision would not have been possible. One survey of northern Catholics in 1968 reported that only thirteen per cent thought the removal of the border would improve their quality of life.

When Basil Brooke stepped down in 1963, the hope was that his successor, Captain Terence O'Neill, would be the one to bring a less nakedly sectarian era to Stormont. Brooke was not just a Protestant and a Unionist but also a bigot, whereas O'Neill was — relatively speaking - a liberal. The Catholic Church was liberalising, too. By 1965, policies brought about by the deliberations of the Second Vatican Council, meant that Catholics were now allowed to enter Protestant churches and take part in their services. Priests were able to speak in Protestant churches and have ministers from other churches do likewise in theirs. For the first time, archbishops from Catholic and Protestant cathedrals could visit on another's places of worship.

Yet as Revd Paisley's fiery words from the corner of Percy Street tell us, all was not well in Ulster.

6

THERE WILL BE TROUBLES AHEAD

Thirteen years in the wilderness of Northern Ireland's amateur leagues ended on 8 September 1985 when Derry City beat Home Farm 3-1 in the League of Ireland Cup first round. From its genesis in 1928, the club's name was both controversial, yet not as controversial as it could be. Its appellation is contentious because it omits the 'London' prefix preferred by the unionist community, despite the city being legally known as Londonderry. Something of a shibboleth; your way of referring to the area is a fairly accurate indicator to the listener as to which side of the sectarian divide you align yourself with. If you receive it, listen carefully next time a BBC broadcast mentions the city and you will hear the presenter use 'Derry/Londonderry' at the top of the segment, then studiously alternate between the two monikers for the remainder of the report. Here more than anywhere, words really matter.

The team itself could have — but did not – adopt the name Derry Celtic, carried by its predecessor club, but aimed to be less antagonistic. Uniquely, the 1928 club drew its directors in even numbers from Protestant and

Catholic communities. Playing in the Irish Football League until 1972, the Candystripes, so called because of their red and white home shirt modelled on Sheffield United's strip, saw their tenure in the northern competition come to a bitter conclusion. As the Troubles escalated they were refused permission to resume playing home games at their Brandywell ground.

THE OPPOSITE OF QUIET

On 9 August, Derry City played Ards at the Brandywell in an Ulster Cup tie, during which they were beaten 3-0 and booed off the pitch by their own fans. Before the end of the month, their 23-year-old forward Lynn Porter had quit the team: it was alleged that he had been part of the rioting that was beginning to become commonplace in the city. Though he denied being involved, pointing to the lack of evidence, the choice had been made for him.

The Brandywell had been the venue for Derry City FC's home fixtures since the club's first season in the Irish League in 1929, previously having been the base of Derry Celtic. Its location on the Bogside, a nationalist stronghold outside Derry's old city walls on the west bank of the Foyle, meant it would become a problem for the Northern Irish footballing fraternity. The situation on its streets spiralled out of control a matter of days after the loss to Ards. A ball would not be kicked by a player in a striped shirt until nearly a month later, on 4 September.

The club's home games against Cliftonville and Crusaders were postponed, as well as two away matches that had been due to take place in Belfast. Every Derry City home game that should have been played at the Brandywell during September was hosted elsewhere. Barricades encircled the Bogside and opposition players were fearful of entering 'Free Derry'. The club's first league game at the Brandywell was finally played on 18 October, ten weeks after the start of the season. This pattern continued for the rest of the campaign, and in March 1970 their match against Linfield was the scene of violence in the stands. Such was the extent of the violence that the return fixture scheduled for the Brandywell never happened: the RUC feared there would be a breach of the peace if it took place.

The 1970/71 season was comparatively peaceful. Access to the Brandywell had become less hazardous and Wolves visited from England in December to contest a Texaco Cup match, a competition created for high finishing teams from these two islands who had nevertheless missed out on European qualification. Even so, some games had to be played elsewhere: Derry City's 'home' tie against Linfield was hosted at the Coleraine Showgrounds and an Irish League game between the two sides at the end of January 1971, as well as their Cup game that March, were the scene of violent clashes.

Derry City went on to reach the final a few weeks later on 3 April, squaring off against Distillery. As was customary, it would be played at Windsor Park but given its location in a loyalist heartland, many fans were rightly sceptical about going there and putting their safety at serious risk. In the end just 180 people travelled to see their team go down to a 3-0 loss.

The following season was to be the last time Derry City completed a full roster of fixtures in Northern Ireland, and the last time that Irish League football would be played at the Brandywell. The Catholic-nationalist populace had very quickly gone from regarding the presence of British soldiers as a protective force against the RUC and the B-Specials, to viewing them as forces of strife and internment. The opening three games of the new season were either postponed or played at another venue because of tensions on the Bogside, although there was widespread violence across the state. Yet it was only to Derry where Irish League clubs would not travel; the violence there seen as in some way different, more political.

Derry City's game against Crusaders at the Brandywell on 19 August 1971 was postponed: the barricades around the stadium to keep Free Derry 'free' did not inspire confidence from the unionist side from north Belfast. The ground was used that Saturday afternoon in any case: the Social Democratic and Labour Party (SDLP) and the Northern Ireland Civil Rights Association (NICRA) held a rally urging participation in a campaign of civil disobedience, with the end goal of shaking up the unjust Stormont parliament, demanding 'British rights for British citizens'. John Hume, a Derry native who would become the second leader of the SDLP and eventually win a Nobel Peace Prize, told those present 'we have pledged ourselves to lead you in a campaign of civil disobedience and passive resistance to bring the system that has governed you for 50 years to an end.'

Though it may seem strange that the rally was held at the ground of a football club already suffering the consequences of its association with a certain strand of nationalism, the fact is it was simply the only large venue on the Bogside. NICRA had been founded in 1967 to demand more power and representation for the Catholic and nationalist people of Northern Ireland. Their aim was not for an immediate united Irish Republic but for a greater piece of the Northern Irish pie for nationalists: a place in the 'democracy' long denied to them by the Ulster Unionist party. The campaign's six point programme demanded one-man-one-vote in local elections, the removal of gerrymandered boundaries, laws against local government discrimination, the allocation of local housing on a points system, repeal of the Special Powers Act and the disbandment of the B-Specials.

When it was eventually deemed safe enough for their fixture against Cliftonville - who had finally cast off their amateur status, having finished at the foot of the Irish League for eleven consecutive seasons — to be staged at the Brandywell, a distinctly meagre crowd of 200 turned up, when 5,000 had been commonplace in the years before the onset of the Troubles. This game, and two others in late Summer 1972, were carried out behind the barricades that lined the outer limits of 'Free Derry' and, as Mike Cronin's article *Playing Away From Home* notes, one local paper reported that 'Cliftonville had second thoughts about accepting the security forces clearance for Brandywell. Even after a trouble free week there were still the remains of barricades on four roads outside the ground, with single lane motor traffic through three of them, and a pedestrian passage in another.'

On 10 September there was further widespread rioting after a British Army Landrover had accidentally run over and killed a seven year-old boy. Amid the stones, bottles and petrol bombs, a shot was fired at soldiers from within the structure of the Brandywell and the police returned fire. The following day, Derry City were due to play Ballymena United and despite Ballymena's protestations, the Irish League ordered that the game should go ahead. Kicking off as rioting continued outside the ground, those inside could hear rubber bullets being discharged and detect the familiar odour of CS gas being sprayed to break up the rioters. Matters only got worse when a group of rioters burst into the ground, covering their faces on their way to gaining access to the Ballymena team bus. When the driver refused to hand over the keys they put it in gear, pushing it through the ground and out of a gate into the street where it was set alight.

The security forces and the Irish League were now firm in their opinion that Derry City could no longer use the Brandywell to host football matches. It seems unlikely that any opponent would have come to play there in any case; the other clubs were by now unanimous in their refusal to travel into 'Free Derry'. The football club had no choice but to play all their home matches at Coleraine Showgrounds instead, but the gate receipts were terrible: a match against Crusaders in the Ulster Cup raised just £33. One of the team's best players, John Rowland, left Derry and went back to England. The signs were inauspicious to say the least; falling revenues and a precarious security situation were not conducive to footballing success.

There was a glimmer of hope at the start of 1972/73 season when the RUC indicated that football could return to Brandywell, but it was extinguished when the majority of Irish League clubs voted against the motion. Derry City were insistent that they should be able to resume home matches on the Bogside, resulting in the forfeiture of the first three home games of their season. Portadown were due to play Derry on 14 October 1972, a game which was scheduled as a home fixture for the Candystripes: once again they applied to have it played at the Brandywell. Once again they were refused.

The day before the game, 13 October, the club issued a statement:

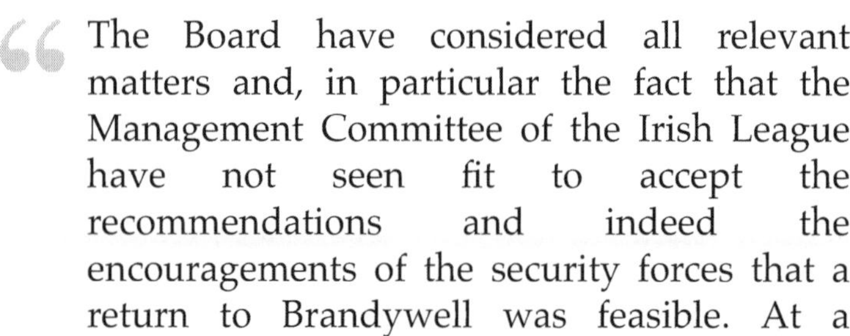

> “The Board have considered all relevant matters and, in particular the fact that the Management Committee of the Irish League have not seen fit to accept the recommendations and indeed the encouragements of the security forces that a return to Brandywell was feasible. At a

> considerable cost to the club, Derry City, for the past three years have kept senior football alive in the interests of the Irish League and indeed the community at large in what can only be described as the most difficult of circumstances. Over the past three years attendances at Brandywell dwindled from 5000 to a few hundred and reached almost vanishing point when City had to move out of Brandywell to Coleraine. A resolution was unanimously passed by the Board of Directors that membership of the Irish League be withdrawn as from 13th October.

Derry had forty-three years of Irish League history, a League championship, three Irish cups and were the first Northern Ireland based team to get to the second round of the European Cup. And just like that, they were gone: replaced in the middle of the season by Larne FC.

FAMILIAR FOES

Glentoran had emerged from the 1969/70 season victorious, running away with the Irish League title by 7 points. For Linfield, something needed to change. They had finished fourth on goal difference as one of a remarkable four sides on the same number of points spanning second to fifth. That something arrived in the form of Billy Bingham, nearing the end of a first stint as part-time manager of Northern Ireland and recently dethroned at Plymouth Argyle.

As luck would have it the first game of the new Irish League season was against their great unionist rival in front of a crowd of 13,000 in gleaming mid-August sunshine. Bingham was a hard taskmaster, demanding his semi-pros train up to five times a week, which meant them working full-time and coming to train with the club in the evening, all for the princely sum of £6 a week. When a player reported he was suffering the effects of a cold and was unable to train, Bingham is said, according to Brodie's *100 Years of Irish Football,* to have replied brusquely, 'I'm terribly sorry to hear about your cold. Now blow your nose and get up here.'

Linfield had qualified for the Cup Winners Cup as a result of their efforts of the previous season as holders of the IFA Challenge Cup, and the first round pitted them against Manchester City. Just three years previously Linfield had reached the quarter-final of the European Cup, going out to CSKA Sofia in the year that Celtic's Lisbon Lions emerged victorious. This time the hope among the Windsor Park faithful was that Linfield would not be disgraced at Maine Road but the team surpassed expectations, achieving what club secretary Harry Wallace described as 'Our proudest hour (and a half).' He was evidently pleased with their efforts, and according to Billy Bingham biographer, Roger Allen in *Billy*, he had beamed, 'For eighty-three minutes we withstood the might of English first division football, and but for an unfortunate injury to Isaac Andrews I firmly believe we would have held out for a 0-0 draw.'

In September, City came to Belfast for the return leg, the precarious security situation meaning visitors had been warned the game might have to kick off earlier than advertised. City manager, Joe Mercer, told reporters, 'The only thing we're frightened of is this man they call Billy Bingham.' He should have watched out for another Billy, too: Millen put Linfield 1-0 up before an equaliser came via Francis Lee. Throughout the match, Linfield hooligans were throwing bottles at Joe Corrigan in the City goal and, in Allen's account, Bingham remembered, 'I was asked to speak to the police but decided to see what I could do on my own...I shouted at them until I was hoarse and it seemed to work, for there was no further trouble.' It had stuck in Corrigan's mind too:

> Behind my goal, bottles and other missiles began raining down from the terraces and the people throwing them made no secret of their intended target: me. It was unnerving to say the least, and Linfield manager Billy Bingham had to come out and plead with the fans not to force the game to be abandoned.

Linfield would soon go 2-1 up through another Millen goal but ultimately went out due to the Manchester club's away goal. The £6 a week semi-pros had narrowly fallen to the £10,000 a year Division One full-timers.

The aforementioned Isaac Andrews, goalscorer in the first leg, was arrested for rioting in the Shankill that same month. As Gareth Mulvenna's insightful *Tartan Gangs and Paramilitaries* brings to light, one year later after a game against Standard Liege where he was Linfield's substitute, a relative of the young man from Orkney Street was one of two men killed at the Four Step Inn, a known haunt of Linfield fans, by a no-warning bomb just after 10pm that night.

There was no shame in going out to an established English side, and Linfield would go on to win the Irish League title, pipping Glentoran to the post by three points. After the league winning match 1,000 Bluemen made there way across to the Oval where they invaded the pitch at the conclusion of Glentoran's match, Allen noting that *Ireland's Saturday Night* (the *Belfast Telegraph's* sports paper) reported it as a 'complete sea of Union Jacks' before a rendition of 'God Save The Queen'. Bingham's stay was destined to be a short one and he departed to manage in Greece, relinquishing his Northern Ireland role in the process.

Despite bringing back winning ways to Windsor Park, when Bingham left there was an element of relief amongst his former players: his training regime had been brutal.

Though Bingham had restored bragging rights, Linfield fans had other concerns. The reconstituted UVF, as well as the UDA (which counted 40,000 among its ranks by 1972), saw younger elements of the Windsor Park crowd as a fertile recruiting ground. This phenomenon, scrupulously documented by Mulvenna in *Tartan Gangs…* became particularly pronounced following altercations between Linfield fans returning to the Lower Shankill and nationalists living in the Unity Flats housing complex.

A riot at the Glentoran v Linfield tie on 12 January 1970 lead to a new chant which, as Mulvenna explains, reflected the increasing militancy among the Windsor faithful:

We took the Oval in half a minute,
We took Coleraine and all that's in it
With hatchets and hammers, Stanley
knives
and spanners
We'll show the bastards how to fight
If you can't beat a Glenman in half a
minute, then you're not a
Linfield fan

Linfield's Irish Cup Final 0f 1970, played at Solitude against Ballymena, witnessed similar scenes and precipitated a harder line from the RUC at the start of the 1970/71 season that September. Linfield fans returning to the Shankill were funnelled through tightly controlled routes to stop them from scrapping with nationalists at interfaces along the way. Instead they waved Union Jacks and sang 'God Save The Queen' as they passed by and republicans, anticipating their arrival, would sing 'The Soldier's Song'.

OUR LOVE WAS ON THE WING

Rumours swirled around Belfast in the Autumn of 1971 that George Best had donated £3,000 to Ian Paisley's DUP. Though Best rubbished the stories, his house was placed under surveillance by the police for his own safety. Manchester United were scheduled to play Newcastle on 23 October at St James' Park, and the bearded winger received a death threat purported to have come from the IRA.

Travelling to the north-east, he was accompanied by two Special Branch police officers who forbade him from going near the windows of the team's coach. Ensconced in the hotel, Best was instructed to eat his meals in his bedroom and at the match the next day forty undercover policemen were dotted around the crowd. 'Whatever happened, I kept moving,' Best told Joe Lovejoy in *Bestie*. It worked. He scored the winning and only goal of the afternoon before two police cars escorted the coach all the way back to Manchester.

One week later a woman who lived near Best's Manchester home was approached by two men asking if they knew where he lived. As they left, she noticed that one man appeared to be carrying a gun. There were further precautionary measures from the police: Best was visited by officers every two hours. Soon afterwards the *Manchester Evening News* received a letter warning that Best would be 'knifed in the back' and would 'never return to England' if he played in his national team's upcoming game against Spain.

Though it would be foolish to attribute one single reason to his growing personal difficulties, this coincided with Best's slide from the top of the game and he would never again consistently produce the form that had made him famous. As Best himself would later write in *Blessed*:

> I was under enormous pressure as it was and having enough problems just keeping my life together, without that. And it wasn't just the threat that bothered me. It was the effect I knew it would have on my family. They were living with the Troubles on a daily basis, which was hard enough for them.

United boss Frank O'Farrell had told Best the club would understand if he did not want to play, 'But I kept coming back to the feeling that I couldn't *not* play, otherwise, where would it all end? And typically of me, having let the team down so many times, when the manager offered me a Saturday off, I insisted that I wanted to play,' he wrote. Nevertheless, Best felt his teammates cannot have been too happy that they had the misfortune of sharing a coach with him: 'I was escorted by a couple of detectives who refused to allow me sit in my normal window seat in case anyone took a pot shot at me.'

To make matters worse, the United team coach was broken into overnight, 'so it had to be checked for any explosive devices and the news didn't make my teammates any less jumpy.' As we know — whoever it came from - the threat never materialised, 'and thankfully, the only shot on target that day was my winning goal.' St James' Park was surrounded by high rise tower blocks, causing Best to muse that it would have been ideal for an eagle-eyed marksman. It was one thing for him to joke about his own demise, though Newcastle manager Joe Harvey's post-match remark — 'I wish they had shot the little bugger!' - was somewhat less tasteful.

INTO THE FIRE

Future Northern Irish international, Terry Cochrane came to Linfield in the early seventies, following a stint with Derry City. It is hard to imagine any player with a more stressful start to their career. His first game in a blue shirt was in September 1972, yet even training was a fear-inducing proposition in those dark days. He recalls in his autobiography, *See You at the Far Post*:

> I well remember training at Windsor Park one Tuesday evening when we heard gunshots at the top of the stand coming from the Andersonstown area of the city. Ivan McAllister was our centre half, but was also a policeman and he promptly ushered us into the changing room. He was able to calm us down because he could clearly see that we were all scared witless — but the mood soon changed when one of the lads remarked that "we couldn't have been playing that bad"

Despite the Killyleagh man's otherwise impeccable unionist credentials, a forty-two game spell at Linfield was over a year later. He had got married, to a Catholic. Her name was Etta Fitzsimons and, as he wrote, 'since she was of a different denomination from me, the Linfield management asked me to leave the club. It actually wasn't their policy to ask a player to leave for this reason, but they felt I would get too much stick if I stayed...I would very much have liked to stay with Linfield as I was really happy there, but it was not to be.' He would go on to join Coleraine under Bertie Peacock, playing 129 times and scoring 41 goals in the same lineup as Pat's brother, Brian Jennings. When his new team beat Linfield to win the Irish Cup in 1975, fans of the Belfast club began throwing projectiles at the victors.

NINETEEN SEVENTY TWO

It was, as Her Majesty might have put it, Northern Ireland's *annus horribilis*. That much we know already. Among the wreckage, though, there was one event which would bring a smile to the faces of both sides of the divide: beating England. 'The Troubles were at their worst,' Terry Neill, the team's player-manager from October 1971 until 1975 recalls in David Tossell's *In Sunshine Or In Shadow*, 'and at Wembley that night, we all felt as a group that it might have given the little province of Northern Ireland a bit of a lift from the day to day problems.'

It was a hope shared by many of those who helped the team to a 1-0 victory (thanks to a goal from Neill), over Alf Ramsey's England that night at Wembley, not least Derek Dougan who wearing the captain's armband for the first time, reflecting in Tossell's chronicle of events: 'Sport, my sport, my soccer, was doing what sport should do and I knew that the possibilities were endless. Here with the victory much had been done...I knew instinctively that we had the power to change minds and hearts.' The dynamic between England and Northern Ireland was something the man from Avon Street had once described as that of a 'stern teacher, and an unruly pupil who never knows for what he is being punished', and for him victory could not have been sweeter.

It's a thread that Eric McMordie pulls at when he reflected on the night of 23 May, in Tossell's biography of Dougan:

> The England game was our biggest result, one you always look back on. I don't think we were under extra pressure because of the Troubles, but we obviously did think it would be a great help and we knew we were getting well supported by the people back home. It felt great to get that result because it helped the country.

Nine months later, Dougan would make what turned out to be his last appearance for his country in a 1-0 loss to Cyprus in Nicosia. Malcolm Brodie had it about right when he opined, 'Internationally, he never made the impact he should have. His international career had longevity, but he didn't have the capacity he showed as a club player. I felt we didn't see the best of him as a Northern Ireland player.'

One of the most remarkable events in the complex narrative of Northern Irish football, is the attempt by a group of players from north and south of the border to shape the landscape for an All-Ireland team. Lead by Dougan, the controversial endeavour could scarcely have come into being during a more fraught social and political era. The most bloody year of the Troubles was barely over. It had witnessed 467 violent deaths, more than 10,500 shootings, nearly 2,000 terrorist bombs and a further twenty-seven tons of explosives had been recovered by the security forces.

The Bogside in Derry had been the scene of a protest march numbering 10,000 people on 30 January, a day that we now know as Bloody Sunday. Twenty-six unarmed civilians were shot by soldiers from the 1st Battalion, Parachute Regiment of the British Army and in the case of fourteen of them, fatally so. Direct rule from Westminster was introduced in late March 1972, after Brian Faulkner, the sixth and last Prime Minister of Northern Ireland, had unsuccessfully requested permission to reconstitute the B-Specials. In July, there was Bloody Friday: the IRA detonated twenty-six bombs in the course of around half an hour, killing eleven and wounding 130 more. Such was the heightened state of affairs, that Irish League teams did not take part in European competition in the 1972/73 season and the Blaxnit All-Ireland cup had become in jeopardy a year earlier when Linfield clashed with fans of Cork Hibernians, chanting 'Up the UVF!'

The national team would play ten 'home' games on the UK mainland between 1972 and 1978 for reasons of safety, too. From the 1972 visit of the USSR until 1975 when Yugoslavia came over, no national team fixtures took place in Northern Ireland. England and Wales eventually came back for Home Championship matches, though Scotland would not return until 1980. Through this nomadic period, Northern Ireland played home games at locations including Coventry's Highfield Road, Craven Cottage, Goodison Park and Hillsborough. The game against Spain - the first to be transplanted across the Irish Sea - was itself a rescheduling of a European Championship qualifier, that should have taken place in November 1971, postponed after the threat was made to Best's life which caused Manchester United to prohibit him from playing and FIFA's ultimate intervention in calling off the game.

Surely only the most foolhardy would try to organise an All-Ireland match in such dire circumstances? Yet that was exactly what the headstrong Dougan sought to do. In the months leading up to the match in July 1973, 163 people had been killed and a hundred more would meet the same fate by the end of the year.

When the players took the field against Brazil at Lansdowne Road in front of a crowd of 34,000, the St Patrick's Brass and Reed Band played 'A Nation Once Again', as, Cormac Moore notes in *Irish Soccer Split* 'entertainment' rather than anthem. Terry Conroy, a Republic of Ireland international who spent the majority of his career at Glentoran and lined up on the wing that night remembered to David Tossell, 'It was the height of the Troubles and we wanted to come together and make a statement that people at this level could get on.' It was a bold gesture.

Martin O'Neill, just 21 at the time, turned out in midfield in Dublin and recalled in Simon Moss' *Martin the Magnificent*:

> Derek sacrificed a lot. He knew what he was taking on — with the game being played against the political and religious backdrop of the time - and his own Northern Ireland career suffered as a consequence. Even then we realised it was very historic, but you would never have known at that stage what the future held. Derek didn't reappear for Northern Ireland. He was getting on a bit in years, but he was still capable of playing international football.

O'Neill was right. For whatever reason, Dougan would never again play for Northern Ireland.

Dougan had not organised the fixture entirely alone, enlisting the help of the FIFA agent and Irishman Louis Kilcoyne. His family owned Shamrock Rovers and Kilcoyne - brother in law of Johnny Giles - had a certain amount of influence over Joao Havelange, who was at the time head of the Brazilian FA and canvassing for support to become FIFA president. He floated the notion of a match against his nation, as part of an eleven week European tour the Brazilians were planning the following year.

When Kilcoyne got in touch with Dougan to tell him the good news, he in turn excitedly brought it to the IFA, who told him they would get back to him. They never did. Though the spirit of cross-border cooperation could certainly have been stronger amongst the men in blazers, on the pitch the situation was far more positive, as Terry Conroy recollected in Tossell's *In Sunshine...*

> There were never any problems between the players. I am a Catholic from the south and Doog was a Protestant from the north but we never had any issues relating to the Troubles. It was never discussed. If you were living in the north at that time you would have found it harder to be friends [with a southern Catholic] - you were dissuaded from it. But it was your environment that dictated what you felt. Doog said he had never experienced any problems with teams of mixed religions in the north. He was no bigot.

Bryan Hamilton, lining up alongside O'Neill in the middle of the park all those years ago, plays down the symbolism of the fixture, preferring to see it in purely footballing terms and telling the same author: 'I think we were all non-political. When Derek asked me to take part in the game, I was looking at it purely from a footballing perspective, and for the chance of playing against Brazil I would have played for the convicts. I saw it as football first, playing Brazil second, and third was the all-Ireland team.'

Evidence of the contentious nature of the fixture is not hard to find. Sir Stanley Rous, the Englishman who was FIFA president until 1974, told Dougan that he was upsetting IFA President Harry Cavan. According to Tossell Cavan was trying 'every trick in the book' to get the game cancelled. It was a lightbulb moment for Dougan, quoted in Tossell's retrospective, 'The pieces on the board came together, and I knew immediately that the man at the top of Northern Ireland soccer had tried to obstruct the possible progress of trust and togetherness.'

As Tossell, writing with Dougan's cooperation, explains: if there was going to be change, then the brass certainly did not want it to be lead from below by the players, 'Harry Cavan tried to get the match cancelled, purely and simply because he felt it was going to be a precedent; the north and south was going to come together after that. It was very selfish.' As the author discovered, Malcolm Brodie later wrote that:

> “the all-Ireland team created quite a stir and caused a bit of antagonism. Officials saw the dangers of unifying the players. It could have meant difficulties for both football associations at FIFA level. It could have led to pressure from them for a permanent all-Ireland team.

In the end, Cavan could not get the game shut down but he did make sure the word 'Ireland' would not be part of the proceedings. On Tuesday, 3 July 1973 the players ran out as the Shamrock Rovers XI at Lansdowne Road to play Brazil, dressed in Shamrock's green and white kit. Lining up in the starting eleven that day were Pat

Jennings, David Craig, Paddy Mulligan, Tommy Carroll, Allan Hunter, Mick Martin, Terry Conroy, Martin O'Neill, Derek Dougan, Johnny Giles and Don Givens. Six men from Northern Ireland, and five from the Republic. The Brazil side they faced was strong with only three players who had won the 1970 World Cup absent, all through retirement.

With all the fuss surrounding the fixture, it would almost be possible to forget that a match took place that day. Brazil took an early lead when Paulo Cesar put away a penalty before the Irish drew level in the twenty-eighth minute through a well-crafted Mick Martin goal. Just before half-time Jairzinho put Brazil ahead and the gap widened in the 51st minute when Cesar grabbed his second and Brazil's third from twenty-five yards. When Rivelino assisted Valdomiro for a fourth it was looking like things might get embarrassing for the boys in green until a cross from Conroy headed home by Dougan restored some respectability. Conroy was to thank again ten minutes from time to make it 4-3, the way it remained at the final whistle.

Despite the loss Dougan, was happy that he had achieved at least partial success, 'What was proved that day at Lansdowne Road was not only could great sporting events be held without security problems, but that an all-Ireland side is a practical proposition.' Martin O'Neill was effusive in his praise of the east Belfast forward, as Tossell discovered: 'Great credit must go to Derek. For him to have that great foresight with the political backdrop of that time was really fantastic. People were telling him to be careful. It was an incredible event.' Likewise, Louis Kilcoyne saw the ball as now being in the court of the respective associations. 'We have done our bit. The next move is up to the legislators, North and South, and I can only hope they will take tonight's lesson to heart. Obviously the players want reunification and the reception given our players surely is proof that the public think along the same lines.'

Dougan confided in colleagues that he thought it might have scuppered his chance of being picked for Northern Ireland, and it transpired that he was never again named in an international squad. Whether this was for footballing or political reasons is hard to judge. After all, he was thirty-five and had failed to score in his last ten internationals, nor had he even been selected for the previous five Northern Ireland fixtures.

Still, he would have few regrets about his part in creating a ninety minute show of unity, according to remarks in Tossell's examination: 'There was no hidden agenda that day as far as I was concerned. I just felt it would be a unique opportunity for us, bearing in mind the Brazil we were facing were the bulk of the 1970 World Cup-winning side. I never realised I would not play international football again, and I only found out when the next squad was announced.' His strong suspicion was that Cavan had told Terry Neill not to pick him again but Tossell believes Malcolm Brodie was not so sure, 'Harry Cavan and him didn't agree, but Harry didn't leave him out. That was a myth. Dougan had an outspoken, cavalier attitude but there was no question of him being boycotted.'

This is further supported by his inclusion of the words of Terry Neill, whose tenure as manager would come to an end in 1975:

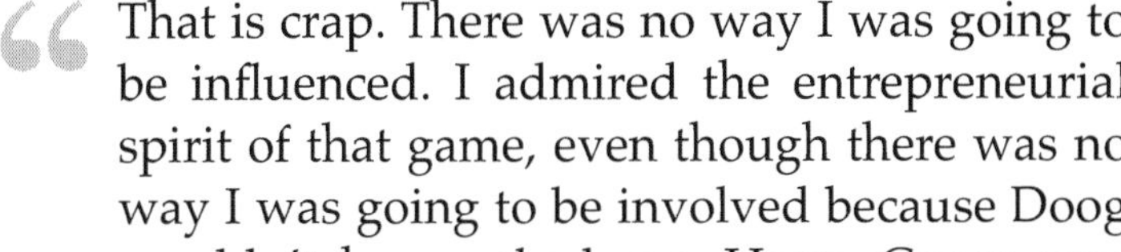

> That is crap. There was no way I was going to be influenced. I admired the entrepreneurial spirit of that game, even though there was no way I was going to be involved because Doog wouldn't have asked me. Harry Cavan was

> never involved in team selection; I would never have tolerated that. Doog either made a mistake or he didn't really know me.

Neill insisted Dougan was left out because he was a disruptive influence and not because of his role in the All-Ireland game. 'There was always something inconsistent with Derek; some demon inside him. He had a need for conflict and could have started an argument in a graveyard. I had a letter from Peter Doherty saying "I know why you have left him out."'

Dougan's international career was over, having gained forty-three caps and a return of eight goals. As *In Sunshine…* grasps, although Terry Conroy, who was unlikely to have had any great insight into the inner-workings of the IFA, he nonetheless recognises that Dougan had been acting with the best of intentions:

> “On this occasion he might have upset a few people from his own side, because they couldn't understand why he wanted to do what he did. Coming from an area that was 100 per cent Protestant, people might have said: "You have got to look after your own side first." That was not in his way of thinking. If there was a problem to be solved he would try to do it.

DISTILLED

Grosvenor Park, the springboard of Dougan's career, had been Distillery's home since 1889, hosting Irish League matches since a year after that when the club entered as founder members. Well, that's almost true. There had been a brief interlude beginning in 1922 that saw the club leave for a new ground at York Park, only to return five years later. The first rudimentary floodlights in Irish football had shone there too, installed for a friendly against Burnley in December 1952. After the demise of Belfast Celtic, there was a brief period where nationalists had looked to Distillery as a potential replacement; its location was certainly convenient and the team were a religiously mixed bunch after the war. While never consistently scaling the heights of some of their bigger Belfast rivals, Distillery and their Grosvenor Park ground were very much part of the furniture.

A young Martin O'Neill was making his name at Distillery, and Peter McParland, managing Glentoran, could already see the potential of the young Irishman, 'I suppose he is the best player Distillery ever produced.' When the Glens played Distillery in an Irish Cup semi-final in 1971, McParland was rightly complimentary, 'That day Martin did as much as anybody to make sure Distillery won. You could see he was at the start of a great career.' In that year's final, O'Neill scored twice to beat Derry City at Windsor Park, and in the first round of the Cup Winners Cup the following season they were pitted against Barcelona over two legs, losing 3-1 in Catalunya and 4-0 in Ulster. O'Neill was the solitary goalscorer for the Irish upstarts, earning him the 'White Pelé' nickname on the Iberian peninsula.

Tragically, the Troubles roared into Grosvenor Park. The ground was firebombed and the club began a nomadic existence, sharing the Skegoniel ground with Brantwood, and later playing their home games at Crusaders' Seaview. The middle of Grosvenor Park became the site of a peace wall, and now sits below the main road which connects the M1 to the rest of Belfast. Distillery left Belfast altogether in 1979, settling in Lambeg on the Ballyskeagh Road. The club's new crest features a phoenix on a football and in 1999 they would eventually become Lisburn Distillery, so as to be more closely identify with their new home.

Months before Grosvenor Park burned down O'Neill was signed by Nottingham Forest, Simon Moss's exhaustive look at O'Neill's trajectory uncovering the words of an impetuous young man 'I got into the first team quite early after coming from Irish football and — amazingly - I got left out after a game or two. I was so big headed I thought, "How can he possibly leave me out of this team?" There I was asking for a transfer within six weeks of arriving at the club.' Eventually he saw sense and stayed with Forest until 1981, spending six of those years under the stewardship of Brian Clough. Not that everything was easy, even before Ol' Big 'Ead arrived:

> When I went to Nottingham Forest it was the early 1970s and the political climate in England was definitely challenging. We had, within months, a situation where the IRA bombing was taken to the mainland, and I don't think before the Troubles in Belfast ever really bothered the everyday Englishman. Now it was on their back door and it became more frightening, it became more hostile and certainly being Irish in those days was a worrying time.

He felt that as an Irish Catholic some of his English teammates viewed him with a certain suspicion, as an agent of the enemy, 'I believed that sport in general or maybe football could transcend politics, but you always felt — especially in those days of 1974 and 1975 - where there were a couple of comments made in the dressing room that suggested you would have an empathy, if not a downright collusion, in events.'

BORN INTO WAR

'To be truthful, I was just too busy playing football and Gaelic football to get sucked into what was going on around me,' Neil Francis Lennon, born in 1971, reflected on his experience of the events of his youth in a Northern Ireland ravaged by conflict in his autobiography, *Man and Bhoy*. It's a place he nonetheless describes as a 'country that was trying to tear itself apart.'

Growing up on an estate that was almost exclusively nationalist, a move to Manchester as an adolescent in 1987 was a shock to Lennon. He was not accustomed to people of different creeds and backgrounds living peaceably alongside one another. Though believing he had avoided the worst of the Troubles through his immersion in English and Irish footballing codes, and good parenting from his mother and father, it would have been impossible for the young Lennon to entirely sidestep the everyday realities of a low-level war that manifested itself in so many forms.

'We were constantly being evacuated from the house because of bomb scares which were usually, but not always, hoaxes,' he wrote in 2011. Lennon remembers one huge explosion which shook the house, just as his sister was carrying a pot of stew across the kitchen, causing her to drop it onto the floor. Though the Troubles did not take any of his family members, one of Lennon's former classmates from St Michael's was not so lucky. It happened on 6 October 1990, by which time Lennon was living in Stockport and commuting to Crewe. His old friend had gone to a secluded spot with a girlfriend when a man approached the car and asked to see his driving licence.

Assuming this man to be a British soldier, he produced it and this proved to be fatal: his Irish Catholic surname gave him away and the paramilitary shot him dead at close range, 'revenge' for an IRA murder at the same spot a fortnight before.

Norman Whiteside, six years Lennon's senior and from the other side of the sectarian tracks, tells a remarkably similar story; the weary mundanity of the Troubles, the unacceptable becoming acceptable. Mulling on his own experience of paramilitary violence, he talks in *Determined* of how he and his friends:

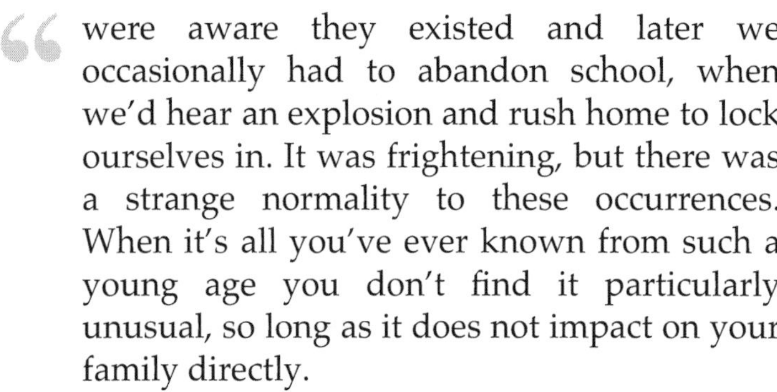

> were aware they existed and later we occasionally had to abandon school, when we'd hear an explosion and rush home to lock ourselves in. It was frightening, but there was a strange normality to these occurrences. When it's all you've ever known from such a young age you don't find it particularly unusual, so long as it does not impact on your family directly.

THE SHANKILL SKINHEAD

The Shankill is the most notable Protestant community outside the east of the city. Wedged into the heart of west Belfast, and surrounded on three sides by avowedly republican neighbourhoods of the Falls and Crumlin Roads, the road itself stretches out for about a mile and a half from central Belfast. In the same way that references are made to the Falls Road, what is usually being talked about when the Shankill is mentioned, is a broader area including the residential streets which intersect and branch off from the main arterial road. During the Troubles, one-third of all deaths occurred in these two districts of Belfast alone.

When Whiteside was growing up there, the greater Shankill area was home to perhaps 70,000 people. Today, the figure is less than a third of that. The Troubles, deprivation and latterly a vicious turf war between the UVF and the UFF are all contributing factors. The skilled working and middle classes who could afford to have moved out to Belfast's suburbs. Those who are left are the poor and unemployed who could not. It's said by Dave Bowler that in the twenties Arsenal manager Leslie Knighton, 'specifically searched for footballers in the drab streets of the Shankill and Falls Road areas' but by the eighties the absence of employment and security meant the area had become increasingly ripe for exploitation by paramilitaries.

'Back then, though,' writes Whiteside of the seventies, 'there was virtually full employment, with the men going off to work at those great Belfast enterprises - Harland and Wolff shipyards, Mackies Metal works, Shorts, the aircraft manufacturer, and Gallahers cigarette factory in York Street.' He makes no apologies for the Shankill. It was what it was and they were who they were, 'a vibrant, hardworking, proud, solid, loyal workforce that left the Shankill each morning, and though, of course, it was not at all culturally integrated, it was wholly integrated socially.'

Such was the communal feel, Whiteside believes, that 'a lot of residents, such as my parents, never feel entirely comfortable away from them and stick close by in these roads and arterial offshoots.' He is realistic enough to accept that things today are quite different from they were in his childhood, reflecting in print how he, 'cannot help but notice the effects of thirty-five years of turmoil. There is a sense that they are an entrenched, embattled people who have been let down by everybody.' He continued, 'The Shankill of the late seventies was not the place it later became. In fact, I think I was only lucky in being born when I was and not twenty years later...'

Not that living at 10 Danube Street was the lap of luxury in one of those 'dilapidated terrace houses that endured on the Shankill until finally they were subject to compulsory purchase orders, condemned and demolished in the late 1970s.' The classic Victorian two-up, two-downs had been left to deteriorate by successive landlords since the thirties until they were, along with similarly neglected properties in the Falls, finally dealt with half a century too late.

'Ironically, although it has become a more dangerous place, there are far more leisure facilities available for the children of the Shankill now than when I was a boy,' he wrote. He is not wrong. Before 1973, Northern Ireland lagged far behind the rest of the United Kingdom in its provision of leisure facilities; a nation of 1.5 million people had not one publicly controlled sports or leisure centre, as John Sudden's *Sport, Sectarianism and Society* explains. In the late 1960s capital grants from the UK government to Northern Ireland for such facilities were a derisory half a million pounds a year, but by 1983 this figure had increased to £7.5 million.

The 1973 Recreation and Youth Service (Northern Ireland) Government Order was the catalyst for change: for the first time district councils in Northern Ireland had an obligation to provide adequate sport and leisure facilities for their residents, unlike their counterparts in the rest of the UK who, despite it being part of their remit, are not bound by statute to do so.

Between 1977 and 1984 fourteen new sport and leisure facilities were built in Belfast. The optimum for a city of its size was eight: the theory being that more were needed in the circumstances to repress the rumblings of a restive population. For similar reasons, when Harland and Wolff's order book began to look decidedly bare in 1975, the British government acquired every share in the company: thousands of Protestant workers suddenly finding themselves out of work at the height of the Troubles was not a scenario they could allow to unfold.

When these new facilities were opened, it was common for there to be an official opening where some Belfast City Council bigwig would turn up and do his (and it was almost always his) ceremonial duties, and then — if the facility was in a republican district - for there to be another 'unofficial' opening a few days later. One such example is that of the Whiterock leisure centre; the city council chose not to invite the local MP and Sinn Fein leader Gerry Adams, so the party arranged a second event where Adams unveiled a plaque inscribed with some words in Gaelic, followed by the hoisting of an Irish tricolour flag.

Sudden writes of how a local DUP councillor, the now deceased George Seawright, was so outraged that under the cover of darkness and brandishing a pistol, he took matters into his own hands and removed the flag. After that, the number of Tricolour flags on display doubled. Such is life in Belfast. Yet because of the sectarian divisions, the city was suddenly blessed with a leisure centre everywhere you turned; individuals on either side of the divide, understandably fearful of venturing into or through an area they knew to be hostile to people like them, and in real need of something right on their doorstep.

These days there is a Norman Whiteside Sports Facility, which includes a Norman Whiteside Football Pitch on Sydney Street West, between the Shankill and Crumlin Roads. It's here that Woodvale FC play their games: they, along with three other Shankill based clubs, Lower Shankill, Shankill United and Albert Foundry, all play in the Northern Ireland Amateur League at various steps on its pyramid. Within the Shankill's borders, Crimea Street is home to a Linfield Supporters and Social Club; if you're a Shankill Protestant you are Linfield, just as if you are an east Belfast Protestant you are probably Glentoran. The area also houses the Ulster Rangers supporters club; devotion to whom is pretty much *de rigueur* for any Northern Irish Protestant.

During Whiteside's time living in the Shankill he started playing for Northern Ireland schoolboys while in his second year at Cairnmartin, training twice a week on Mondays and Wednesdays. This meant leaving the 'safety' of the Shankill for the first time, in order to navigate his way on buses to east Belfast, where he would meet up with his schoolboy teammates. It was a pretty big deal, as he writes:

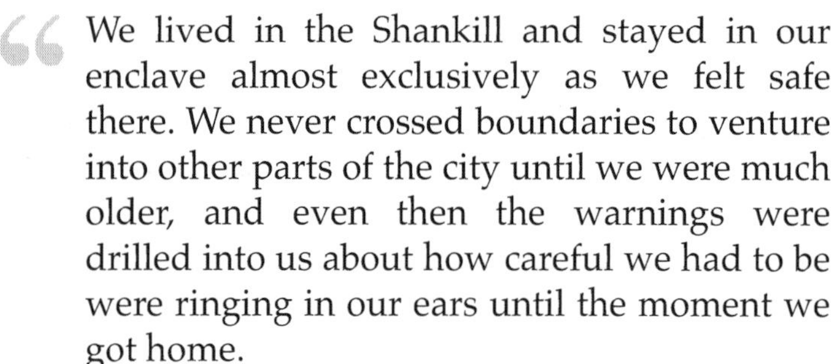

> “We lived in the Shankill and stayed in our enclave almost exclusively as we felt safe there. We never crossed boundaries to venture into other parts of the city until we were much older, and even then the warnings were drilled into us about how careful we had to be were ringing in our ears until the moment we got home.

The trip home would often prove challenging: more buses would be going up the Crumlin Road, a Catholic area that flanked the Shankill. It was hostile territory for the young Whiteside. 'Because of the segregation, you could tell the religion of a person on that bus by which stop he got off at,' he wrote, going on to explain the survival strategy he had devised, 'If you were to avoid a kicking after the first few stops on the (Catholic) start of the road, by a Catholic youth who was staying on the bus as it went on to Ardoyne, you had to be very canny about how you got the bus to stop, at any of the three stops which led towards the Shankill. The last thing you would do is stand up a good distance before your stop, pressing the bell and thereby announcing your religion.' In such guile he was not alone, his story reminiscent of the tale told by George Best about his route to and from Grosvenor Grammar School, which improved his sprinting capability, if nothing else.

VOLATILE

Lord Mountbatten, second cousin once removed to Queen Elizabeth II, was killed on 27 August 1979. The IRA had planted the fatal bomb on a leisure boat on which Mountbatten, his fourteen year-old grandson Nicholas and a local fifteen year-old Paul Maxwell were sailing in Mullaghmore, County Sligo. Another passenger, Baroness Brabourne, would later die of her injuries. Yet it was an event that took place that same day which was to add to the body count. What is now known as the Warrenpoint massacre saw the IRA's South Armagh brigade ambush the British Army, using two roadside bombs at Narrow Water Castle. The resulting loss of 18 soldiers made it the deadliest attack on British forces during the Troubles.

Pitch Battle V - Dundalk 1-1 Linfield, 29 August 1979

A match was scheduled to take place two days later between Linfield and Dundalk of the League of Ireland, in what would now amount to a Champions League qualifying game. Dundalk would go on to come agonisingly close to beating Glasgow Celtic in a later round which would have set up a historic tie with Real Madrid.

Yet it was what occurred outside the white lines of the pitch that night, which would have a greater impact on the future of Irish football. Crowd trouble had been expected as soon as the draw was made, with Linfield appealing to their supporters to be on their best behaviour and not to bring any alcohol on the sixty buses which transported the fans across the border. There were fears among the Dundalk faithful that there could be worse scenes than had occurred during the visit of Glasgow Rangers eleven years previously, which sadly turned out to be well founded. The simmering tension, which had only been further stoked by events forty-eight hours previously, boiled over into tangible violence. Twelve Linfield fans were arrested for fighting in one pub, while another local hostelry had its windows kicked in. Dundalk fans, for their part, threw stones at the Linfield buses as they arrived in town.

All of this was before a whistle had been blown or a ball kicked. Searching supporters coming into Oriel Park for improvised weaponry proved pointless since there was a ready supply of rocks on the ground to be used as makeshift missiles. The game began in what the official Dundalk FC website today describes as a 'war zone'. An eight foot barbed wire fence which had hitherto separated the fans was torn down by Linfield fans, who climbed up floodlights to better display their Union Jacks. The Irish tricolour flag was burned and there were running battles with the *Gardai*, already policing the event in numbers higher than any other sporting occasion outside Dublin. Well over one hundred people were injured, including fifty-six *Garda*. Derek Corbett, club secretary for the visitors, implored fans over the tannoy to 'stop throwing stones. It is the name of Linfield FC that you are damaging.'

The match was blighted by stoppages, with the second half kick-off delayed by trouble during the break. Only minutes later the game was paused again after a Linfield goal prompted its fans to invade the pitch. Almost immediately after it was restarted, a stone thrown from the stands struck Linfield's Terry Hayes, playing at right-back that day and now a sports therapist at the club. This meant another suspension of play. Eventually, around twenty minutes before the final whistle, the *Gardai* successfully chased the Linfield fans out of the ground altogether, brandishing batons. To settle scores, the fleeing Linfield partisans broke every window they could along the Carrick Road. Meanwhile, inside the ground the match continued — almost a sideshow at this point – and Dundalk equalised.

An *Irish Press* editorial in the immediate aftermath reported, 'In the wake of Mullaghmore and Warrenpoint the game was played in an atmosphere of hatred. It should be added that both teams gave a fine display of football and sportsmanship despite the frightening conditions.' A hastily produced UEFA report implicated Linfield as the sole culprits of that night, despite protestations that Catholic supporters of Cliftonville had travelled down intent on inflaming tribal passions. Linfield were told to pay for the £5,000 of damage to Oriel Park, as well as the costs of holding the second leg at a venue outside of Ireland, and Dundalk were issued a much lesser fine for failing to properly police the match. The second leg was arranged at the home of the since dissolved HFC Haarlem in the Netherlands, Dundalk progressing thanks to a Cathal Muckian brace and a fruitless night for the Blues in front of goal.

FANS ON THE RUN

The streets of Northern Ireland were littered with sectarian shrapnel during the seventies, and the terraces were too: those Cliftonville fans who had travelled down to Oriel Park in Dundalk were just beginning to make a name for themselves as the 'Red Army', an ultras section of the Solitude club's supporters. They had been cajoled into existence a year earlier by clashes with Glentoran fans, and further violence provoked by loyalists purporting to be supporters of their Irish Cup final opponents Portadown, which had necessitated the intervention of riot police.

Today Cliftonville is associated with the city's Catholic and nationalist communities as it has been since the seventies. The area went from being a lower middle-class Protestant district (and home to Belfast's Jewish community), to a majority Catholic area in the space of a few short years. Suddenly, there was again a club that Catholics could support and it quickly became theirs. According ti Henry McDonalds excellent *Colours,* the academic Peter Shirlow remembers going to Solitude in the early sixties and 'seeing Cliftonville fans wearing Rangers shirts and scarves to the games. But just as the makeup of the city was rapidly changing, so too was the demography on the terraces.'

Before the shift in support, the club had drawn support from the loyalist Torrens area but the name Cliftonville became so strongly associated with Irish nationalism, that when the Cliftonville Cricket Club was burned out of its premises in north Belfast in 1972 and relocated to the suburbs in Greenisland, local loyalists thought it must be a papist institution and daubed it with anti-Catholic graffiti. The Cliftonville Road itself was a dangerous place to be, not because of football fans but because it was a notorious hunting ground of the Shankill Butchers. They were as grim as the name suggests; an ultra-violent offshoot of the UVF who would grab people they suspected of being Catholic at random, beat them senseless then hack at their throat with a butchers knife.

Rioting at football matches in Northern Ireland intensified after 1980, particularly following the first hunger strike at Long Kesh began that winter. In his book *Colours: From Bombs to Boom,* McDonald recounts how Cliftonville's Red Army would regularly travel to away games by train. One such occasion took them to Coleraine with a complimentary RUC escort: each time the train stopped members of the Red Army would jump out onto the platform, run to the station wall in whichever Protestant town they had alighted and scrawl UTP (Up The Provos) on it, then kick any unsuspecting men on the platform and rush back onto the train before it departed.

Though little reported elsewhere, the Red Army's battles with the loyalist fans of rival teams at the tail end of the seventies and the early eighties, were the worst incidences of football-related violence anywhere in the UK. As McDonald reports, when Cliftonville were drawn against Larne in an Irish Cup semi-final at the Oval on St Patrick's Day 1979, the match ended in a 2-2 draw, but it was the replay four days later that some unlikely hooligans pounced: just before the Red Army went inside, they were met with a volley of abuse from a gaggle of loyalist old ladies. As intimidating moments go, it probably ranked fairly low, until one of them ran from her house with a shovel containing hot coals, which she proceeded to launch in the direction of the Cliftonville crowd.

Linfield were a familiar foe, off the pitch as well as on it. The Blues won the Irish League title in 1979, taking the opportunity to display the Gibson Cup at their next match. By McDonald's recollection, particular satisfaction was derived from brandishing it towards the Spion Kop where the Red Army were ensconced: the Cliftonville faithful chanted that Linfield centre-half Peter Rafferty was a 'dirty baldy bastard' when he took the pitch, and before long stones and broken up bits of terrace were being lobbed towards the Linfield fans at the north side of the ground. Lines of RUC men separated the hordes from one another, as the Linfield crowd sang songs praising the Shankill Butchers, the UDA and the UVF. After Cliftonville had sealed a 2-0 victory, the scenes inside the ground were repeated on the streets outside, across the A1 into the Donegall and Falls Roads. Cars, ambulances and RUC Landrovers were not spared from the bombardment, as stones and bottles flew across the main road connecting Belfast and Dublin.

A week later, the clubs met again in the Irish Cup final at Windsor Park and fans fought each other on the pitch before the match had even kicked off. You would have thought the match would be postponed, but it was not. You would have thought that the police band might decide that playing 'God Save The Queen' was not the best idea, but they did not. As the British anthem played while the teams lined up, McDonald notes that old hands within the Cliftonville crowd urged their fellow fans to 'sit down, sit fucking down.' Which they all did, gladly. That day Cliftonville won the Irish Cup for the first time in 70 years.

Occasionally, there was humour. *Colours* notes with amusement a match in December of 1979 that witnessed a small number of Cliftonville fans blow up an inflatable Santa Claus and tie a club scarf around its neck. They held him up triumphantly and soon the Cliftonville - and, eventually Ballymena - crowd sang in unison 'One Daddy Christmas, there's only one Daddy Christmas.'

Early the following season, Cliftonville's north Belfast

rivals, Crusaders, took to the field, keen to settle scores after being defeated by their neighbours in the County Antrim Shield. The RUC had seen fit to put 1,000 officers on d duty. McDonald's account talks of how that day there were three times more police at Crusaders' Seaview ground than there had been at Ibrox the previous Saturday when Rangers played Celtic, ten times as many as when Arsenal played Manchester United the same day and fifteen times more than at Anfield when Liverpool played their first home game of that season against West Brom.

These were serious rivalries, yet there is no more consequential duel than the one between Linfield and Glentoran. McDonald's compelling narrative explores how, when Glentoran had played Benfica in the early rounds of the European Cup in 1968, Linfield fans turned up at the Oval to support Eusebio and co. — hoping the Glens would get stuffed. When Benfica did score, a crowd of hundreds of Linfield supporters cheered them on from the City End, ultimately disappointed when the first leg ended 1-1. The enmity had always been there but the Troubles changed Irish League football crowds; the terraces became harder, harsher places. Linfield fans began to abuse Catholic players within the Glentoran team, taunting the Glentoran fans as 'fenian lovers' and the Oval became the 'Vatican City'. Windsor Park was a cauldron of sectarian hatred.

It was the worst of times for Northern Irish football.

7

DANNY'S BOYS

Danny Blanchflower's first match in charge of Northern Ireland was George Best's return to the international fold after an absence of three years. There had been plenty of reasons to leave him out, not least a World Cup qualifying match against Bulgaria where he had been sent off for punching an opponent. A year earlier when Terry Neill had called him up to play against Scotland at Hampden Park, Best simply did not show up. Neill recalled in Lovejoy's *Bestie* how:

> "George had done a runner from Manchester United, and nobody knew where he was. There was a national hue and cry, and I had the press and television cameras virtually camped in my bedroom at the team's hotel in Troon. It wasn't something the players talked about, but we all loved Bestie, and we put up a protective wall and held on, saying nothing...We would rather he had been with us, but we weren't annoyed that he wasn't.

> We were worried about him, each of us in his own way.

Falteringly plying his trade with Fulham at Craven Cottage, Best had been picked out of desperation rather than an overarching master plan. Indeed, in Bowler's *Danny Blanchflower,* his new manager is said to have remarked that 'George has no tactical awareness. He is such a great player that he must play, but it means that to get the right balance in our 4-2-4 system I must play fourteen players!' In the run-up to his return against the Dutch, Northern Ireland had been abysmal; five games without a win, and three Home Championship fixtures where the Ulstermen had failed to even score, going down by 1 to Wales, 3 to Scotland and 4 against England under part-time player-manager Dave Clements, based in New York so he could play for the Cosmos.

When the IFA decided it was time for Clements to move on, they took their cue from a *Belfast Telegraph* poll conducted during the dreadful Home Championship series, which indicated that the fans wanted Blanchflower to take over the hot seat. He was given a contract running to the end of June 1978, including World Cup qualifiers against Holland, Belgium and Iceland. 'At least let's give the people some hope,' he said upon his appointment, reflecting the commonly held view that the qualifying group was a no-hoper, which gave the team license to play with nothing to lose. 'Let's be honest,' he had continued, 'there is nothing but difficulties in the path of Northern Ireland. We have got to accept that. It takes time to change habits and many of those players will be loath to do this. Still, we must do something if we are to get better, to get out of the rut.'

In preparation for the first of those games, the team played a behind closed doors match against Luton Town, which they won 2-0. It seemed to pay off when Best played well in Rotterdam against the Dutch, reinforcing the perception that he could (perhaps only) perform at the peak of his powers, when facing the highest calibre opposition. Drawing 2-2 away against a side that contained Wim Jansen, Johan Neeskens and Johan Cruyff was highly creditable and it certainly stuck in the mind of Sammy McIlroy, who later described it to Teddy Jameson as a 'fantastic result. And the beam on Danny's face was worth all those years to see, because we were in the lion's den, expecting to get turned over and we got an absolutely unbelievable draw.' Some indication of the gulf in quality of players available to the two teams back then is found, when we consider who scored Northern Ireland's goals: Chris McGrath and Derek Spence. Who? Exactly.

Blanchflower's gung-ho approach had borne fruit against the Netherlands but, as Bertie Peacock pointed out in Bowler's narrative, 'We didn't have the players that we would have liked to have had to play the way he wanted to play — when Billy Bingham took over, he played the percentage game, which was the only way Northern Ireland could have got success; but Danny wouldn't play that way.'

Before the game against Belgium, there was another secretive match against Luton. Best was picked again and seemed to be finding this new way of doing things a breath of fresh air, apparently declaring: 'It's fun to play for Ireland under Danny. He says the same things as Sir Matt Busby used to at Old Trafford: "Go out and enjoy yourself on the field." The only difference is he takes twice as long to say it!' It may have been enjoyable but it was not a winning formula the second time around: Danny's boys fell to a 2-0 defeat in Liege in front of 25,000. Blanchflower was trying to implement a playing style that would have worked well in the fifties or early sixties, but was hopelessly outdated for the late seventies. He would not be told though: Bowler notes that he proclaimed, 'It's better to lose having a go than be defeated concentrating on defence as Ireland has done so often.'

Next up was a friendly against West Germany in April 1977, a game where Pat Jennings was deemed to be at fault for Northern Ireland's heavy loss. Malcolm Brodie wrote a scathing piece in the *Belfast Telegraph,* but it was the headline 'AUF WIEDRSEHEN, PAT' which struck a particularly cruel tone. We know, of course, that Pat would retain his claim on the shirt for another nine years but the criticism stung at the time, especially as he believed that it was not he — but Blanchflower's tactics - to blame for the deluge of balls in his net. Frustratingly for the players, as Jennings notes in eponymously-titled autobiography, 'Danny wouldn't change the style. We wanted to, because it's no fun standing at the back watching the ball fly past you. I wanted a good defensive unit around me, and to start from there, but he wouldn't change his principles. We had players like Allan Hunter, who was as good as anyone in Britain, and he didn't want to be carrying the ball up to the halfway line while everyone dropped back.'

Football was more sophisticated than during Danny's days as a player, and although it was not as tactically advanced as it has become today, players needed to be responsible for more than one phase of play. This did not suit the Blanchflower agenda, as Jennings explained in one passage:

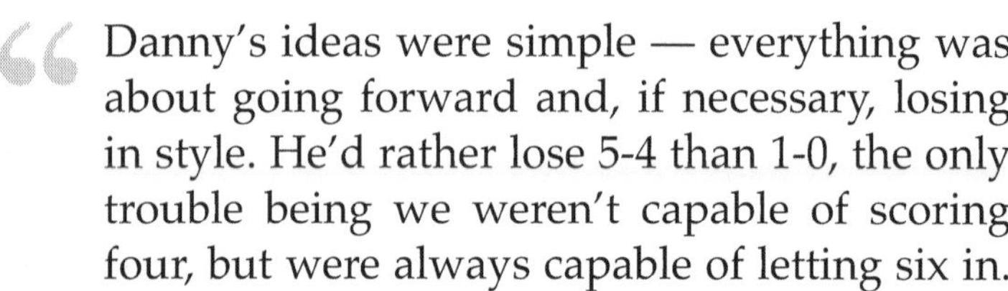

> Danny's ideas were simple — everything was about going forward and, if necessary, losing in style. He'd rather lose 5-4 than 1-0, the only trouble being we weren't capable of scoring four, but were always capable of letting six in.

> You had to entertain and hope that we might just win. Which wasn't much good for me as a goalkeeper. A lot of the players weren't too keen on that, especially as things went on, because you don't want to keep getting hammered...We weren't good enough to take the game to the likes of West Germany, and I don't think his tactics were right for us. It didn't suit our players.

Gerry Armstrong concurred with the goalkeeper's view in conversation with Jamieson for *Whose Side...?*, 'Danny was brilliant to be with because Danny was just full of beans and full of enthusiasm and he made you laugh. But sometimes he liked to be too adventurous and as a result you got your backside kicked in a couple of times, which didn't do the morale much good.' Worse was to come after the Home Championship, a 1-0 loss to Iceland in Reykjavik.

Blanchflower's naïve, almost boyish vision of how football should be played was failing. It might have worked in the primary school playground but it was not effective on the international stage in the late seventies. The return fixture against Iceland in Belfast did bring the first win of the Blanchflower era, but caused him to channel a Euro 2016 Cristiano Ronaldo in forthrightly declaring, 'That's not the way I would have played under the circumstances. They only came to save their face, not to entertain, but I suppose that's the name of the game today.'

Three weeks later, George Best would play his final competitive game in the green of Northern Ireland, the last of his 37 caps coming during a 1-0 loss to the Netherlands at Windsor Park. It was an international career that had produced its distinguishing moments, but the inescapable fact is that sometimes George just was not taking it all that seriously, as his former Manchester United roommate David Sadler testified to Joe Lovejoy, 'It was a real joke for George, playing for Ireland. He had fantastic matches, like when they played Scotland and it was George Best against eleven Scotsmen, but the fact of the matter is that Northern Ireland were never going to qualify for the World Cup, and that definitely got to him.'

The truth was that a few years later they would — without him - but that is a story for later. If nothing else, Best was able to enjoy himself on international duty as Derek Dougan, his sometime roommate on foreign trips reflected in David Tossell's book on the Doog, 'In the Irish squad he's treated as he likes to be treated, not as a celebrity but as an equal. He can muck in, horse around, feel for a while his Irish background and make contact with his roots.'

HOME TRUTHS

November 1977 saw the Belgians come to Belfast and a change in approach yielded a 3-0 win though, as Pat Jennings later wrote, it was not a manager approved alteration: 'At Windsor Park, the crowd dictated the way we played. If you had a full house in Belfast, they didn't want to see me rolling the ball out to the full-backs, they wanted the ball in the other half, and so we played a more direct game and we had some good results from that.'

One policy implementation, that was the source of particular pride for Blanchflower, was the introduction of Irish League players to the squad. His hope was that putting these hopefuls in the shop window would secure them moves to England, and Bowler mentions in a self congratulatory tone how the manager had asked:

> 'Have you ever seen a time when there was so much movement in Irish football? We have brought in a few young players, we have had quite a few transfers, there had been cash for youth, a policy development at this level and there is sponsorship which is going into the game at a phenomenal rate. We are all working on the right lines.'

Moving in a positive direction was well and good but the 1978 Home Championship series saw 1-0 losses to England and Wales, and a draw with Scotland, whose minds were elsewhere: bound for the World Cup in Argentina. The draw for the 1980 European Championship qualifying put Northern Ireland in a group with contained England, Bulgaria, Denmark and the Republic of Ireland.

Significantly, this would be the first time the two teams on the island of Ireland would play each other, and their meeting in Dublin opened proceedings. Clearly, there were fears that the match could become another focal point for sectarian activity, not so much on the pitch as off it. Evidence of this is in Pat Jennings recollection of how the team 'got a police escort through Dublin, it flew through there. The security guys had us picked up as soon as we went over the border and took us through to the hotel. I've never driven through Dublin so fast!' The one blot in the copybook occurred in Belfast when, as Jennings describes, 'some idiot threw a stone which laid out the Republic of Ireland midfield man Gerry Daly.'

Although security surrounding the game and its buildup was high, Pat Rice emphasises in Bowler's recital that the players did not carry sectarian baggage onto the Lansdowne Road pitch with them:

There was no ill feeling between the players. We actually had a vote at one time as to whether there should be one team for Ireland, as they do in rugby union, and the players all said that we should, but the actual governing bodies turned that down. When it came to the game though, nobody wanted to lose! It was inevitable that the game was a nil-nil.

Blanchflower saw this result, a point away from home, as a disappointment and announced that he would step down after the qualification matches or the tournament in Italy, if his boys made it. He thought it was time for a younger man to take over, and in *Danny Blanchflower* it is evident that his former teammate Peter McParland was not surprised by the decision in view of the bigger picture: 'By 1976, when he took over, he knew he could get in among his own people, among the players and inspire them. But I think it was always likely to be a brief stay for him.' Another colleague from the great 1958 World Cup team in Bertie Peacock reflected, 'Peter Doherty and Bill Nicholson both had that bit of grit, something stable in the middle of the field, but Danny was a cavalier fella, loved to go forward - Keegan at Newcastle epitomised everything Danny liked.'

The Tottenham legend seemed to have come to the realisation that his ideas were not likely to bring success, with a team of limited technical ability but was unable to embrace the pragmatism flowering in the South. The time of Jack Charlton's reign at the helm of the Republic's dressing room was not too far off and he would make judicious use of the grandparent rule allowing him to pick ostensibly English players with Irish ancestry. For Danny and the IFA however, it was an issue of pride; they thought the team should be made up of bona fide Ulstermen. This limited the pool of available talent, with only Pat Jennings in the Blanchflower era likely to have made the England squad. As Jennings himself put it 'the cruel truth is that the Irish team wasn't equipped to make it work.'

In the years before a twenty-four team Euros, or even a sixteen team tournament, Northern Ireland's distant second place in the group behind England was not enough to secure passage to the finals. Though there were wins over Bulgaria, Denmark and the Republic on the way, Danny had not been able to scale the mountain that winning the group represented, but in the words of Jennings, he 'restored a bit of pride, but it was really Billy Bingham who transformed our fortunes, with the right kind of tactics.'

For Jennings, Blanchflower was a good man, if not a good manager: 'If I'd wanted to win for any of the managers I'd played under — and there have been some lovely fellas, like Bertie Peacock, who was a real gentleman - it would have been for Danny. There wasn't an ounce of badness in him, he just wanted what was good for Irish football, but it wasn't to be.' He had instilled some positivity into a demoralised and hapless outfit, as Pat Rice concluded in remarks found in Bowler's exposition, 'What he really did was to brighten up Northern Irish football. All of a sudden there was a lot of happiness, joviality about the camp, a great spirit and sense of comradeship among the players, and I think that stood the team in good stead after he left.'

Just how would the side fare in a post-Blanchflower era?

8

KING BILLY RIDES BACK INTO TOWN

The team had spent the build up to the 1982 World Cup training at the University of Sussex, the unusually hot temperatures on England's south coast that Summer ideal preparation for their upcoming Spanish sojourn. While in Brighton, the travelling party stayed at the Metropole hotel beside the Brighton Grand where some two years later the IRA would detonate 20lb of gelignite, resulting in the death of five Conservative officials at the party's summer conference.

One man would not be catching the flight, though there had been a 'nearly' moment for George Best in the months before the tournament, with talk of him going to Spain as a 'supersub'. He was thirty-six and turning out for San Jose Earthquakes, sanguine about his omission years later in his portrayal by Joe Lovejoy, 'I had half a chance to go, I suppose. Billy Bingham was the manager, and the Irish media, and general public, put him under a bit of pressure to take me with them — sentimental stuff, really.'

Among the squad Bingham *had* chosen, the mood in

the camp was one of cautious optimism, reflected in Martin O'Neill's observation that 'I honestly feel we have the spirit to do something special in Spain.' Billy Bingham's preparations for the tournament — including making the players guzzle ten pints of water a day - involved using the *Estadi Ciutat de València* (home of Levante) as their base, although Valencia's second club were practically bankrupt and required the IFA to pay some of their bills to keep the lights on, and in Whiteside's autobiographical words, 'get the ankle-high grass cut.'

Arrangements behind the scenes were well underway too. The IFA had freighted crates of Guinness over to the team hotel in Valencia, which Whiteside wryly observe was 'no doubt more with the blazers in mind than the tracksuits.' Bingham and his wife owned a chemist, providing the suntan cream for the side's training camp in Sussex and their Spanish escapade. The manager had also done a deal procuring identical sunglasses for the entire squad, later noting, 'We'd had a few days sunshine. We'd trained very hard, we were fit and ready and off we went.'

Ready they may have been but as Sammy McIlroy remembered, 'No one gave us a chance.' Gerry Armstrong recalled similar to Teddy Jamieson, 'I think it was Jimmy Greaves who did a piece saying, "Well done to the Irish and my old mate Pat Jennings and Gerry. Good luck to them for qualifying. They ain't going to be there long. Just bring a toothbrush and a spare shirt and you'll be okay." That type of thing.'

Simply titled 'Yer Man', the official song ahead of the tournament featured the players alongside Ireland's 1970 Eurovision winner Dana, belting out inspired couplets such as 'Viva Northern Ireland/We're off to Spain'. They had reached this point by virtue of finishing second in a group containing Portugal, Sweden, Israel and Scotland, who topped the table. It was against the Israelis on 14 November 1981 that passage to the finals was secured with a 1-0 victory at Windsor Park. Though his emergence was overshadowed by political realities — it was the height of the republican hunger strikes at Long Kesh - there had been a new player on show that night: wee Norman Whiteside.

He had not even made his United debut; that would come against Brighton on 24 April the following year, still not seventeen years-old. It had been a meteoric rise. His place in the Northern Irish starting eleven, according to Bingham, was cemented by a twenty yard goal he had scored at training in Sussex. So it was that he became the youngest player to take the field at a World Cup finals, aged just seventeen years and forty-one days old, in Northern Ireland's opening fixture against Yugoslavia.

The 0-0 result against the Yugoslavs on his debut was creditable, if uninspiring, and the inability of the Spaniards to beat Honduras the previous day meant that the group was wide open. Just off the South American coast, British forces had secured victory against their Argentine foes in another type of battle altogether. Margaret Thatcher's decision to allow the 'home' nations to compete and possibly face the South Americans on the pitch had been vindicated.

Three days later, on 20 June, the Spanish defeated Yugoslavia 2-1 in Valencia: not only did it put them in a strong position on home turf, it opened up the prospect of the Northern Irish being able to put some fresh air between themselves and the rest, if only they could get a win over Honduras the next day. In front of 15,000 fans in Zaragoza, Gerry Armstrong put the Ulstermen ahead after ten minutes and their potential to progress from the group rose from possible to likely. That is, of course, if they could maintain the lead. The team held out until the sixtieth minute when Honduran substitute Eduardo Laing levelled the tie. Suddenly their prospects were not looking so rosy. With the score 1-1 at the final whistle, Bingham's boys would have to get something against Spain, and hope that the result of the Yugoslavia-Honduras fixture did not inflict fatal damage to their campaign.

These were the days of two points for a win, meaning that a Honduran victory would put them on four points. The same result for the Yugoslavs would see them on three, so merely drawing against the Spanish would not be good enough for Whiteside and company: winning was their only option. The team started the tournament at 150-1 outsiders, so unfavoured that the administrators had only seen fit to take three sets of shirts to the tournament. It was time to show them up for their lack of faith.

Back in Zaragoza once more, the Yugoslavs triumphed over Honduras, courtesy of an eighty-eighth minute Vladimir Petrovic penalty. As things stood, it was they who would secure their place in the next round and the Irish who would be boarding flights back to Nutt's Corner. Imploring his players not to concede an early goal, Billy Bingham oversaw an extremely physical first half. Crucially, though, nothing had made its way into Pat Jennings goal. Then, very early in the second half, something incredible happened. Gerry Armstrong picked up the ball thirty-five yards from the Spanish goal, escaped the clutches of three opponents and laid the ball off to Gerry Hamilton on the right wing. The Burnley forward shed his markers and put the ball in front of Armstrong, who struck it with his right foot low into Luis Arconada's net. The man from Fintona had just rocketed himself into Northern Irish folklore as well as enabling one of the most famous passages of football commentary to this day: 'And Arconada......Armstrong!'

A blow had been struck, but with forty-seven minutes on the clock the game was still far from over. A couple of minutes later Sammy McIlroy's gashed leg meant there was no choice but to substitute him. Things only got worse ten minutes on, however, when Mal Donaghy found himself tangled up with Jose Antonio Camacho, the force of the challenge causing the latter to collide with the advertising hoardings. Donaghy's night was over, sent off. Northern Ireland's had just begun. An agonising moment during injury time, when a cross was floated high into the Northern Irish box required the intervention of Pat Jennings to tip it over the bar before Juanito could make contact. Finally, the whistle sounded. Northern Ireland had topped the group, a point better off than Spain and Yugoslavia.

Bingham invited the jubilant supporters to party with the players back at the Sidi Saler hotel, a journey delayed because a dehydrated Armstrong was required — yet unable to immediately produce - a urine sample after the game. As Jamieson reports, Martin O'Neill, installed as captain by Bingham, saw it as 'one of the most memorable nights...where we shared great moments with Northern Ireland supporters. In fact there were about thirty-five in my bedroom at half past three in the morning.' Asked what would happen next he declared, 'We'll probably win the World Cup.'

Whiteside remembers the result *even* being well received in the Republic, too. Simon and Garfunkel were touring and, per his recollection, 'were actually cheered at their Dublin reunion concert when, maybe not knowing which side of the border they were on, they dedicated "The Boxer" to Yer Men.'

Norman's brother had decided to come over but having used up all his holiday for the year told his painter and decorator bosses that he was sick, a tale that was blown wide open when he was shown on Ulster TV walking along a Valencian beach. The regional TV franchise was also responsible for bringing together Whiteside and Hamilton's mothers to watch the next game, in what the Shankill man later described as a 'symbolic show of unity' featuring a young Eamonn Holmes, as Hamilton's parents hailed from Mica Drive on the Falls. The United new boy had phoned his mother after the win and she had told him of 'people dancing up and down the Shankill.'

The IFA made hurried arrangements for accommodation for the next fixture, having not expected the team to make it this far. The squad and the security guards assigned to protect them from the Basque separatist group ETA ended up staying in the defeated Yugoslavs hotel, literally passing them in the corridor. There was also a rushed order to Adidas for the green home kit, as they had only needed the white one for the three group games.

On the field, the next round would consist of a three team group with the top team making it through to the semi-final. Northern Ireland's first game would pit them against Austria. Harland and Wolff, as well as the Sirocco rope works, put on overtime shifts on Wednesday in order that their workers could leave early on Thursday to watch the match on television later that day. For those back home, this was something to savour: Whiteside's *Determined* contains the fascinating gem that more video recorders were hired in that week in Northern Ireland, than had been for the royal wedding the year before.

Each of the three-second round games in Group D would take place at Atletico Madrid's *Estadio Vicente Calderón*. The first of these was between Austria and France, settled by a thirty-ninth minute Bernard Genghini goal. The French would need to be tamed but first up were Austria. Middlesbrough's Jim Platt deputised for the injured Pat Jennings in goal, while Brighton's Sammy Nelson moved into the left-back berth vacated by Donaghy due to his suspension. Austria knew they had to win this game and were desperate to score. For Northern Ireland, a positive result would mean their match against the French a few days later would effectively be a quarter-final with both teams going for a win.

Each side had the chance to seize the initiative before the Northern Irish took the lead in the twenty-seventh minute. Sammy McIlroy sent the ball to Gerry Armstrong on the right, still inside the Irish half. He was able to lose two Austrian defenders on his way to the byline, and a precise cross on to Hamilton's head at the far post put the ball beyond Koncilia. Shortly after half-time John McClelland was unable to deal with a ball floated into the box, which fell to Walter Schachner who struck it against the post. Jimmy Nicholl was there to put it out of play, but when the corner was taken, Herbert Prohaska found Ernst Baumeister on the edge of the box, his low shot was completed by Bruno Pezzey to draw them level.

The Austrians were flying and a rapid move allowed Walter Schachner to put the ball past Platt. Mercifully, the goalscorer was adjudged to have been offside but with twenty minutes to go Austria won a free kick 25 yards from the Irish goal. They played it short to substitute Reinhold Hintermaier who fired it past Platt, putting the Austrians in front. Bingham's players were used to troubles of one sort but this time theirs lay squarely on the pitch.

They were down but not out. Building patiently from midfield paid off in the seventy-fifth minute, when Armstrong ran at the Austrian defence once again. His shot from outside the area deflected off Erich Obermayer towards the onrushing Jimmy Nicholl, who was in space on the right hand side. As the keeper bore down, Nicholl swept the ball across to the far post, where it came off Hamilton's head again before landing in the empty net. It was not the win that would strengthen Bingham's hand but the team had avoided defeat. The decisive match against the French would take place three days later on 4 July, causing dissent from Ian Paisley because — you guessed right - it was a Sunday.

All of Bingham's famed motivational skills would be required if his side were to progress at the expense of France. Whiteside recalled that his manager's team talks were 'tailored for the Northern Ireland football team, and were about our country, its people, what they'd gone through over the past decade and what our being out there meant to them.' Jennings returned between the sticks and Donaghy was reinstated after serving his suspension. A draw would be enough for France but for the second time in three games the Irish needed a win and nothing less would do.

The French were the form side of the tournament, gathering momentum after losing their opening game of the tournament to England. They exerted early pressure on the Irish, who were thankful that Pat Jennings was able to save attempts from both Michel Platini and Dominique Rocheteau. Now it was Northern Ireland's turn to raise their game, a break on the right from Whiteside made its way to O'Neill, who exchanged the ball with Armstrong before firing past Jean-Luc Ettori. Goal! But...the linesman had his flag up. Video replays seemed to suggest the Irish captain was justified in questioning the call but, well, that's football. Then, shortly after the thirty-minute mark, Platini made a run which saw him reach the byline before cutting the ball back to a waiting Alain Giresse. He had time to take a touch before slotting it past Jennings to open the scoring.

Early in the second half, Marius Tresor found

Rocheteau on the left, and a skilful turn took out Jimmy Nicholl and set the Frenchman running towards Chris Nicholl. As he neared the eighteen-yard box, he switched from his right to left foot and powered the ball low beneath Jennings at his near post. Rocheteau should have grabbed a couple more, before a free-kick out wide on the left side of the pitch was played short to him, his deft touches to switch the ball from right foot to left then back again as he beat Jennings ended any realistic hopes the Northern Irish harboured of getting the result they needed.

Armstrong was able to score a consolation goal with the assistance of Whiteside, but when in the closing minutes the Irish pushed forward, dreaming of the impossible they exposed themselves to the French counter-attack. With ten minutes left on the scoreboard, Giresse picked out Jean Tigana on the right wing, and his quick cross expertly met his compatriot's forehead to put the result beyond doubt.

A weary side unaccustomed to the heat had wilted in the Madrid sun, but could justifiably regard themselves as one of the world. Only four other players scored more goals than Gerry Armstrong's three goal tally in the tournament. Yet it was O'Neill's disallowed goal that lingered longest in the memory, as he wondered what could have been: 'Television replays prove I was a yard onside,' he had told the *Irish Times*. 'Then a couple of minutes later, Giresse scores and they win 4-1. But if my goal had stood, I think we had a chance. It still rankles with me greatly; not being in the record books as scoring in the World Cup is soul destroying.'

The players had decided between themselves that rather than divide their prize money on the basis of appearances — £600 for the first XI, £400 for the substitutes and £200 for unused squad members - they would split it equally. 'It was excellent for morale,' Whiteside wrote, 'but I remember thinking about it as I bounced up and down on the left touchline, and caught a glimpse in the stand of Bobby Campbell clutching a burger in one hand and lifting a beer to his mouth with the other.' Pat Jennings also wrote positively of the decision:

> The four Irish League players, all part-timers who earn only peanuts from football, were particularly pleased with the reward. And I was especially delighted for our third-choice goalkeeper, George Dunlop of Linfield, who had been made redundant from his full-time job in Belfast shortly before the World Cup.

Bingham, the first Irishman to be involved in two World Cups, was pleased 'the championship has been a marvellous boost, not merely to the team but to all the people of Northern Ireland.' Speaking of his players and their various backgrounds he was quoted in the *Sunday Telegraph*:

> the team could not have done what it had if I had eleven Protestants in it or if it had eleven Catholics. Martin was a wonderful captain for us. He wanted the responsibility and he was such a bright fellow, I knew he was the man for the job. And he played alongside Sammy McIlroy in the centre of midfield, a Protestant. Elsewhere in the team you had Gerry Armstrong, from the Falls Road, and Norman Whiteside, from the Shankill. It didn't matter to us.

O'Neill was the first Catholic to be appointed captain

of the Northern Irish team, a decision that was clearly not without controversy *outside* the dressing room, as Bingham told the same newspaper:

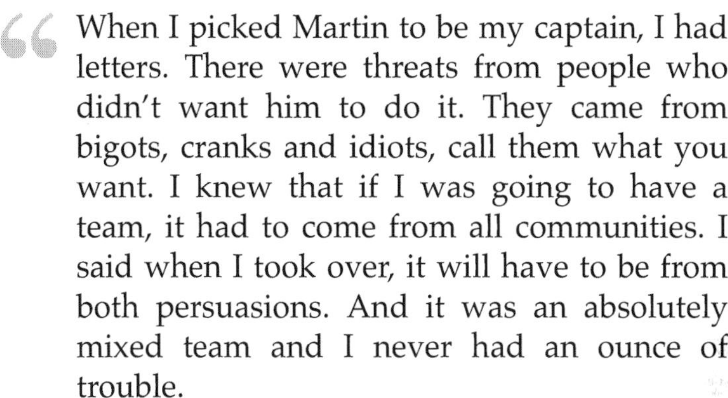

> When I picked Martin to be my captain, I had letters. There were threats from people who didn't want him to do it. They came from bigots, cranks and idiots, call them what you want. I knew that if I was going to have a team, it had to come from all communities. I said when I took over, it will have to be from both persuasions. And it was an absolutely mixed team and I never had an ounce of trouble.

In his typically considered manner, O'Neill hoped that football could be a welcome distraction in fraught circumstances, musing to the *Daily Mail*, 'If it doesn't sound too self-righteous, we hoped we could give our wee place a lift, Myself, I would say being a professional footballer shielded you — to an extent - but not in every way. There was bombing in England too. To be Irish in England then was never unbelievably bad, but it was uncomfortable at times.' Maybe he was right: the sectarian murder rate had been running at one every three days before the tournament yet in the two and a half weeks between the team's first and last games, the Troubles claimed only one fatality.

OUT OF THE WEEDS

By 1984 moves were afoot to get Derry City back into football. A new board were trying to find a ground without the territorial baggage that came with the Brandywell. They put forward five sites: two were on the Bogside of the Foyle and three on the Waterside. None were acceptable to the authorities. The Irish League AGM rejected their strongest and final application to rejoin on 11 May 1984, once again citing the objections of the security forces as justification.

In *Playing Away From Home* we find Robert Ferris, club Chairman and a unionist, reflecting wearily 'we seem to have come to the end of the tunnel without achieving anything. We feel that the police's decision has far reaching implications not only for Derry City, but also for potential investors in the club. If the police feel they cannot provide security for senior soccer in the city, then what will industrialists think when they are weighing up the possibilities of investing here?' They could only conclude that they were being shunned for reasons other than football, because of who and what they were perceived to represent.

For Derry stalwart and socialist, Eamon McCann, quoted in David Hassan's fascinating *A People Apart,* this was merely a continuation: 'They resigned from the Irish League in 1972, after several years of what they regarded as discriminatory behaviour by the football authorities in Belfast and they were right, absolutely right. And some of it was sheer religious bigotry. They didn't want to come to the Bogside to play their football.' Yet historically the football team had an open and inclusive outlook; when a Catholic board member left, he would be replaced by another Catholic. When a Protestant one left, they would do likewise. The playing staff was mixed, unlike that of other notable clubs who faced no censure. Derry were in a no-win situation.

The club would eventually tire of being spurned by the Northern body year after year, turning their attention instead to a league they believed would be more receptive to their advances. The League of Ireland was in the throes of being restructured in 1984, creating a twelve team top tier, and a ten team second tier. Derry could hardly jump straight into the first, so they would have to pay their dues in the second. The FAI council considered their application, and were supportive of it, yet unable to move until the IFA and the Irish League gave their consent. FIFA would need to give their nod of approval, too.

Having been granted special dispensation by the IFA (who, having refused Derry for the previous dozen seasons, could hardly now try to cling on to them) and the world governing body, Derry City successfully gained entry to the new league. Further permission from UEFA allowing the club to steward their own games was granted; the consensus being that the presence of RUC officers in such a vehemently republican area would be, at the very least, counterproductive. What did the FAI think about the security situation, the lack of any official police presence at the games? Eddie Mahon, the club's PR spokesman, was frank in conversation with Teddy Jamieson, 'You see Dublin? Dublin knows shit all about the north.'

FIFA's permission had come in October 1984, with the proviso that it was to be a one-off occurrence, accepting that their situation under IFA auspices was untenable. Derry's location four miles from the border with the Republic minimised any security or logistical issues that would have made a similar move by a Belfast side impossible. It was made clear by all parties that this arrangement would not be countenanced for any other Northern Irish club, and all but three League of Ireland clubs voted in support of Derry City joining them, with the exception of Limerick, Shelbourne and St Patrick's Athletic. Their objections were apparently motivated by concerns about the financial burden travel to Derry would put on their budgets.

By 1 February 1985 the final stages of Derry City's reemergence were complete, and the construction of a team of local talent supplemented by ageing English journeymen looking for one last run out began. Eddie Mahon, talking of the club's ethos in Mike Cronin's *Playing Away…* stated:

> we will not be asking people where they go on Sunday or for whom they vote. We are purely and simply a football team — nothing else. We are not in the business of attracting people from any specific side of the fence. We want football supporters and nothing else. Politics should be kept outside the ground. As a club we want no involvement with politics. In fact we are doing our best to avoid the topic at all times.

This was a noble aim, but when Derry City resumed matches later that year a supporter from the Protestant Waterside, in comments found in Cronin's paper on the subject, was sceptical, 'Look at the game against Shamrock Rovers [in a friendly] last year. The majority of the crowd were only intent on annoying those people who were not of their own religious persuasion. They seem to me to have found a vehicle for their bigotry which they have searched for years to get. I want no part of that scene.'

One player, Alan Harrison, was signed by Derry City from Ballymena - of all places! — before the season began but had put in a transfer request by December. It should be said that this denigration was not necessarily coming from Derry's fans; Harrison's family lived in east Belfast and were getting severe grief from local loyalists. He got his move, returning to the Irish League for Glentoran.

The phoenix club's opening game of 1985/86 season, their first senior fixture for fifteen years, was played against Home Farm at the Brandywell in front of 7,000 fans. A commemorative record, 'Derry are Back', was released, but most unusually of all for a match in Northern Ireland, was this: it was played on a Sunday. This was a club on the rise, garnering attention from across the Irish sea and beyond: Brian Clough brought his Nottingham Forest team for a friendly, and talked glowingly of the experience on *Football Focus*.

Tony O'Doherty, a sometime commander of the Free Derry Police who played for the club in their first season in the League of Ireland, and went on to manage the team in the nineties recalled to Jamieson how Clough 'came on and said they'd just played in a midweek friendly with 10,000 people and not one policeman, and that's how people should be.' This served to intensify interest; suddenly more reporters from outside the island of Ireland were coming along in search of a story.

The reborn club was a huge hit. This was about football but also identity. It was about showing the IFA and other Irish League clubs how small-minded they were; they were little teams getting gates of a few hundred, while Derry City were pulling in 10,000 every other week.

In two seasons, the club won promotion to the League of Ireland Premier Division and reached the final of the FAI Challenge Cup in 1989, beating Cork City 2-1. It was an event Eamonn McCann, talking to David Hassan, saw as hugely significant for a city of its relative size. He explained how Derry:

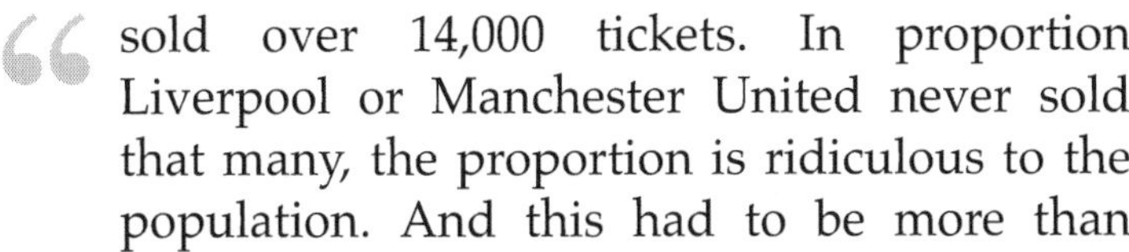

> sold over 14,000 tickets. In proportion Liverpool or Manchester United never sold that many, the proportion is ridiculous to the population. And this had to be more than

> about football, it just had to be more than about football. And I believe here was a team based in the Bogside, celebrating a sort of all-Ireland dimension of existence, broke away, free from the bastards "up there"

On the pitch, the team were going places. Away from it sectarianism still sizzled: after the cup final disgruntled loyalists carrying Ulster flags waited for returning Derry fans in coaches as they came across the border into Northern Ireland and proceeded to throw stones at the vehicles. Meanwhile an attempt to schedule a benefit match that same year with Linfield failed, because fans of both clubs saw a 'friendly' between these two avatars of the sectarian divide as a contradiction in terms.

When Derry faced Benfica in the European Cup first round early the following season as League of Ireland champions they became the first team to represent two national leagues in the same tournament. They had done so as Northern Irish champions in 1965 when they had played FC Lyn of Oslo and then a one-legged away tie against Anderlecht in the first round proper. Derry did the League and Cups treble in 1989 and the final of the latter was played outside the political border of the Irish Republic for the first time, at the Brandywell.

Pitch Battle VI - Linfield 2-1 Donegal Celtic, 19 February 1990

As the pages of the calendar flipped from the eighties to the nineties, the sectarian football situation in Belfast was undoubtedly worsening. The Irish Cup draw scheduled a February 1990 tie between Donegal Celtic and Linfield. Despite the former being named after one of the three counties of Ulster not within the Northern Irish border, the club is actually based on Suffolk Road in the Lenadoon area of west Belfast, the entrance to the clubhouse shielded by a masonry wall two foot deep. Since Donegal Celtic had been drawn first the game should have been a home one for them but the RUC had no intention of allowing that. Under their advice, the IFA decided it should be moved to Windsor Park, where officers felt they could better police the game.

The west Belfast outfit were not willing to settle for what they saw as administrative discrimination, and attempted to obtain a high court injunction to reverse the ruling, their legal team contending that the IFA had acted in 'an arbitrary and cavalier fashion.' This judicial action failed, however, when the RUC reiterated their position, that the only way they could ensure the safety of players and fans was if the game was played at Windsor Park. Predictably, there was serious crowd trouble among the 10,000 fans anyway; forty-eight policemen and fifteen civilians were injured, and the police fired plastic bullets in an attempt to quell the pitch-side unrest, serving only to inflame passions. Archival BBC footage even shows Celtic's goalscorer, Brendan Tully, being kicked on the pitch by an invading fan. A night of bus burning and rioting in nationalist areas of Belfast followed. The familiar sectarian stench that had wafted across Belfast football grounds for one hundred years had not been blown away just yet.

The nationalist press saw the IFA as deserving of the lion's share of the blame for how the situation had unfolded. As Sudden notes in *Sport, Sectarianism and Society,* commentators writing in the *Irish News* saw the governing body as having a smug attitude that made no effort to take on board the views of the Donegal Celtic hierarchy. Even the conservative unionist *News Letter* opined 'the problem is not readily solved by the expedient switching of the venue!' going as far as to criticise the actions of the IFA and the RUC's policing methods. SDLP councillor, Dr Joe Hendron, described the police tactics as 'absolutely crazy and indefensible.' In his thorough account of Linfield encompassing this period, *Every Other Saturday,* Daniel Brown recognises it was a sentiment echoed by his *Sinn Féin* counterpart Máirtín Ó Muilleoir, who criticised the RUC for 'the way they fired into such a large crowd', saying it was like 'shooting fish in a barrel.'

The following season, Donegal Celtic were drawn against Ards. Once again it was scheduled as a home fixture for the west Belfast side but the RUC decreed that they should travel twelve miles south east of Belfast to Newtonards and play the game at the home of their opponents. Instead, Donegal Celtic decided to withdraw from the competition and at the end of the season applied to join the League of Ireland, bidding to follow Derry City out of the Irish League and into greener pastures. This request was denied, the rationale being that while Derry is a mere four miles over the political border, having sides from the Republic travel into the heart of Belfast every other weekend would probably not be conducive to peaceful order. A letter writer to the *Irish News* was scathing, fuming:

> The spineless organisation [the IFA] has failed abjectly in its responsibility since the departure of Belfast Celtic in 1949, to reassure all fair-minded people that it is an organisation which is prepared squarely to confront the sectarian elements within its jurisdiction, which patently do not espouse equality of opportunity in the playing of football....soccer will continue to stagnate in the foetid waters of sectarianism.

As if the sectarian fire was not already burning red hot, on 5 November 1991 UFF paramilitaries threw a hand grenade over a wall at Windsor Park into the area where Cliftonville fans were as 'retaliation' for an IRA bombing three days earlier at the military wing of Musgrave Park Hospital, where two soldiers were killed and eighteen civilians injured.

Less than a year later, Linfield manager Eric Bowyer was quoted in a fanzine saying that he could not envision signing a Catholic, claiming that not only would it make life difficult for Linfield but for the player too. On its own this should not have been a controversial observation, but his making it explicit proved to ignite debate around the issue, which was his intention. Bowyer would later clarify to Daniel Brown, 'part of me wanted this to open up because I wanted to sign Catholic players… I didn't see any sense in cutting half of the population off.'

Club secretary, Derek Brooks, reiterated his employer's policy was not to 'exclude from its staff anyone by reason of colour, race or religion' but many refused to take this at face value. Father McManus of the Irish National Caucus (INC) in the United States, demanded that the IFA sever ties as tenants of Windsor Park and threatened to disrupt Northern Ireland's preparations should they qualify for the 1994 World Cup, to be held in the USA. As Brown records, he also said that, 'Linfield must be expelled from all soccer games…[the club's] publicly stated position is the equivalent of an American coach saying he could not hire a black or a Jew.'

According to Brown, McManus' INC lobbied IFA sponsors Coca Cola, urging 'Irish Americans, as well as lovers of peace and justice' to boycott their products, though their contribution to the IFA for advertising hoardings at Windsor Park was never in doubt. Another company, Thorn Security, ended their own sponsorship deal with Linfield because of downturn in the economy and *not,* Brown asserts — as was widely reported at the time - because of the INC's activities. Nevertheless, Linfield were an institution on the defensive, holding a press conference declaring themselves a non-sectarian organisation and stating:

> People of all classes and creeds are welcomed at Windsor Park, both for Linfield games and for internationals, and the Management committee strongly refute the scurrilous and unfounded allegations made by Father McManus and his associates in their campaign to have commercial sponsorship withdrawn from soccer in Northern Ireland.

The club produced a list of seventy Catholics who had played for Linfield through its history, although only a handful had done so after the late 1940s. What they would not do, as Brown's *Every Other Saturday* makes clear, was apologise for their unionist links, which were part of a 'quite legitimate ethos...which [was] just as strong today as it was in the early formative years.'

Among Catholic players who had taken to the field for Linfield in the modern era, all were from outside Ireland. In conversation with Daniel Brown, an apparently bemused Coyle had wondered if the club had signed another player behind his back, and when informed of their subject said he, 'didn't ask the lad, "By the way what religion are you?"' when asking him whether he wanted to sign. Coly himself was subjected to both racist and sectarian abuse by Glentoran fans, who threw banana skins and nectarine peel at him throughout an entire match with Linfield. Coyle was reported in the press at the time as saying that while Linfield had played Cliftonville 'several times and they are always tough games. But the Cliftonville fans didn't bring this sort of thing into it.'

Linfield's limitation on signing Irish Catholics, self-imposed or otherwise, had the bizarre effect of making the league fairer by denying them access to obvious talent. Yet not long after Bowyer's remarks, Linfield attempted to sign Jim McFadden - a Catholic who lived in New Lodge - from Cliftonville, but he declined, despite rumours Linfield would quadruple his current wage, fearing not only for his own safety but that of his family. As Brown points out in *EOS...*, the player told the local press 'the climate was simply not right... It would be difficult to envisage any Catholic player from Northern Ireland signing for Linfield, although I could see a Scottish or English Catholic playing for them.'

Change would arrive sooner than he had expected: Chris Cullen signed as Linfield's first local Catholic since the war, followed by Dessie Gorman, the first Catholic arrival from the Republic at Windsor in the half century since Limerick man Davy Walsh. When Martin Bayly was added to the roster later in the season, Linfield could now count three Catholics among their squad.

PITCH BATTLE VII - Northern Ireland 1-1 Republic of Ireland, 17 November 1993

Just as domestic football in Belfast and Derry was the site of a febrile atmosphere, so too was the international game. Windsor Park had been reduced to a 10,000 capacity for non-domestic competition, owing to its state of disrepair, meaning Northern Ireland's fixture against the Republic in a World Cup 1994 qualifier would be contested in front of a reduced crowd. The Hume-Adams initiative, with the aim of moving towards a peaceful settlement to the Troubles, had commenced just weeks before but the build up to the game was most certainly not one of love and understanding.

On 23 October 1993, posing as fish salesmen, IRA volunteers Sean Kelly and Thomas Begley bombed Frizzell's fishmongers on the Shankill Road. Their target was a UFF volunteer by the name of Johnny 'Mad Dog' Adair, a paramilitary and Neo-Nazi. The IRA men believed he was in a meeting room above the takeaway, though it transpired that this was not the case. It was too late. The bomb went off and nine people were killed, including two children. This was the biggest loss of life in Northern Ireland for six years, and included that of Begley. Perhaps unsurprisingly, a week later UFF members entered a bar in Greysteel, County Londonderry. It was the day before hallowe'en and one gunman is reported to have shouted 'Trick or Treat!' before opening fire. Eight people were killed in the attack including seven Catholics and one Protestant. Margaret Thatcher declared her belief that there would be no peace in her lifetime.

Before the qualifying campaign had even started, Republic manager Jack Charlton had been dismissive of Northern Ireland's chances. Though the possibility of progression for his own team had vanished, this was the chance for Billy Bingham to exact his revenge and thwart his southern neighbour's chances of reaching the World Cup final, characterising Charlton's men — only four of whom were born in Ireland - as mercenaries. The home leg at Landsdowne Park had seen Bingham's boys go down 3-0 to chants of 'One team in Ireland' from the home fans.

There had been talk of relocating the game to London or Rome, and security concerns eventually dictated that Charlton's side took to the skies to travel the one hundred miles from Dublin to Belfast, their coach from the airport populated with Special Branch officers wearing FAI tracksuits. Small children gathered around the vehicle making gun signs with their hands and yelling 'Fenian bastards!' Though the FAI had purchased 400 tickets for their fans at Windsor Park, they decided that, with the ground surrounded by a ring of steel, they would not sell any of them. Around fifty Republic supporters chose to go anyway, interspersed among the 'home' fans.

The grossly sectarian 'Billy Boys' chant was heard from the stands, as well as songs about exalting the perpetrators of the Greysteel massacre. The Irish tricolour was not flown, nor *Amhrán na bhFiann* sung. Alan McLoughlin started on the bench for the Republic and recalled in Jamieson's *Whose Side…*, 'the safest place to be was on the pitch not sitting by the sidelines, so when Jack said "Get your gear, you're going on," I was a bit relieved to get off the bench.'

The *Irish Independent*'s report the next day was evocative, describing how:

> the old wooden stand creaked and rumbled to a raucous, unholy anger. Forefingers jabbed fiercely into the tense night air and harsh, Shankill voices dredged up the bile that poisons this sad city….And there was a faintly surreal glare, as the kindly grandfather shape of Billy Bingham paraded the tramline with wrist sweeping provocation to the assembled.

During debate in *Seanad Éireann*, the atmosphere that night was described as an example of 'the depth of the bigotry and hatred in what may be only a small segment of the population…is precisely the atmosphere or environment which permits violence. Having seen and listened to that we can understand how and why people are murdered. The display was absolutely irrational.'

Alan Kernaghan turned out for the Republic that night. Born in England, he grew up in Bangor, watching all of Northern Ireland's qualifying games for the 1982 tournament from the stands, and even playing for Northern Ireland up to Under-15 level. Kernaghan had dreamed of turning out for what he considered his country although neither he nor his parents were born within its borders. At the time the IFA were sniffy about calling up such players, even if their grandparents had been born within its jurisdiction (something allowed since a rule change at FIFA's 1964 congress in Tokyo) and were fully compliant with FIFA regulations. The FAI, famously, had no such qualms. So it was that man who in his younger days had been a ball boy at Windsor Park was part of the Republic squad.

Kernaghan explained to Jamieson, 'I had no problems pulling on the Republic shirt. I was simply furthering my career. There was always a lingering tension on the periphery. Some Republic of Ireland fans and journalists didn't like it. I dealt with it as I deal with it now. It doesn't matter to me.' He continued, 'It was non-stop abuse. My every touch was booed and whistled. My dad and brother were there, but fortunately my mother did not go that night. I was f'd and b'd everywhere.' The man who had once only wanted to pull on a Northern Ireland shirt was called a 'Fenian bastard' and 'Lundy' by a crowd he had once been part of.

As Moore's *Irish Soccer Split* makes clear, the *Irish Times* columnist Fintan O'Toole heard it all too. 'To be a Republic supporter in that stand,' he wrote:

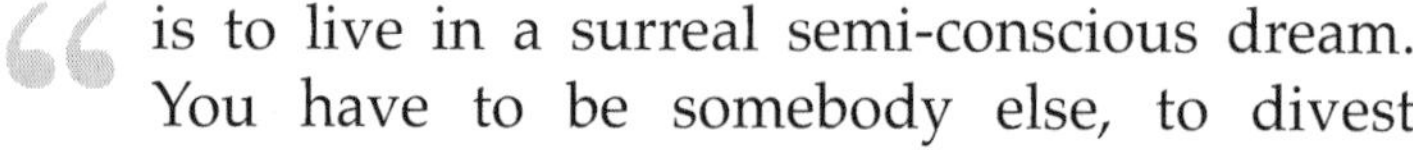

> is to live in a surreal semi-conscious dream. You have to be somebody else, to divest

> yourself of your voice and still your reaction. To put your conscious, waking self into a state of suspended animation, like a machine with the power on but all the controls turned right down, lest it leap out and betray you. With the Billy Boys left and right, with the screams of "Fenian scum" and the palpable waves of hatred breaking over your back, you have to act a role. You have to think and feel like them, to be outwardly a Billy Boy yourself.

It was that other Alan - McLoughlin - who levelled the score with ten minutes to go and propelled Jack Charlton's side to the World Cup in Billy Bingham's last game in charge of the Northern side after thirteen years at the helm. It was the end of an era. Billy from Bloomfield had played for Northern Ireland over a period of twelve years then, across two spells, managed them for a further seventeen.

Sammy McIlroy, who spent seven years as one of Bingham's charges and would eventually take on the mantle of manager himself, described to Jamieson how upon taking on the job a second time his boss 'really had nowt to lose...because we weren't winning. So he was digging people up from the third division. Big John McClelland from Mansfield, John O'Neill, a young lad from Leicester, Mal Donaghy, all these people coming in. Chris Nicholl we got through parentage and this team started to bond.'

Gerry Armstrong, talking to the same author, concurred with his teammate's observations:

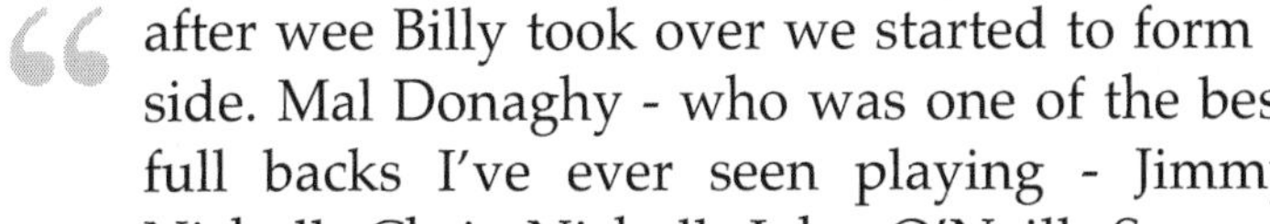

> after wee Billy took over we started to form a side. Mal Donaghy - who was one of the best full backs I've ever seen playing - Jimmy Nicholl, Chris Nicholl, John O'Neill, Sammy

> Nelson. The defenders we had were good defenders. It was all based around Pat Jennings who was the kingpin. He gave us that confidence and belief and whenever we made a mistake he made some unbelievable saves. We started being really tough to beat. We weren't scoring many goals — which has always been a problem for us - but we kept it tight at the back and we weren't going to concede many.

The relative success of Bingham's team, as is true of any Northern Irish national side throughout footballing history, relies on individuals coalescing to be more than the sum of their atomised parts. This was something he was able to impress upon them, as McIlroy recognised in talking to Jamieson,

> Tommy Cassidy would start a game because maybe he wanted an extra passer in there. Or maybe David McCreery would start a game where the opposition had a player who needed to be nullified, and little McCreery was one of the best at that, 110 per cent fit, brave as a lion. He would do that job. Bingie had one or two people in that squad who could do certain jobs. That helped us get the results needed.

Bingham, fond of referring to himself as Anglo-Irish, had run a tight ship on the pitch, and despite the civil strife that had engulfed Northern Ireland throughout his reign had maintained a cohesive dressing room. White-side has memories of nights before home games at Windsor Park, telling Jamieson the team would 'go to the

Culloden Hotel and sit up and not go to bed and sing. Well, I'd not be singing, but Martin and Gerry would be singing. There'd be Proddy songs, Catholic songs, Irish songs. It was just one big happy family.' Conversely, the winger also remembers that when the team returned from important international matches, and were invited to Stormont to meet local dignitaries, all the Catholic players would gravitate towards John Hume and all the Protestants to Ian Paisley, which is hardly surprising in the circumstances.

When the team beat West Germany 1-0 during qualifiers for the Euro '84 tournament, it was the first time Germans had lost at home since the war. Whiteside scored the goal that day and it marked Gerry Armstrong's fiftieth cap and revenge for the 5-0 defeat inflicted on the Irish on his debut. After the game, Bingham bought everyone a drink, telling them that there were six Catholics and five Protestants in the team that night. Whiteside was realistic enough, however, to realise that when Mal Donaghy invited him to come for a drink at a Celtic social club in west Belfast, it would probably have been a bridge too far in the fraught atmosphere of 1980s Ulster.

Though on pitch relations appear to have been largely cordial, sectarianism from the stands of Windsor Park really began to take hold during international ties, in a way that simply had not been the case during the middle part of the twentieth century. Unionists in the crowd would happily cheer on Pat Jennings in one breath, and in the next break into 'The Billy Boys' with its lyrics about being up to one's knees in Fenian blood. In his autobiography Jennings remembers his earliest appearances for the team he had supported since he was a boy, replacing Harry Gregg:

 It was a sufficient ordeal for a teenager to be

> playing for his country, so it was a nasty shock to find that my home crowd wasn't exactly rooting for me. The worst stick came from the staunch followers of Linfield, who thought that their club goalkeeper Willie McFaul - who later played for Newcastle United - should have been picked. Being a Catholic was no popularity boost.

Being a Catholic was one thing but being a Catholic who played for Celtic was the unforgivable sin. Days before his twenty-second birthday, Anton Rogan would make his home debut for Northern Ireland in the Spring of 1988, greeted by the sound of jeers from his 'own' fans. Sadly, the west Belfast born full back had expected it, 'I got called into the international squad and I was on the bench against Poland at Windsor Park. Billy Bingham said I was coming on, and when I stood on the halfway line a lot of people started booing me. I wasn't really surprised, because I played for Celtic.' More dispiritingly still, it would not be the last time he was subjected to this sectarian stupidity.

In the weeks before Rogan's home bow three IRA men were killed by the Special Air Service in Gibraltar. Then days later UDA paramilitary Michael Stone (once pictured with Rangers stars Tore Andre Flo and Ronald de Boer at Ibrox, albeit unwittingly on their part) attacked mourners at the Republican funerals for those same men at Milltown Cemetery, killing another three people. When those killed by Stone were being buried a few days later, two off-duty soldiers were murdered in west Belfast after inadvertently driving into the funeral cortege. 'I was aware of things when I went onto the pitch and I knew what I was going into before I went onto the pitch,' Rogan recalled, continuing, 'It wasn't rocket science to know it was going to happen. I was the first Celtic player to play for Northern Ireland for a long time. Belfast was a hard place to be, there were a lot of things going on that were very unsavoury....Once it happened, I just had to get on with it and 90 per cent of the fans were fine.'

Though in a previous era, Bertie Peacock and Charlie Tully - Celtic players both — did not receive abuse, these were very much not normal times: goalkeeper Allen McKnight, a Protestant who came through Distillery's ranks before heading to Celtic alongside Rogan, faced similar treatment during his ten appearances for his country. Though the crowd at Windsor Park was not exclusively Protestant during this time, the trajectory was clear and the stadium had become unwelcome territory for Catholics, with 'Taigs Keep Out' graffiti daubed on walls near its entrance.

Having secured qualification with their victory over the Northern side on that dark night in Belfast eight months earlier, Jack Charlton's Republic of Ireland were drawn in the infamous 'group of death' alongside Mexico, Italy and Norway. Their first task was to get something out of their matchup with Italy, which they duly did through Ray Houghton's left-footed strike in the eleventh minute. Supporters had gathered in The Heights Bar in Loughinisland, County Down to witness the occasion, a highlight of Irish footballing history. Yet six of those present would lose their lives that night, civilians gunned down for the crime of watching a football match. Members of the UVF had burst into the bar with assault rifles, firing indiscriminately on the patrons inside because the pub was known to be frequented by Catholics.

Taking responsibility for the massacre, which saw the wounding of five more, the UVF claimed it was retaliation for an Irish National Liberation Army (INLA) attack on loyalists in the days before. It was a tragic punctuation mark to a turbulent period in Irish history yet a little more than two months later the IRA would declare a 'complete cessation of military operations' after twenty-five years of armed struggle.

Was a brighter future for Ireland and Irish football to come?

9

GOOD FRIDAY'S ALRIGHT FOR FOOTBALL

Early indicators did not portend well. In October 1996 a match between Portadown and Cliftonville was abandoned, after supporters of the travelling team and the buses they had arrived in were attacked by a mob throwing stones, and brandishing placards emblazoned with the words 'No Republican Scum in Mid Ulster'. The Cliftonville fans were prevented from even entering Portadown's Shamrock Park by the Loyalist Volunteer Force, and when the team's players realised what had happened they refused to reappear for the second half. David Hassan wrote that one Cliftonville supporter said that, much as he loved his team, he would never watch them again fearing it was 'only a matter of time before somebody is killed and no football match is worth that.'

Unionist politicians and loyalist paramilitaries were exploiting the travelling Cliftonville fans as part of a wider battle, which involved the rerouting of Orange marches to avoid nationalist areas including, infamously, one destined for Drumcree Church in Portadown.

Earlier in the season, Cliftonville fans were heading for

a cup match with their north Belfast rivals, Crusaders, to be played at the Oval in east Belfast due to it being a semi-final. The Solitude faithful had made the journey scores of times before, but this time it was different. Controversy during the marching season relating to Orange parades which traversed nationalist areas had reached fever pitch, and it was fatuously suggested by Unionist representatives that football fans simply walking across the city to a football match were in some way comparable: Jim Rodgers of the Ulster Unionist Party cynically claimed that rather than football fans, they were *Sinn Féin* activists intent on causing trouble, and Glentoran chairman David Chick went as far as to say that perhaps Cliftonville should withdraw from the Irish League. Their fans were prevented from reaching the ground by loyalist vigilantes and Cliftonville fell to a 4-0 defeat.

And yet. Within the fandoms of the respective Belfast clubs, things were changing: Henry McDonald's *Colours* highlights that a Cliftonville fanzine featured a column by the correspondent ODG; which is to say Ordinary Decent Glenman. Following the events at Portadown, academic and Linfield fan Peter Shirlow recalls 'genuine anger in the stands at Windsor' at how their fellow football fans had been treated.

THE SETTLEMENT TRAIN

On 10 April 1998, the culmination of a series of paramilitary ceasefires and intense negotiations between Northern Irish politicians and the British and Irish governments resulted in the Belfast Agreement, better known today as the Good Friday Agreement. This set up a new system of government in Northern Ireland, while ensuring it remained part of the United Kingdom. New cross-border structures were created to foster cooperation with the Republic, and the third strand of the accord would also subtly alter the relationship between Dublin and London over how the future of Northern Ireland would be overseen.

The Troubles had raged for the best part of thirty years, and Northern Ireland had been a tinderbox on the island of Ireland since its inception some seventy-seven years previously. The events of Easter 1998 would not end division in Ireland but open conflict would — hopefully - be a thing of the past.

Northern Irish football's own Good Saturday moment came about later that year. Linfield were permitted to play at Solitude again after a twenty-nine year ban by the security forces, on the basis that Windsor Park was easier to police. The 21 November match was to kick-off at 11am and the crowd capacity was capped at 1,500 of which, Daniel Brown reminds us, only 500 could be Linfield fans. In the event, only 325 took up the opportunity and every single junction on the route to the ground was sealed off. Upon their arrival they were welcomed by Cliftonville fans congregated at the Waterworks end of the ground, with Linfield fans taking their place at the opposite side. Their hosts held aloft a banner proclaiming 'Céad Míle Fáilte LINFIELD' and another one conveying the same sentiment in English: 'A Hundred Thousand Welcomes LINFIELD'.

Though Linfield's historic return to Solitude was a giant step forward, the previous Saturday Donegal Celtic had been due to contest a cup semi-final, in which they were drawn against a representative team from the RUC. They had been scheduled to play them in a similar fixture in 1996 but had withdrawn. This time, however, the players had voted by a majority of 23-1 in favour of playing despite the fact that one player's father had been shot dead by an RUC officer just six years before. Even *he* wanted to play.

The decision was condemned by *Sinn Féin* politicians, including Gerry Adams, who conceded that while it was a matter for the club, 'no Nationalist, indeed no democrat, should have anything to do with the RUC.' The club called an Emergency General Meeting of all members, where once again a majority were in favour going ahead with the fixture. Rumours emerged, however, that some players were 'visited' by republicans who made their feelings clear, allegedly telling players that their safety could not be guaranteed if they were to frequent local bars.

Celtic had little choice but to withdraw. Two years later they would issue a civil bill against the Irish Football League, who had refused to admit them to the bottom rung of the footballing ladder, despite their meeting all the necessary criteria and being regarded as a very good amateur side. They did so with the support of the Equality Commission, a body which owed its existence to the Good Friday Agreement. Before the bill had been lodged with the court, admission to the Irish League had been, as the Equality Commission put it:

> “at the behest of member clubs, voting on applicants and those seeking re-election, rather than allowing in teams based on the merits of their playing achievements. The result has largely been maintenance of the status quo and feelings of frustration and anger amongst those clubs that see themselves as unfairly excluded.

Finally, on 30 May 2002, Donegal Celtic and Lurgan Celtic Bhouys were admitted to the second division for start of 2002/03 season. It was another watershed moment in Northern Irish football.

SAME OLD, SAME OLD

One rivalry had not changed throughout the momentous changes across the province: that of unionist Linfield and unionist Glentoran. Post Good Friday their enmity maintained its same intensity, McDonald reminding us that Glentoran fans welcomed their visitors with barbs such as 'In Your Shankill Slums…' and 'I go down the pub, I drink ten pints, I am getting plastered, I drink ten more and then go home, beat up the wife, I'm a dirty Linfield bastard.' Before Linfield had begun to sign Catholic players again, Alan Bairner's *Soccer, Masculinity, and Violence in Northern Ireland* points out, the club's fans would taunt their east Belfast neighbours with chants of 'No Fenians on our team...No not one', to which the Glenmen would retort, 'Gerry Adams is your MP,' referencing the fact that many of the Windsor Park club's fans resided in his Belfast West constituency.

Such is the passion of their intra-unionist antagonism that there are even Glentoran fans who refuse to attend Windsor Park for international games, on the basis that it would mean them going to the stadium of their hated foes. Though the employment landscape has changed in Northern Ireland, as it has across most western nations, historically Glentoran fans tended to be the shipyard workers and plane makers of east Belfast. Linfield fans tended to be engineering and linen workers. A depressingly modern illustration of the contestation between the two institutions is documented in the pages of *Colours* involving the UVF-UDA feud of the new millennium in which a man was stabbed in a loyalist social club off the Newtownards Road. The UVF hierarchy were worried that one of theirs had gone rogue and taken matters into his own hands, but it transpired that both men were in the UVF - indeed in the same battalion — but had fallen out over football: one was a Glenman, the other a Blue.

OUT OF THE ULSTER FRYING PAN

Domestic football had witnessed a profound shift, with clubs bridging the sectarian divide, but what of the national team? It had certainly become a more resolute monument to Britishness than it had been before the mid-eighties. Most evidence suggests that rather than reverse the drift towards sectarianism in the stands, the Good Friday agreement actually accelerated it. A section of the loyalist community felt — whatever the reality - as though it was losing everything it held dear, and the Northern Irish team was one rock it could cling to.

As the late Derry football journalist Frank Curran explained to the academic Gerry Hassan in 1999:

> Northern Ireland football games in fact have now almost become a spectacle, a platform for political declarations. Before most of the "Troubles", a majority of people in Derry would have supported the Northern Ireland soccer team. The "Troubles" have changed so many things, football included.

The turn of events at Windsor Park during international fixtures would even see some moderate unionists begin to find the situation at these matches distasteful, so the notion that nationalists of this era would embrace this twisted entity was out of the question. Supporters of the Republic who might once have seen Northern Ireland as their second team now looked upon them with active disdain.

For an avowedly sectarian minority of the Northern Irish support, the feeling was entirely mutual and would extend to the hounding out of Neil Lennon. In March 2001, the Celtic midfielder had been abused by a section of the Windsor Park crowd during a game versus Norway, chanting 'We've got a Provo on our team!'

As Lennon describes in his autobiography *Man and Bhoy,* 'There wasn't a massive crowd at the game, maybe 7,000 or so, and the minority might only have been 500 or 600, but to me the proportion booing me didn't matter — one per cent would have been too much for me.' He did not see it as a spur of the moment reaction by the home fans, believing that it was:

> completely premeditated by a part of a hard core of support which could not stomach seeing a Catholic Celtic player turning out for "their" country…I had played thirty-five times for my country before that night, and had a good relationship with most fans who knew I gave my all for Northern Ireland. So what had happened to make things so different? Answer: I now played for Celtic.

Sammy McIlroy hooked him at the break with the Irish 3-0 down. The game was McIlroy's eighth in charge, and he initially attempted to downplay the sectarian abuse that had come from the stands, saying it was simply because he was now a Celtic plater. McIlroy himself accepts that he may have misjudged the circumstances, reflecting to Jamieson later, 'Neil was a fantastic professional. He was a good footballer and we couldn't afford in them days to bring religion into anything because we had to play our best players. That night against Norway I was so mad about our preparation - our non-preparation - and what happened to Neil. But I could have handled it better.'

For Lennon, this was an understatement to say the least. He wrote that:

> after the match, Sammy tried to play things down and was so blasé in interviews that unfortunately he gave out the wrong message. It was as though he did not understand what lay at the heart of the whole situation. He indicated that everyone got booed at some time or another in their career — a remark that angered my family in particular, as they were the ones who had been forced to live with the appalling graffiti…

The Lurgan man was whisked away in an unmarked RUC car, unable to watch the second half as the vehicle sped through the streets of east Belfast. 'Here I was,' he wrote, 'minutes after playing for my country, getting a police escort through its largest city — it was beyond satire and in the realms of madness.' His manager and mentor, Martin O'Neill's advice was to go back and give it another go, despite Lennon expressing the understandable opinion that he did not want to play for Northern Ireland again, especially at Windsor Park. O'Neill told him that if he did quit, he might regret it.

The IFA's community relations officer Michael Boyd said he would be calling for action, issuing a statement announcing, 'The time has come for the IFA to send out a strong message that this sort of behaviour cannot be tolerated. Banning these people is what the majority of decent supporters want.' Unfortunately, as Lennon observes, 'He was promptly contradicted by a different IFA spokesman who was quoted as saying: "Obviously we are very disappointed by the reaction of a section of the crowd. But there is very little we can do about it...It might have been Rangers supporters coming over for the match, because we'd read press reports before this match that Rangers supporters were planning to attend to give Neil Lennon a hard time."'

In their next game, Northern Ireland were beaten by the Czech Republic, during which Lennon played and was cheered loudly by the crowd as he entered the field. He reflected 'it was incredibly heartening that ordinary football fans were prepared to stand up and be counted on my behalf.' The events of the previous tie against the Norwegians seemed to have galvanised the nascent *Football For All* campaign, and there was an effort to drown out the worst elements within the midst of the supporters.

On 20 August 2002, McIlroy was confident enough to name Lennon as his captain for the game against Cyprus the following night, a game sponsored by the Northern Irish Community Relations Council. His other options - Stephen Lomas, Michael Hughes and Gerry Taggart - were either injured or not available for selection. 'It was the obvious thing to do to make Neil Lennon captain. He was my most experienced player,' McIlroy told Jamieson. Lennon had captained the side as a substitute before, under Lawrie McMenemy, but he was a Leicester player then.

This time, though, something dreadful happened. When McIlroy had told him he would be captain earlier in the week, Lennon was 'delighted'. At a press conference, McIlroy proudly extolled his virtues, 'Neil is a leader; he has been captain for Celtic as well. It's a good honour for him. I hope he enjoys it and that his performance rubs off on the rest of the lads.' Lennon was keen to put what had occurred the year before behind him and the team, 'I certainly was honoured, and my family were also proud and delighted for me. At a press conference I emphasized that the unpleasant events of the Norway game were in the past and that I preferred to look forward.'

Northern Ireland was four years post Good Friday agreement and Lennon thought things had moved on. But hours before the game the BBC received a phone call, purporting to come from the LVF. It said that Lennon would be 'seriously hurt' if he was on the pitch at Windsor Park that evening. Lennon explained in his autobiography, 'He [McIlroy] told me straightforwardly that there were two police officers from the newly named Police Service of Northern Ireland outside waiting to talk to me.' McIlroy told him there had been a phone call, 'I knew immediately what the call was, and my heart sank into my boots.'

The manager himself remembered to Jamieson:

> we had done the team talk, the lads were having their pre-match meal and we get a phone call at the hotel. If he plays he gets shot. I mean, this was unbelievable. So I have to go to Neil, I have to speak to Neil and say, "Listen, this is what happened. Whatever decision you make I'm 100 per cent behind you." Obviously the kid can't play because he's got a family.

The two police officers who formally told Lennon - one man, one woman — remain anonymous, as is protocol in Northern Ireland. He asked them 'how genuine the threat was and they said that nine out of ten of these calls prior to sporting events were hoaxes.' They were very clear that they could not, and would not, tell him what to do. 'My first reaction, nevertheless, was that I should play on,' he wrote. Lennon remembered that 'this time Sammy McIlroy reacted well and sympathetically. He said that if the call had been about his son, he would want him to go home.'

The Celtic Park man immediately phoned the club's security adviser, whom he knew well, and was counselled that he should get back to Glasgow as quickly as possible. 'My father said that of course I could not play and he would come and get me...A few minutes later I was in his car and on my way home to Lurgan.'

A couple of Lennon's teammates wanted the IFA to pull out of the match, as Keith Gillespie - whose mother had grown up on the same street as Martin O'Neill in Kilrea - remembered in *How NOT To Be A Football Millionaire*, 'Sammy called a meeting to explain the situation and, while we chose to go ahead with the game, I really don't think anyone was in the mood. It finished 0-0. Fitting, because there were no winners that day.'

Lennon was no longer in the stadium. He had a young daughter and concluded that he could not 'in all conscience put them [his family] through that strain again.' Neil Lennon's Northern Ireland career was over.

THE CELTIC DIMENSION

The team had been captained by a Catholic before, although Martin O'Neill's assertion that he had 'only got booed because [he] was crap', when *he* wore the armband, is a slightly generous reading of the situation from a gracious man. What is certainly true, is that the worst elements of the Windsor Park crowd had become too loud to ignore. The compounding factor in their bigotry seemed once again to be Lennon's being on the payroll at Celtic Park.

Gerry Armstrong had played two decades earlier against the backdrop of a far more turbulent Ireland yet he was never abused by his own fans. 'I never got that. Never. Neither did Pat or Martin as far as I know, maybe because we were a good team and successful and doing things. I don't know. I don't know.' The Fintona native, who had only started playing football while serving a disciplinary ban from Gaelic competition, remembers turning out for Northern Ireland against Uruguay, 'We beat them 1-0 but Anton Rogan was getting booed every time he got the ball. He was always 150 per cent effort, always, and he cut a couple of them in two and he ended up scoring the winning goal. And I would say 95 per cent of the fans went crazy when he scored the goal and cheered him off the park. But you were always going to have a small element who were going to go "Ah, but he's still a Catholic player."'

Condemnation of this renewed surge of sectarianism from the stands came from Michael McGimpsey, an Ulster Unionist MLA in South Belfast. He declared the notion that:

> anyone should issue threats to one of Northern Ireland's players, simply because he has signed for a particular team in the Scottish Premier League is appalling. Let no one be in any doubt that this type of thuggery has absolutely no place in sport, and that to fail to condemn it is to fail to support our national team. We don't need, or do we want, this sort of behaviour, especially at a time when the entire football family is pulling together for the future well-being of our game.

Given positive developments off the field, however

fitful, many expected that this would not happen anymore. O'Neill reflected, 'I thought it would have gone past this stage; that they would like him no matter who he played for if he gave his all.'

Keith Gillespie, in his autobiography, admits that 'religion was part of the banter. The louder Protestant lads, like Alan McDonald, Phil Gray and Tommy Wright, would be taking on the vocal Catholics, fellas like Gerry Taggart, Jim Magilton, Steve Morrow and Michael Hughes.' When Northern Ireland were preparing for a home tie they would stay at the Chimney Corner hotel, and

> on our way to training we'd go through some fierce Unionist and Nationalist strongholds. Our bus would pass the Shankill Road...and the Catholics would pipe up about what a shithole it was. We'd then move along and pass the Divis Flats at the bottom of the Falls Road....and the Protestants would hit back with their own insults.

It was, though, he says 'all good natured. There were no cliques based on religion. Some of the boys came from areas that were heavily involved in the conflict. Phil Gray's family hailed from the Shankill, while Jim Magilton came from the Andersonstown area...' The Larne-born man says that though 'there were plenty of harmless insults for the sake of banter...the bottom line was that nobody cared what side of the community the person sat next to them was from.'

A KICK UP THE ERSE

This was a stark wake up call. When the *Football for All* campaign had been instigated at the turn of the millennium, with the aim of eradicating sectarianism at Windsor Park, it was hoped the IFA had finally got the proverbial kick up the backside it needed. That was optimistic; a panel had been convened in February 2000 to advise on the way forward for football in Northern Ireland, but its recommendations were not implemented until 2004 with suggestions from certain quarters that the deep roots in unionist structures of some of the IFA administrators meant that heels were dragged for longer than necessary. Counterintuitively, the fact that the British government was putting pressure on them do something did not sit well either.

When change did come, however, it proceeded at pace. Private security guards were employed to mingle with the crowd and identify the guilty parties, while supporters groups were largely successful in their attempts to drown out sectarian chants like 'The Billy Boys', with drum beats and songs such as the now ubiquitous 'We're not Brazil, We're Northern Ireland'. As football writer Keith Bailie wrote in the *Blizzard* a decade later, 'it was positively naff, but at least it was positive.'

From selling just 15,000 replica shirts during the qualifying campaign for World Cup 2006, that figure rose to 65,000 for the Euro 2008 qualifiers and supporters club branches rose from eleven to forty-five. Former IFA president Jim Boyce recognised 'there was a time...when some of the chants at Windsor Park disgusted me. I was not alone either. Dignitaries were becoming reticent about attending games, and people from both sides of the local community were writing to me saying they would not be back.'

Just as comity off the pitch was rising, results took a nosedive. In a strange way this seemed to galvanise the anti-sectarian effort, creating a bond between the unfortunate souls wedded to their hapless team. When Lawrie

Sanchez took over as manager in January 2004, Northern Ireland had not scored for the two years and five days since a Steve Lomas header had found the net. Put another way, it had been 1298 minutes, twenty hours spanning thirteen games; a record for a UEFA member. During this time allied UK-US forces had invaded Iraq and its embattled dictator had gone into hiding, leading to wags developing a meme, involving Saddam Hussein emerging from his bunker to ask his potential captors, 'Have Northern Ireland managed to score a goal yet?'

Having secured the job after the IFA failed to agree terms with Jimmy Nicholl, the Windsor Park faithful were cool on Sanchez, who had qualified to play for the national side through parentage, making three appearances under Billy Bingham during his on-field career. He was unable to bring a win in his first game in charge, but he brought that other most elusive thing: a goal. It was something to build on.

Born in Lambeth to an Ecuadorian father and a Northern Irish mother, his new charges were ranked 124th in the world when Sanchez was appointed. His was an era of reinvention and — eventually - significant improvement, perhaps best remembered for three fixtures against England, Spain and Sweden. Though Sanchez had stabilised the situation, progress — as is often the way - was not entirely linear; a disastrous tour of the Caribbean in the Summer of 2004 was best summed up by a 1-1 draw with Barbados, during an end of season jaunt which one player saw as nothing more than 'a pain in the arse.'

The first in that trio of historic victories was the tie against the English at Windsor Park (now reduced to a capacity of 14,000) in 2005; Sven Goran Eriksson's side paying their first visit to the province in eighteen years. In their preceding games, the Northern Irish had drawn 0-0 with Austria and lost 4-0 to England at Old Trafford. Yet it was a friendly against the Maltese, a month before welcoming the English to Belfast, where something clicked, as Gillespie wrote that, 'If there was a real turning point for Lawrie, it was a friendly with Malta a month later. It finished 1-1 and I was sent off by the English ref, Mike Riley, for a silly scrap with one of their lads. They were a poor side and Lawrie tore into us afterwards. He made it clear that the two games in Belfast were vital…'

Gillespie prepared for the home fixture against England as he always did, by smothering his shirt in 'Vicks' to aid his breathing. Wayne Rooney, Steven Gerrard, Rio Ferdinand and Frank Lampard were in the English eleven whereas, as Gillespie admitted 'we had a mixture of lads from up and down the divisions in England and Scotland.' *The Sun* had run a sweepstake ahead of the game, where the potential scores ran all the way up to 14-0 for England. It's fair to say that Northern Ireland were not fancied to get a result. 'Laurie's pre-match team-talks rarely lived long in the memory, but he got the tone right,' Gillespie conceded. 'As we were standing up to leave the dressing room, he played the David Bowie song, "Heroes" on the stereo.'

Whether it was The Thin White Duke's lyrical inspiration or Sanchez's tactical masterplan, something had clicked: 'The atmosphere was incredible,' Gillespie continued, 'just like the special nights in the '80s that I spent with Dad on the Kop. Our first objective was making it to half-time scoreless, and we managed to do that relatively comfortably.' Reflecting on the first half, the winger recalled that 'the English were frustrated. In fact, I probably could have got Wayne Rooney sent off.'

The second half was something else, though:

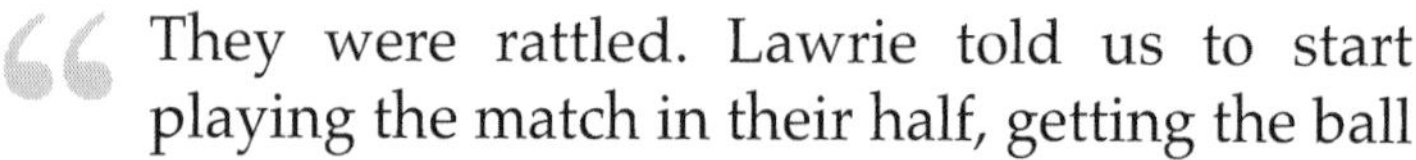

> They were rattled. Lawrie told us to start playing the match in their half, getting the ball

> forward as quickly as possible. All the training ground work was built towards this. In the 73rd minute, it paid off. We pegged them back, and their keeper, Paul Robinson, hoofed the ball towards the halfway line. Steve Davis judged the flight better than Lampard, and found the space to chip David Healy into space. He did the rest, right in front of the Kop.

For Sanchez, the victory was particularly sweet: 'It was nearly 80 years since England had been beaten in Belfast and to be in a competitive fixture too made it even better.' Paul Prentice, the team's massage therapist and a part time fireman, believed 'it was the turning point in Northern Ireland football at international and local level. It used to be years ago that everywhere you looked kids were wearing Manchester United, Liverpool, Rangers or Celtic jerseys, whereas now everywhere you look they're wearing Northern Ireland.'

During the nineties, to wear a Northern Ireland shirt on the street was tantamount to admitting you were a bigot. So loaded with negative connotations had supporting Northern Ireland become, that when Windsor Park played host to reigning World Cup holders in 1999 the stadium was not sold out. Many of those who did show up racially abused Marcel Desailly, Lilian Thuram and Patrick Viera and sang 'The Billy Boys', a paean to a Catholic-murdering Protestant gang of 1920s Scotland. Now a sea of green had replaced the red, white and blue. Bigotry had not been eliminated, but progress had been made.

Against a team of superstars, the hard-working pros had achieved the near-impossible: it was Northern Ireland's first home victory versus England since 1927, and David Healy's goal ensured he would be talked about for decades, possibly centuries to come. The striker celebrated in his own way: alone in his hotel room with a chicken sandwich and a blackcurrant and lemonade. It was the least George Best moment in Northern Irish footballing history. The man from Killyleagh had even earned a new chant to the tune of 'Away in A Manger', 'The Stars in The Bright Sky Look Down on Hea-lay.'

HOT AND COLD

Three hundred and sixty-four days later Spain were the visitors to Windsor Park. The qualification campaign had not got off to a great start; Sanchez had their tie with Iceland marked down in his notebook as a home win but, as Gillespie ruefully noted, 'we were three down at half-time and that was that. They beat us fair and square, and it hurt.'

Yet four days later there was reason for optimism. Spain had drawn first blood through a Xavi strike, only for David Healy to equalise. When David Villa made it 2-1 to the Spaniards, Healy once again drew level. Then, in the eightieth minute the man from Killyleagh completed a hat-trick in front of the Kop, lobbing Iker Casillas from 25 yards. Gillespie remembers the last 10 minute as a backs to the wall affair, but the team held on and Jonny Evans - only called into the senior side for his debut after the disappointing collapse against Iceland days earlier — had a debut to savour.

'Looking back now,' wrote Gillespie in *How NOT…*, 'it was an even better result than we realised. They were building a team that would go on to dominate international football for six years, winning two European Championships and a World Cup.' The match was the catalyst for a change in approach within the Spanish camp, but also ignited a hopeful flame within the Northern Irish ranks, 'It was a magic time to be a Northern Ireland player. From a situation a few years previous where only 3,000-4,000 people were attending games, we could have sold the ground three or four times over.'

The same was true of the playing staff, too 'everyone was starting to believe. Lawrie might have got the specific results wrong, but a top-two finish in the group — and automatic qualification for Euro 2008 - began to look very possible.' Next up was a 0-0 with Denmark 'with the backing of our biggest away support in over 20 years, and then we took full points from Latvia at home and Liechtenstein away, before another famous win at Windsor against Sweden put us top of the group.'

Healy's 13 goals during the campaign was a new record, surpassing Davor Suker's 12 during qualification for Euro 96. Reflecting years later, Northern Irish football writer Keith Bailie wrote of the kid from Killyleagh, 'George Best might be the greatest player to come from Northern Ireland, but David Healy was Northern Ireland's greatest ever player.'

THE BIG MAN UP TOP

'Northern Ireland is doing fantastically well — just like the DUP. They win all their big games and they have a superhero called Healy; we win all our big games and we have a superhero called Paisley!' And there was you thinking Tony Blair's professions of support for Newcastle United were cringeworthy. Ian Paisley Junior had uttered those words two days after Northern Ireland emerged 2-1 victors over Sweden in March 2007. His utterance came on the back of a historic press conference; which saw his father sit alongside Gerry Adams to announce a power sharing agreement between those polar opposites on the sectarian spectrum: the Democratic Unionist Party and *Sinn Féin*.

Whereas the Good Friday agreement had been birthed in the cradle of the by now (slightly) more moderate Ulster Unionist Party and its nationalist counterpart the SDLP, the intervening decade had seen sectarian attitudes harden. The prevailing expectation was that the politics of Northern Ireland would gradually come to more closely resemble Britain or Ireland, with a majority coalescing around the centre ground.

In reality, the hardliners won the day: in 2001 four in ten voters opted for either Sinn Fein or the DUP, yet by 2006 this figure was six in ten. The political settlement of the late nineties had, mercifully, largely removed active warfare from the streets, but it was replaced by a codified sectarianism that is arguably more deeply entrenched than it was before the Good Friday Agreement. In one study, seventy-two per cent of respondents would not use health centres in communities they perceive as being dominated by the other community, and sixty-two per cent of those receiving Job Seeker's Allowance would not sign on in their nearest Jobcentre because it is in a neighbourhood that would endanger their own safety. Where sectarianism used to be demarcated at the butt of a gun or the switch of an improvised bomb, now it had been institutionalised.

CRYSTAL BALL

Gillespie recalled that Sanchez had predicted Northern Ireland finishing second with his forecasts, including precise score-lines, 'I guess he wanted us to believe in that vision, but we had to come to realise that the oddness was just part of his personality.'

The team's upward trajectory had elevated Sanchez's profile in the game and his contract with Northern Ireland was hardly lucrative, so it was unsurprising when Fulham, facing the final five games of the 2006/07 Premier League season, decided to bring him in on a caretaker basis with the permission of the IFA. Their top flight status assured, the south-west London side opted to employ him permanently at a crucial point in Northern Ireland's European qualifying campaign. 'Football is a selfish game and for those reasons, the lads didn't want Lawrie to leave,' Gillespie wrote of the man whose methods had eventually convinced him, 'I was genuinely disappointed. It turned out the IFA had made a brilliant call appointing him, and the really sad thing is that his departure didn't work out well for either party.' Sanchez was sacked by Fulham six months later, Northern Ireland's dreams of qualification similarly doomed.

The departing manager had left them with a strong chance of progressing to the tournament in Austria and Switzerland; ranked in thirty-third place by FIFA, the end of Sanchez's tenure had seen them jump ninety-one places higher than where he had found them on his arrival.

In Nigel Worthingon's first match in the dugout against Liechtenstein, the optimism from Gillespie and others appeared to be well founded, winning 3-1 courtesy of two from Healy and a first for Kyle Lafferty. The side was in control of its own destiny as it went into matches with Latvia and Iceland. Yet it was also within their power to blow it. Which they did. 'Nigel baffled us in Riga,' wrote Gillespie, 'at half-time, it was 0-0 and we'd played reasonably poorly, but there was time to turn it around. Nigel burst into the dressing room, livid, and announced that if we didn't buck up our ideas, then we wouldn't be allowed to go for a drink that night. What kind of thing was that to say at half-time during an international?' In the second half, Chris Baird put it into his own net and Northern Ireland had ceded their position of strength, 'and yes, we ended up having a few drinks that night anyway, looseners before the journey to Iceland which had suddenly taken on an extra relevance.'

Lacking intensity against Iceland, the home team lead at the break. David Healy did his bit to equalise from the spot, and the team surged forward in search of the additional two points 'but in classic Northern Ireland style,' Gillespie wrote, 'disaster struck. With two minutes left, we gifted the Icelandics a comical winner. I should know. I bloody scored it.'

'We'd blown it,' he lamented. The figurative and literal green shoots? Northern Ireland had finished third, bested only by Spain and Sweden. An Irish League player, Peter Thompson, had even got on the scoresheet in a 4-1 win over Georgia; the first time this had happened in twenty-five years. Then, in 2008 the Windsor Park faithful won the Brussels International Supporters Award, just six years after the shameful treatment of Neil Lennon.

OLD FOES

In 2005 Linfield and Derry City finally played a friendly at the Brandywell. It was probably too soon: the 300 travelling Linfield fans were attacked with bricks and stones and the team bus was damaged. It was the first time they had faced each other on the Bogside since 1969. After the fundraiser for the financially stricken Derry City ended in a 1-1 draw, Linfield manager David Jeffrey, a member of the Orange Order, was quick to point out that his team should no longer be perceived as an anti-Catholic entity, 'It's not a case of us having one or two token Catholics.

Half our squad are Catholic. Half are Protestant. All are footballers.'

Jon Clifford, a senior steward at the Brandywell, reflected in Hassan's *A People Apart* how:

> It's a very closed community in Derry. It all goes back to the "Troubles" when they had to stand shoulder to shoulder at the bottom of the Rossville Street to take on the police and the Army and the 'B' Specials and whoever else was coming at them. At one stage you were defending your area for three days and you had to do your bit. That determination to oppose is still there on the terraces of the Brandywell.

Following the initial burst of enthusiasm which had greeted Derry City's return to senior football some two decades previously, the club had fallen on harder times. Crowds dwindled from their initial high point in the late eighties, and the club has effectively folded twice due to financial difficulties, most recently in 2009.

The club are viewed as outsiders even by some in the League of Ireland. 'To this day we are the only club in the entire world who play outside our political jurisdiction,' Eddie Mahon said to Teddy Jamieson. While Berwick Rangers are an English team who play in the Scottish leagues, and several Welsh teams are part of the English football pyramid, they are — for now - all ultimately governed from Westminster.

It had been mooted, during contentious periods, that Cliftonville might follow Derry City out of the Irish League but this was never a practical proposition. In any case, as Stephen McKillop, a board member at Solitude in the early aughts asked of Jamieson, 'What's the alternative? Do we pack up and say "we're going home." Playing in the League of Ireland isn't a viable option. And there's a thing — we're the oldest club in Ireland, we were founder members of the IFA, our ground is the oldest ground in the Irish League. We were playing before any of the rest of them, fucking sure we're not going to be the ones to leave.'

Would they have even been welcome 'down south'? On the Republic's conflicted relationship with the North, Mahon sounded weary when telling Hassan 'generally people in the south don't want to know about people in the north. That has spilled into football. I think they believe we are going to be throwing petrol bombs at the dressing rooms or something.'

It is only Cliftonville of the major Irish League teams which has a predominantly Catholic following. Ballymena, Coleraine, Crusaders, Glenavon, Glentoran and Portadown could be regarded as having a mainly Protestant support, and Linfield exclusively so. This can partially be explained by historic demography, in as much as most of the senior clubs of today were established more than a century ago, in predominantly Protestant towns, and today these towns retain a similar ethno-religious make up.

For ardent devotees of Portadown and Glenavon, there is a perverse enmity towards Linfield - the richest and most commercially viable of all Irish League clubs — who are seen as undeserving holders of the title of *the* preeminent Protestant club. As the great Malcolm Brodie explained in his *100 Years of Irish Football*:

> there is no other football club in Ireland quite like Linfield. They are loved and hated. Loved by thousands of fans — some of whom have had their ashes scattered at Windsor Park,

> while others were buried in their Linfield regalia. Hated down the years by the opposition with an implacable enmity, a fierce and relentless sporting rivalry has always existed between Linfield and all other teams.

Though they are a part-time club in a far below average European League, the Blues have a status that rises above their lowly berth, due to the lasting sectarian nature of football in this part of the world, even as the nineties saw the signing of a growing number of Catholic players.

STAND YOUR GROUND

There is an underground wall in Belfast City cemetery which very deliberately separates the bodies of deceased Protestants and Catholics. Territory, and the location of flagship buildings within Northern Ireland, are never far from the headlines. It was no different during the search for a site for a stadium suitable for the modern footballing era. Though Windsor Park - with its name derived from a residence of the British royal family and an image of a castle adorning the Linfield badge — was held dear by Bluemen and a certain type of loyalist, many Northern nationalists are understandably simply not willing to watch the football in an arena imbued with so much cultural baggage.

It was (and is), as one astute observer described it, the home of 'Ulster Unionism at play'. The problems facing the IFA were threefold: its physical location, its psychological weight and, more prosaically, the dilapidated state of the stands. The mooted solution to this was a proposal to construct a new 45,000 seater stadium on the land where the Maze prison had once stood, its last inmates vacated in 2000. The government still owned the real estate and in almost any other nation it would have been a *fait accompli*. Why would you not build on some vacant land that you already held the deeds for?

Context and contestation are once again our watchwords: the idea was that this would be an arena for not just football but rugby and Gaelic football too. The GAA was initially wary, viewing the IFA with a long and deeply held suspicion. The feeling was likely mutual. Beyond the governing bodies, unionist politicians had their hackles raised, fearing that it would become a totemic site for nationalists wishing to commemorate Bobby Sands and republican hunger strikers in general. In remarks found in Bairner's *The cultural politics of remembrance*, the DUP's Sammy Wilson claimed that it would amount to 'provision of a shrine to hunger strikers at the Maze - something which is already happening and which is being promoted by *Sinn Féin*.'

Fan groups had their own concerns too: the Amalgamation of Northern Ireland Supporters Clubs had been assured it would be a neutral space, but felt it would become a 'ghoulish tourist attraction' which would be unlikely to entice the average sports fan. These worries partly stemmed from the plan to retain one of the infamous H-Blocks - H6, where the hunger strikes were planned — as an International Conflict Transformation Centre.

A move that would have symbolised a new beginning was ultimately impossible, the past was remaining all too present. Warren Feeney, who went on to manage Linfield and whose own father and grandfather had turned out for the Blues, was against the switch, preferring instead that Windsor Park be redeveloped: 'Northern Ireland should continue to play at Windsor Park, with the South and

Railways stands being re-developed, rather than move to a new stadium.'

In May 2008, the decision against building the multi-purpose stadium had been made, with no agreement over the presence of the Conflict Transformation Centre. Though there had been other potential sites, including the North Foreshore of Belfast Lough, the Titanic Quarter in east Belfast and East Belfast FC's Danny Blanchflower Stadium, the Maze had been the only site deemed viable. The three sporting bodies had committed to using the new development in a proportionate manner, but it was only the IFA who *needed* to take immediate action and faced a dilemma over what to do next.

MORE THAN WORDS

The IFA had undoubtedly learned some lessons, but remained either unable or unwilling to make progress on other issues. Foremost among these is that of the anthem where, unlike Scotland or Wales, Northern Ireland has opted not to sing its own song. Instead, it retains the British one also favoured by English teams on sporting occasions, 'God Save The Queen'.

Watch any televised Northern Ireland match in which Northern Ireland are playing, and you will generally see six or seven of the team belt it out with a gusto not usually observed among their English counterparts. The other four in the lineup will be looking decidedly sheepish. Niall McGinn, a Catholic, told researchers Darragh McGee and Alan Bairner in their study of the issue, *Transcending the borders of Irish identity?*, that for him it is a case of:

> “Just put your head down and try to get through it...Just keep it down. I mean you

> have boys like Michael O'Connor and Sammy Clingan who are Catholic boys from Belfast and they just keep their heads really low so as to not make a scene but also to show that as Catholics they must be respected.

The malign influence of sections of the crowd had happily been all but neutralised and this is a credit to the IFA. Where they remain culpable in the eyes of many current or potential nationalist players born in the contested counties, is around British-unionist imagery and symbolism. Michael Boyd, Community Relations Officer at IFA, is aware of this perception, quoted in Hassan's *North or South?* as seeing it as a 'potential "banana skin" for the IFA. We need to treat the problem like a mirror, and ask the hard question as to why some players from Northern Ireland would rather play for the Republic of Ireland - then we need to remove as many of the barriers to inclusion as we can.'

Those were fine words but there has been no action. Eddie Mahon, former goalkeeper turned chronicler of Derry City FC, believes that Northern nationalist players sense that the Northern Ireland team had, in his words to Hassan, 'more of a British ethos or a Protestant ethos' and that:

> over the years Windsor Park hasn't been a very friendly place for Irish Catholics. Anybody who has ever played for Celtic like Allen McKnight and Neil Lennon have had to pack it in because they have got booed out of Windsor Park. So obviously with a background like that, you don't even have to be political, you just don't want any aggravation and a lot of these young guys

> have a far greater chance to get capped for Northern Ireland than the south but they don't want the aggravation of going up there [to Belfast] and being booed off the pitch.

One of those 'young guys' was Shane McEleney. He explained his decision to opt for the Republic, emphasising to Alan Bairner and McGee that 'without a doubt, my main influence for going down south was the way that I was treated by them [the IFA], as at that age you need to feel welcomed but they never did that...I definitely would not consider ever going back to Northern Ireland because of their treatment of me and that basically, Protestants will always be selected over Catholics if at all possible.' His brother Patrick was of similar mind, explaining to the same author 'before I played for Northern Ireland [at junior level], I knew that I would have to go through 'God Save The Queen' and all that. But before my first game, one of the coaches went around each of us, warning us that we better have our heads held high during the anthem. I remember him saying that we better be proud to represent our country.'

Another player who made the decision to opt for the Republic, having represented Northern Ireland up to Under-18 level, is Eugene Ferry. Asked by Bairner and McGee about his footballing allegiance he says, 'It would always have been the Republic as I supported them as a boy. But then when I got called up to the Northern Ireland team, I didn't care so much about that. I would say "I don't care that my pride is with the Republic, I'm only playing football for them."' He continued:

> we always supported the Republic of Ireland since I was a boy...Given that I'm from the Creggan area of the city, I would always see

> boys running around in Republic shirts. If anyone ever wore a Northern Ireland shirt, they would have known about it. They would have been given dogs abuse on the streets.

The goalkeeper's experiences in the Northern Irish junior setup share startling parallels with those of Shane and Patrick McEleney, as Ferry expounded, 'It's not right to say it but it was always the Protestants that were favoured over the Catholics. It was just a sense you got with the managers always talking to them much more than they did to us....Even with the Belfast lads, they would always take an interest in how they were doing at school but would never ask me, or the other Catholic lad.' That Protestant coaches would have little knowledge of Catholic schooling is hardly surprising; in 1992, long after most of them had finished their education, there were only two integrated secondary schools, and eight integrated primary schools in the entirety of Northern Ireland.

Though Ferry's sporting career has since fizzled out he remembers 'being watched by them [the loyalist supporters] who are just ready to shout abuse at you simply because of the fact that you are Catholic. Like I usually always bless myself before matches but up there I was sort of afraid that they would be watching me...you are always aware of it when you are playing.' After choosing to represent the Republic of Ireland Under-19 side, he told Bairner and McGee that he felt:

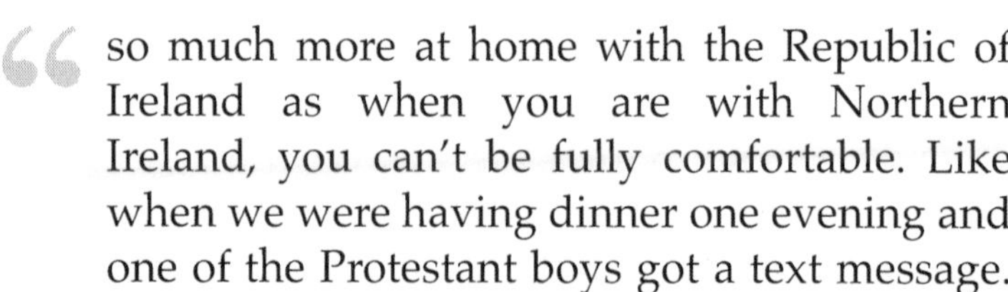

> so much more at home with the Republic of Ireland as when you are with Northern Ireland, you can't be fully comfortable. Like when we were having dinner one evening and one of the Protestant boys got a text message.

> It was the 'sash' that rang on his phone...that really does influence you to go down south as there is none of that political kind of thing.

Shane McEleney's reflections are in accordance with those of his fellow Derry native, 'deciding to represent the Republic,' he told McGee and Bairner in *Transcending the Borders...?*, 'has given me something new and to be honest, it gets me away from all the political problems you have up here [in Northern Ireland]. The thought of now being able to represent "my country" makes me feel great....I do see the Republic of Ireland as my country.' For Ferry, talking to the same authors, it was simple, 'I'm a Catholic you know what I mean and I feel a lot more pride for the Republic of Ireland...It's just political sort of stuff you know. You feel very proud standing for the *Amhrán na bhFiann* as it represents your country, even if that isn't the way some people see it.' Not that players make these decisions from a place of naïveté, as McEleney perceptively realised 'going to the Republic is what I really want to do but daunting in a way, as you don't know how you will be received there either...coaches might not take to you because you are from the north. Being from Derry, you are kind of stuck somewhere in the middle — a kind of halfway house.' Interestingly both McEleney brothers, having not featured in Republic of Ireland senior lineups, would now consider a call-up from Northern Ireland despite their previous statements.

For some of these Northern-born footballers, declaring for the Republic is not derived from 'nationalist essentialism', but is directly rooted in their experience of playing in and for Northern Ireland before they reached adulthood. Others have chosen a path of pragmatism, as was the case for Niall McGinn and Paddy McCourt. Though McGinn, born in Dungannon, did not hesitate to answer the call from the IFA offices in Windsor Avenue despite his nationalist sensibilities, he elucidated 'when it comes to football matters, you don't really think about whether it has to be the Republic of Ireland as "my country". That is kind of different to your football stuff. You don't really take that into consideration when it's about football.'

'Obviously coming from where I do, I would have loved to go and represent the Republic of Ireland,' the winger said to his academic interlocutors, his upbringing in a nationalist community meaning that as a youngster he 'would always be out on a Saturday playing a soccer game and then going on the Sunday to play Gaelic...To be honest I really loved doing that. Even now I would have liked to play Gaelic but it's just too difficult.'

For McCourt, conversing with McGee and Bairner, his call-up was a decisive moment: 'When I got called up to play for Northern Ireland, I decided then that they would be my team. I wasn't going to go here and then there as I wouldn't want to be seen as someone who did a u-turn. I mean you pick a country to play football for and mine just happened to be Northern Ireland.' Emphasising the pragmatic aspect of his opting for Northern Ireland, he explained, 'when you begin playing football, you set out to play at the highest level and if that chance comes with Northern Ireland, then you have to take it. I was thinking about the career of Paddy McCourt and what would present the best opportunities.' McGinn was motivated by the same desire, 'when Northern Ireland called me up, if I had of (sic) said no, I would rather hold out for the Republic, I might never have got that opportunity. So I'm glad that I took the chance. You can't really think about stuff like that. If the chance comes then you have to grab it and use it to enhance your career.'

When spending time back in the community he grew up in McGinn reflected, 'I get the odd joke when I'm home about me playing for them, but it was just a matter of making the boys know that I'm only there to play football and that's the only thing. They have even now started to watch the games; although I know they are only supporting me and wanting me to do well.' When Ferry spent a couple of years as part of IFA teams he 'felt as though I had to call "them" [Protestants] all "orange bastards" and all. You feel like you sort of have to put that on even though it's not really what I think. These boys don't understand what it's like to sit and chat with Protestant boys and wouldn't understand if I explained so I just don't...I just tell them what I think they want me to say.'

Both McGinn and McCourt had reason to reconsider the wisdom of opting for Northern Ireland when, in 2011, they received bullets in the mail with a Northern Ireland postmark. Their manager at Celtic, Neil Lennon, got one too.

GONE SOUTH

The trend of Northern-raised players opting for the Republic became particularly pronounced from 2002 onwards. Indeed, in correspondence uncovered by Hassan, McCullough and Moreland in *North or South?*, one writer in the letters pages of the *Belfast Telegraph* mused:

> It is only a matter of time before other players from all backgrounds in the North [Northern Ireland] follow Darron [Gibson]'s example and opt to play international football in a plush modern stadium in front of 50,000 plus multicultural, apolitical fan base, away from the decrepit environs of Windsor Park and the monoculturally supported IFA team.

Gibson had represented the IFA side at Under-16 and -17 levels but controversially switched his footballing allegiance. The Irish FA were up in arms, yet FIFA tacitly condoned the state of affairs, despite the fact it seemed to contradict their rules governing player eligibility. Not wanting to become involved in such a thorny issue, FIFA's rulings were open to interpretation. The world governing body's 2008 intervention supposedly clarifying that any player 'wishing to play for Republic of Ireland must have been born there, or have a parent or grandparent born there, or have lived there without interruption for two years', was practically meaningless in the context of the Good Friday Agreement, with the Irish birthright it bestows upon those from the island of Ireland and the codified provision for 'parity of esteem' between Irish and British cultures.

Raymond McCartney, a former hunger striker turned *Sinn Féin* MLA, vehemently defended players right to do so, demanding the Northern Irish football authorities:

> “stop putting obstacles in the way of nationalists opting to represent the Republic of Ireland...The IFA must send out a clear message that it will respect the rights of Irish nationalists as Irish citizens in their own country. The Good Friday Agreement recognises the right of Irish people living in the north to their identity and it is not up to the IFA to deny them that right.

It would not be long before another high profile 'defector' from Derry would reignite the debate once more.

10

KICKING WITH BOTH FEET?

'It's probably the wrong thing to say but it was just a stepping stone in my career,' James McClean explained of his time in the Northern Irish underage setup, 'You don't really feel at home. I think any Catholic would be lying if they said they did feel at home, seeing all those flags and hearing the songs and chants.'

The fresh-faced Derry native had been called up to Giovanni Trapattoni's Republic of Ireland squad for a friendly against the Czech Republic in the Spring of 2012. Though there is probably nothing that could have persuaded someone with the ardent Irish republicanism held by McClean that he should represent any other nation, the issue remains a live one. Months before McClean pulled on the green and white of the Republic, Michael O'Neill had become manager of the green and white team from the North, emphasising that his reign would be about 'making the national team fully inclusive.' He was as aware as anyone that the IFA administered team was losing some of its brightest hopes to its neighbours.

The twenty-two year old McClean was merely the most recent high-profile example of that phenomenon. Though his own political convictions are stronger than those of most footballers, he acknowledged that O'Neill's appointment could help smooth the way for others in the future: 'That needs to happen. It's important that it does. Michael is a great manager and was supportive of the decision I made. Catholics should feel more welcomed and part of it when called into the Northern Ireland squad.'

Though current Northern Ireland internationals from nationalist backgrounds understandably have their careers in mind, and refer only obliquely or indeed not at all to such matters, ex-professionals have no such concerns. Among them are former Northern Ireland legend Gerry Armstrong. He stressed that something needs to change, having spoken 'to a lot of nationalist families and kids who play and represent Northern Ireland at under-17, under-19, and under-21 level, and obviously it is an issue that needs to be discussed.'

It is a sentiment which ex-Norwich midfielder, Paul McVeigh, capped twenty times and a staunch advocate of a new anthem willingly corroborates, 'It could be a reason for someone not to play for Northern Ireland and really we want to encourage young players coming through to want to play for Northern Ireland.'

There is still much work to be done. Future prospects in the Arsenal and Aston Villa academies from Derry and north Belfast have, in 2017, declared their allegiance to the Dublin association amid accusations of poaching by what Michael O'Neill has dubbed the 'morally poor' FAI. His hackles were raised because the IFA invests time and money into these players, receiving no recompense when they declare for the Republic.

ONE NIGHT IN BELFAST AND DUBLIN

> *Incredible night for Irish football !!!Congrats Martin & Michael O'Neill & both teams.Beating the World Champions in Dublin so Amazing !!! - @M_McGuinness_SF*

Four years after McClean's controversial switch, former Northern Ireland internationals managed teams from either side of the border into Euro 2016, the first time that both Irish sides had qualified for the same tournament.

Capped thirty-one times, Michael O'Neill is an Ulster-born Catholic who had been a promising Gaelic football star as a schoolboy, representing his native County Antrim GAA Minors before his soccer career took flight with Chimney Corner. He was an unused substitute during the infamous Windsor Park fixture in 1993. 'Things have moved on,' he told an *Irish Times* journalist in the run-up to the team's European extravaganza, 'the atmosphere is fantastic now and it is going to be fantastic going forward, a really positive atmosphere for the players to play in. We have left a lot of the past behind us.'

O'Neill's squads regularly include Liam Boyce, a Catholic who blesses himself as he enters the pitch, as well as Josh Magennis, a Protestant from Bangor. The two often room together on international duty and, Boyce said to the *Irish Times*, 'get on like a house on fire.' Though the young man from Divis in north-west Belfast went to a Christian Brothers school, he maintains that many of his former classmates supported Northern Ireland back then and continue to do so today.

Conor McLaughlin, currently plying his trade for Fleetwood Town, went to the same school as Boyce and since his debut in 2011 has only positive things to say about the reception he has received from the Windsor faithful, 'From the first time I've played here the atmosphere has been unbelievable. I love coming back to Windsor,' he told the *Irish Times* Gerry Moriarty. The team's performances, particularly in the European qualifiers, probably have something to do with this, as McLaughlin acknowledges, 'I reckon we've helped that side of things.'

O'Neill's first game in charge was a humbling 3-0 home defeat to Norway, followed by a 6-0 loss to the Netherlands in his second outing. Jonny Evans had not played in a winning Northern Irish team for two years, Chris Brunt had not tasted victory wearing a green shirt in four. The qualifying campaign for the 2014 World Cup was bruising and the fans were angry, beginning to wonder whether the former Shamrock Rovers boss was the one to arrest the decline precipitated by the Worthington era. His last result in charge had been a 3-0 defeat in Italy, cementing Northern Ireland's fifth in a six team Euro 2012 qualifying group: played 10, won 2.

Key to his ability to do so would be man management of one individual in particular, County Fermanagh's Kyle Lafferty. Described by the chairman of Italian Serie B side Palermo as an 'unruly Irishman' and an 'out of control womaniser', the forward, along with West Brom's Chris Brunt were sent off during a close match with Portugal in September 2013. As Lafferty describes it in the *Blizzard*, 'he [O'Neill] sat me down the day after I was sent off...it's difficult when you've got a good relationship with someone and a guy you respect is saying things that hurt you. But when I went away and had a think about it, I knew he was right.'

During the qualifiers for the 2014 tournament, Lafferty could boast more red cards — one - than goals, yet the

Euro 2016 qualifiers saw him score seven times in nine appearances, picking up just two yellow cards. He credits his international boss for this reversal of fortunes: 'I had to grow up sometime. The team and the country needs the Kyle Lafferty with the head screwed on, not the clown. The transformation is down to Michael.'

Northern Ireland would lose just once on their qualification journey for the tournament in France and banana skins which would have sabotaged them in times past were dodged. 'Home to the Faroes, it's the kind of game we don't win,' full-back Gareth McAuley had joked. But they did, and comfortably. Victory over Greece courtesy of two Steven Davis goals and a draw with Finland in Helsinki saw Northern Ireland through to Euro 2016 as winners of Group F. A friendly win against Slovenia in the Spring of 2016 meant the team had gone ten matches unbeaten, a new record and one which O'Neill was pleased to claim from Billy Bingham, who had given him his debut as an eighteen year-old.

The campaign also witnessed another first when Windsor Park hosted an international match on 29 March 2015. Why? Because it was a Sunday. Leaflets were distributed by Presbyterian ministers on Olympia Drive, warning of Satanic incursion into the national game, a rebuke the fans took in their stride when at 2-0 up they began to sing 'We're supposed to be in church.' The IFA protested that there was little they could do: until 2014 fixtures had been arranged on a mutually agreeable date between national associations but were now ordained by a UEFA computer.

From having won just once during O'Neill's first eighteen games at the helm, seeing the team slip to an all-time low of 129th in the world rankings, Northern Ireland were now setting sail for their first major tournament in thirty years. Given Northern Ireland's limited resources, O'Neill had no choice but to fashion a team from hard-working pros earning their money in unfancied towns across England and Scotland with a few Premiership names dotted around the squad for good measure. Such a side could not hope to compete by taking the game to their opponents in a group containing Germany, Ukraine and Poland. Instead, blessed with half of the West Bromwich Albion backline, O'Neill's men were happy to cede possession, having less of the ball than any other side which progressed to the second round.

Ahead of their first fixture in France, Northern Ireland had conceded a solitary first half goal in their previous twenty-one outings, though ultimately Arkadiusz Milik's fifty-first minute strike for Poland was enough to determine the outcome of the tie. Though it had been a dogged defensive display, Steven Davis off target shot was their only attempt at goal. Four days later the nation of less than two million took on Ukraine, population 45 million, and won. Goals from Gareth McAuley - who has now notched as many goals for his country (nine) as George Best - and Niall McGinn gave the Northern Irish a deserved win, ensuring they remained competitive heading into the final group game with Germany.

This time, the Enniskillen-born goalkeeper Michael McGovern delivered a career-defining performance to hold Joachim Löw's men to a single goal despite having an astonishing seventy-nine per cent possession, setting up a nervous wait as players and fans alike scrutinised the table of third-placed group finishers from which only four teams could emerge, their passage secured by virtue of Turkey's 2-0 victory over the Czech Republic. Results elsewhere meant their second round opponents would be Wales, Chris Coleman's side having navigated their way to the summit of Group B by virtue of their own efficiency and the fecklessness of Roy Hodgson's England.

Thirty years to the day since arguably their greatest ever result — the Armstrong! Arconada! victory over Spain in Valencia - the fourth oldest football association in the world squared off against the third most ancient. Though the most obvious Welsh threat was posed by Real Madrid's Gareth Bale, ultimately it was an unfortunate own-goal by another Gareth - McAuley - which decided one of the scrappiest ties in recent memory. Will Grigg, despite not kicking a ball in earnest during the entire tournament, was deemed to still be on fire by the travelling faithful, and Northern Ireland ascended to twenty-fifth in FIFA's rankings, making the leap from punchline to punching above their weight.

While one O'Neill spearheaded the North into the tournament, his near-namesake Martin, eighteen years his senior, had been in charge of the Republic's side since late 2013. His side would also progress to the round of 16, sadly falling to a less than stellar French side, despite seizing the initiative through a third minute penalty. The tournament was also occasion for him to renew his acquaintance with *World Soccer* correspondent Paddy Agnew. Both had grown up in Kilrea, separated by dint of their parents religious proclivities and would not establish a connection until they had departed Northern Ireland. Agnew, the son of devout Presbyterians, would go on to become the Vatican correspondent for the *Irish Times,* and chose the tournament to laud O'Neill as a 'talented guy...there are a lot of northern Catholics who are very driven, very focused and very successful because they have come out of the apartheid background and it made them what they were.'

With both teams enjoying periods of relative success on the field, the possibility of a united Ireland team is as remote as it ever has been, only likely if the majority of nationalists as well as unionists in Northern Ireland decide that they want to be part of the Irish state, while also being welcomed in by voters in the Republic. The idea that a putative united Ireland football team could exist in advance of this — despite *Sinn Féin*'s opportunistic call - is fanciful and logistically fraught. Though the idea that the borders around Ulster's fourth green field could be erased is not as far-fetched as it might have seemed, even a couple of pre-Brexit years ago, it will surely be decades before it could be considered a realistic outcome.

Though the totemic nature of the Northern Ireland football team as a symbol of Britishness is waning, it is still something for the unionist community to hold on to, to be able to point to as a marker of differentiation; to be able to hold up as proof that Northern Ireland exists as separate entity, distinct from the island itself. The continuing conflict in Northern Ireland, largely *sans armes*, is as much about religion as it ever was — not a lot - but rather, as it always has been, about national-cultural identity. Much of Northern Irish Protestantism in 2017 is what the academic Alan Bairner describes as a 'form of secular, non-Christian Protestantism', or what his peer Norman Gillespie calls a 'mixture of selective theological dogma, anti-Catholicism and pragmatic loyalism.'

SPEAK UP

The anthem was a salient issue in Northern Irish youth football once again in 2016. The suggestion that it be dropped from before matches in the Milk Cup tournament was mooted by one player's mother, who contended in the *Irish News* that:

> this is meant to be a cross community football tournament where all the young players feel

> welcome, and we were all proud when my son made the team, he's worked really hard and our entire family want to go and support him...but it's almost as if we are not wanted or purposely made to feel unwelcome. Why can't a neutral anthem be played, my wee lad doesn't understand why he's being asked to stand for a British national anthem when all he wants to do is play football. Why are politics being dragged into a youth football tournament at all?

The clamour for answers to such questions grows ever louder, and if the IFA is serious about inclusivity at all levels of Northern Irish football, it will have to respond to them. Speaking at the team's homecoming event for the returning Euro 2016 team, Michael O'Neill reiterated that he 'want[ed] every young boy, wherever they're from in Northern Ireland to play for Northern Ireland.' His optimistic tone was tempered by a tweet from *Sinn Féin*'s Raymond McCartney, writing 'He might but they won't.'

While the truth is that for some, no changes short of the dissolution of the Northern Irish state would be enough, it is also true that the path for those who do chose to operate within it could and *should* be made smoother. Matt Lowry of the *Our Wee Country* fanzine concurred, 'I don't think we should play it. A sizable (sic) minority don't like it. If the English change it, we will have to also. It's ridiculous, we're not playing as Great Britain. I know of some people who won't go into the ground, who stay on the concourse until the anthem is played.' For the IFA to avert their eyes while this is the case suggests that, at best, there is an ambivalence towards those nationalists supporting Northern Ireland.

Predictably, political figures beyond the footballing

sphere continue to wilfully miss the point. First Minister Arlene Foster waffled before the tournament:

> We have a national anthem, as you know, but I'm also very conscious that we don't want to get into the politicisation of sport because sport is something that unites people. Right across Northern Ireland people are getting behind our sporting heroes. We have a national anthem. I don't think there's any need to tinker with that, but it's something we're all looking forward to into the summer and the sporting exploits of our heroes. I don't see any reason to change it...but as I say I don't want to get into politicising sport because it's something that unites everybody.

The plain fact is that sport does not unite everybody and the anthem itself is inherently political, which feeds into a sense of disunity.

Sinn Féin's Pat Sheehan, a West Belfast MLA, recognised that 'on its own, it's not going to make a massive amount of difference [changing the anthem], but there are a range of options that the IFA could put in place, that would make Windsor Park a more welcoming sports stadium for all of the community. I feel there is still a chill there [at Windsor Park] and I think the playing of God Save the Queen plays into that.'

STALEMATE

The anthem was not played before the Glentoran v Cliftonville Irish Cup final at the end of the 2012/13 season, despite the DUP threatening to take the matter to court. Their one time chairman and former IFA President Jim

Boyce's suggestion that 'a football anthem should be played at all World Cup and European games, like in the Champions League, instead of the national anthems' would be worth consideration by the relevant governing bodies, too.

Though singing 'Danny Boy' to the tune of 'Londonderry Air' — as is done at the Commonwealth games - is another possibility, Gerry Armstrong's study of the issue signposts the predictable obstacles that such a change would entail:

> there's one view that thinks the move could bring a few more Catholics back to international matches at Windsor Park. But on the other hand it has become clear there would be a significant number of dissenters among the fans who have supported us through thick and thin. The research I've done points to a conclusion I had foreseen all along — there is no point, no benefit, when it comes to bridging the yawning gap in society here.

PASTURES OLD

A twenty-nine month redevelopment costing £35 million also saw the Windsor Park's ownership situation change. Rather than pay rent to Linfield as tenants the IFA in effect now have shared ownership of the revamped ground, first used some 111 years earlier when it played host to a match between the Blues and Glentoran, generating £100 in gate receipts.

The crumbling edifice of which Jurgen Klinsmann had remarked in 1996, 'Ah, East Germany 1983!' had seen names as varied Alex Higgins and Ruby Murray grow up in its shadows. It was replaced by a stadium fit for twenty-first century football: on Saturday, 8 October 2016, a capacity 18,500 fans were present for Northern Ireland's World Cup qualifier against San Marino. The days of the 'Taigs Out' graffiti have hopefully consigned to the dustbin of history, the hateful scrawls subsumed by murals of Northern Ireland's greatest players across the eras.

Plans are also afoot for the redevelopment of Glentoran's Oval ground, with £10 million of public funds ring-fenced for use by the east Belfast club, a state of affairs reflecting the quasi social democratic, welfarist infrastructure that is Northern Ireland. The state is partly financed by a subvention from Westminster to the tune of around £10 billion every year in recent memory. These financial settlements are the price of peace, pots of money wrested from Conservative and Labour governments largely willing to underwrite the status quo so long as the guns stay off the streets.

Much to the chagrin of Derry residents and local politicians, this has largely been spent in Belfast, although Derry City FC have received a small amount of government cash as part of the redevelopment of the Brandywell over the course of 2017. This has necessitated a season of 'home' fixtures hosted in Buncrana, County Donegal, despite having the GAA's Celtic Park on their doorstep. Derry City's last season at the old Brandywell witnessed a mob carrying iron bars outside the ground before a match with league champions Dundalk, resulting in injury to a teenage fan of the visiting club, though the PSNI continues its 'hands-off' approach where a more involved strategy would undoubtedly only serve to provoke more persistent violent incidents.

The city itself betrays a legacy of abandonment and isolation; the logical outcome of decades of unionist dominated bodies pursuing a policy of neglect against

Northern Ireland's most significant nationalist conurbation. It's hardly surprising therefore that the Foyle constituency is ranked third highest in a UK list of 'jobless blackspots', less than an afterthought for a Conservative government which appears to regard the 1.8 million residents of Northern Ireland - Protestant, Catholic or otherwise — with almost complete disdain.

The 2016/17 season saw a Linfield side managed by David Healy narrowly pip north Belfast's Crusaders (from the largely Protestant Shore Road) to the NIFL Premiership title — their first since 2012 - after the Crues surrendered a nine-point lead. Healy's men clinched the trophy on the last day of the season at Crusaders bitter rivals Solitude ground in front of a crowd of 2,129 fans. Overall, Irish League attendances are on the rise — up twelve per cent year on year - reflecting the game's shedding of its deepest sectarian elements, which had discouraged so many from turning up in the worst of times. Domestic football in Northern Ireland retains a working class nature, in a way that English or even Scottish football does not and ticket prices are capped at £10 (which would not even get you into most sixth tier games in England). As the one-hundredth year of the Northern Irish state approaches, the cleavage in Irish League football is no longer whether a player is allowed to play for this club or that one, but can still be observed within fanbases and the peace lines which often mark them.

Belfast continues to be a footballing hotbed, boasting four of the semi-professional NIFL Premiership's twelve teams. In the suburbs, Lisburn Distillery are once again climbing back up the Irish League pyramid, having arrested a precipitous decline in fortunes. The city's grand shipbuilding yards, once the largest in the world, are no more; the last vessel to be launched from the Harland and Wolff slipway was the MV *Anvil Point* in 2003. From its first ship *Venetian* to what is likely its last, Harland & Wolff constructed 1,651 vessels over 144 years, an average of 11 ships per annum. These days the company specialises in building offshore oil rigs and wind turbines, employing around 500 workers. Not insignificant, but a fraction of its former workforce.

The footprint of the old yards is now reimagined as luxury apartments and a high tech office district named — apparently without irony - the Titanic Quarter. The giant yellow gantry cranes are enshrined by statute as part of Belfast's furniture, listed as historic monuments is 2003. Goliath was even coaxed out of retirement in 2007, recommissioned for construction of Derry's Foyle Bridge and the Ha'penny Bridge in Dublin. Move outwards from the centre and the city is still pockmarked by several dozen 'peace walls' — some more than 30ft tall - which divide nationalist and unionist neighbourhoods, a buffer against the low-level disorder which can erupt at these fractious interfaces. Their continued existence is seen as tragic yet necessary in a city where schooling remains delineated on whether you consider yourself a P or an RC.

Following the snap Stormont election in March 2017, the city that has been a byword for loyalty for the British crown for two centuries or more has ceased to be majority-Unionist 105 years since Edward Carson etched that first signature on the Ulster Covenant with his silver pen. That same election brought *Sinn Féin* within one seat of the Democratic Unionist Party across Northern Ireland, throwing unionism into a collective psychological crisis to which the prognosis remains unclear.

In the run up to the poll, former Ulster Unionist Party leader Mike Nesbitt graciously declared that he would attend Northern *and* Republic of Ireland matches, but his party were reduced to less than a dozen of the newly restructured ninety seat assembly, calling time on his reign at the top of the party that ruled Northern Ireland as its fiefdom for fifty years in the twentieth century. Weeks after *Sinn Féin*'s surge, former IRA commander and Deputy First Minister Martin McGuinness passed away from the rare illness which had rendered him a gaunt and frail figure. His fellow 'Chuckle Brother', Ian Paisley, had met his maker on 12 September 2014, 102 years to the day since the revolver shots had rung out over Celtic Park.

One thing is for certain, there is still very little that is normal about Northern Ireland.

BIBLIOGRAPHY

Books

Allen, Roger *Billy: Biography of Billy Bingham* (Viking, 1986)

Best, George *Blessed - The Autobiography* (Ebury Digital, 2012)

Bowler, Dave *Danny Blanchflower: A Biography* (Orion, 2013)

Brodie, Malcolm *100 Years of Irish Football* (Blackstaff Press Ltd, 1980)

Brown, Daniel *Every Other Saturday* (Motelands Publishing, 2016)

Brunt, Heather Jan *Lawrie Sanchez: The Northern Ireland Years* (Appletree Press Ltd, 2007)

Byrne, Peter *Green is the Colour: The Story of Irish Football* (Andre Deutsch Ltd, 2012)

Cairns, Stiofan *Adventures in Sectarianism: An Offbeat Tour of Northern Ireland* (Wider Horizons, 2014)

Cameron, Stephen *Belfast Shipbuilders: A Titanic Tale* (Colourprint Books, 2011)

Campbell, Tom *Celtic's Paranoia . . . All in the Mind?* (Fort Publishing, 2012)
Clarke, Liam and Johnston, Kathryn *Martin McGuinness: From Guns to Government* (Mainstream Publishing, 2011)
Clavane, Anthony *Does Your Rabbi Know You're Here?: The Story of English Football's Forgotten Tribe* (riverrun, 2012)
Crerand, Paddy *Paddy Crerand: Never Turn the Other Cheek* (HarperSport, 2014)
Cochrane, Terry *See You at the Far Post* (Clive Scoular, 2014)
Corry, Eoghan *The History of Gaelic Football: The Definitive History of Gaelic Football from 1873* (Gill & Macmillan, 2010)
Cullen, Donal *Freestaters: The Republic of Ireland Soccer Team 1921-1939* (Desert Island ebooks, 2012)
Doherty, Peter *Spotlight on Football* (Art & Educational Publishers, 1948)
Dougan, Derek *The Sash He Never Wore* (HarperCollins Distribution Services, 1974)
Duffy, Ron *Until the Troubles Started: A Brief Political History of Northern Ireland* (Createspace, 2013)
Flynn, Barry *Political Football* (The History Press, 2011)
Garnham, Neal *Association Football and Society in Pre-partition Ireland* (Ulster Historical Foundation, 2004)
Gillespie, Keith *How NOT to be a Football Millionaire - Keith Gillespie My Autobiography* (Trinity Mirror Sport Media, 2013)
Gordon, David *The Fall of the House of Paisley: The Downfall of Ian Paisley's Political Dynasty* (Gill & Macmillan, 2009)
Gregg, Harry with Anderson, Roger *Harry's Game: An Autobiography* (Mainstream Publishing, 2002)
Hanna, Ronnie *The World at Their Feet: Northern Ireland in Sweden* (SportsBooks Ltd, 2008)
Hannigan, Dave *The Garrison Game: The State of Irish Football* (Mainstream Publishing, 1998)

Jamieson, Teddy *Whose Side Are You On?* (Vintage Digital, 2011)
Jennings, Pat *Pat Jennings: An Autobiography* (Harper-Collins Publishers Ltd, 1984)
Jess, Mervyn *The Orange Order* (The O'Brien Press, 2012)
Lennon, Neil *Neil Lennon: Man and Bhoy* (HarperSport, 2009)
Lovejoy, Joe and Best, George *Bestie: A Portrait Of A Legend* (Sidgwick & Jackson, 2012)
Marshall, Evan *Spirit of '58: The incredible untold story of Northern Ireland's greatest football team* (Blackstaff Press, 2016)
Macdonald, Henry *Colours: Ireland - From Bombs to Boom* (Mainstream Publishing, 2005)
Martin, Ivan *David Healy: The Story So Far* (Appletree Press Ltd, 2007)
Martin, Ivan *Green and White Army: The Northern Ireland Fans* (Appletree Press Ltd, 2008)
McCluskie, Tom *The Rise and Fall of Harland and Wolff* (The History Press, 2013)
McGuirk, Brian *Celtic FC - the Ireland Connection* (Black & White Publishing, 2010)
McLoughlin, Alan and Evans, Bryce *A Different Shade of Green: The Alan McLoughlin Story* (Ballpoint Press, 2014)
Milburn, Jack *Jackie Milburn: A Man of Two Halves* (Mainstream Publishing, 2004)
Moore, Chris *United Irishmen: Manchester United's Irish Connection* (Mainstream Publishing, 2000)
Moore, Cormac *The Irish Soccer Split* (Atrium, 2015)
Morris, Terry *Vain Games of No Value?: A Social History of Association Football in Britain During Its First Long Century* (AuthorHouse, 2016)
Moss, Simon *Martin the Magnificent - The Future of Irish Football* (John Blacke, 2014)

Mulvenna, Gareth *Tartan Gangs and Paramilitaries The Loyalist Backlash* (Liverpool University Press, 2016)
Neill, Terry, Scovell, Brian and Harris, Harry *Revelations of a Football Manager* (Sidgwick & Jackson Ltd, 1985)
O'Connell, Sue *The Man Who Saved FC Barcelona: The Remarkable Life of Patrick O'Connell* (Amberley Publishing, 2016)
Ryan, Caroline Oceana *Adventures in Belfast: Northern Irish Life After the Peace Agreement* (Ascension Times Publishing, 2014)
Schofield, Shaun *There's Always One: Ten Years of Watching Northern Ireland (June 1995-June 2005)* (Diable Vert Publications, 2006)
Sugden, John *Sport, Sectarianism and Society* (Leicester University Press, 1995)
Thompson, Tom *Auld Hands: The Story of the Men Who Made Belfast Shipyards Great* (Blackstaff Press, 2013)
Tossell, David *In Sunshine or In Shadow: A Journey Through the Life of Derek Dougan* (Pitch Publishing (Brighton) Ltd, 2012)
Westcott, Chris *Norman 'Black Jake' Uprichard* (Amberley Publishing, 2011)
Whiteside, Norman *Determined: The Autobiography* (Headline, 2014)
Wilson, Richard *Inside the Divide: One City, Two Teams . . . The Old Firm* (Canongate Books, 2010)

Journal articles

Bairner, Alan and Shirlow, Peter *Loyalism, Linfield and the territorial politics of soccer fandom in Northern Ireland* (Space and Polity, 1998)
Bairner, Alan *Soccer, Masculinity, and Violence in Northern Ireland* (Men and Masculinities, 1999)
Bairner, Alan and Walker, Graham *Football and Society in*

Northern Ireland: Linfield Football Club and the Case of Gerry Morgan (Soccer & Society, 2001)

Bairner, Alan *Political Unionism and Sporting Nationalism: An Examination of the Relationship Between Sport and National Identity Within the Ulster Unionist Tradition* (Identities, 2003)

Bairner, Alan *Titanic Town: Sport, Space and the Re-imag(in)ing of Belfast* (City & Society, 2006)

Bairner, Alan *From Sands to Sanchez: The Making of a National Sports Stadium For Northern Ireland* (Entertainment and Sports Law Journal, 2007)

Bairner, Alan *The cultural politics of remembrance: sport, place and memory in Belfast and Berlin* (International Journal of Cultural Policy, 2008)

Bairner, Alan *The Ulster Boys: reflections on masculinity within Northern Ireland's protestant community* (2008)

Bairner, Alan *Sport, the Northern Ireland peace process, and the politics of identity* (Journal of Aggression, Conflict and Peace Research, 2013)

Brown, Daniel *Linfield's 'Hawk of Peace': pre-Ceasefires reconciliation in Irish League Football* (Soccer & Society, 2016)

Cronin, Mike *Playing Away from Home: Identity in Northern Ireland and the Experience of Derry City Football Club* (National Identities, 2000)

Curran, Conor *Networking Structures and Competitive Association Football in Ulster, 1880–1914* (Irish Economic and Social History, 2014)

Curran, Conor *Irish-born players in England's Football Leagues, 1945–2010: an historical and geographical assessment* (Sport in Society, 2016)

Garnham, Neal *Association Football and Politics in Belfast: The Careers of William Kennedy Gibson* (The International Journey of the History of Sport, 2007)

Hassan, David *An Opportunity for a New Beginning: Soccer,*

Irish Nationalists and the Construction of a New Multi-Sports Stadium for Northern Ireland (Soccer & Society, 2006)
Hassan, David, McCullough, Shane and Moreland, Elizabeth *North or South? Darron Gibson and the issue of player eligibility within Irish soccer* (Soccer & Society, 2009)
Hassan, David and O'Kane, Philip *Terrorism and the abnormality of sport in Northern Ireland* (International Review for the Sociology of Sport, 2012)
Hassan, David *A People Apart: Soccer, Identity and Irish Nationalists in Northern Ireland* (Soccer & Society, 2002)
Laverty, David and Garnham, Neal *Football in Inter-war Northern Ireland: Ballymena Football and Athletic Club Limited - Religious and Political Exclusivity or Civic Inclusivity* (The International Journal of the History of Sport, 2010)
McGee, Darragh and Bairner, Alan *Transcending the borders of Irish identity? Narratives of northern nationalist footballers in Northern Ireland* (International Review for the Sociology of Sport, 2010)

Quarterlies and Periodicals
Godfrey, Mark (Editor) *The Football Pink: Issue 6*
Wilson, Jonathan (Editor) *The Blizzard, Issue 8*
Wilson, Jonathan (Editor) *The Blizzard, Issue 17*
Wilson, Jonathan (Editor) *The Blizzard, Issue 20*
Wilson, Jonathan (Editor) *The Blizzard, Issue 21*

Newspapers, websites and any other media as credited in the text.